THE CROP CIRCLE
Enigma

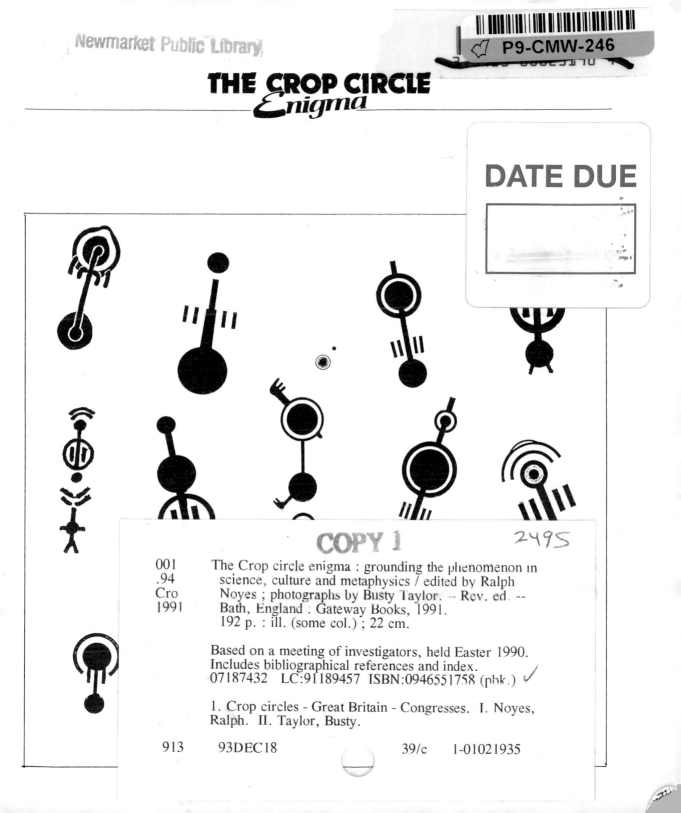

THE
CROP CIRCLE
Enigma

GROUNDING THE PHENOMENON IN SCIENCE, CULTURE AND METAPHYSICS

EDITED BY RALPH NOYES

PHOTOGRAPHS BY BUSTY TAYLOR

GATEWAY BOOKS

First published in 1990
by Gateway Books
The Hollies, Wellow,
Bath, BA2 8QJ, UK

© Gateway Books 1990
Revised edition 1991

Distributed in the USA by
The Great Tradition
11270 Clayton Creek Road,
Lower Lake, CA 95457

Cover photographs by Busty Taylor and Alick Bartholomew
Jacket and book design
by John Douet of Wimborne, Dorset
Set in Berner 10pt on 12 by
Photosetting and Secretarial Services of Yeovil
Printed and bound by
Butler & Tanner of Frome
Colour plates by Tabro Litho of Huntingdon

British Library Cataloguing in Publication Data

Noyes, Ralph
The crop circle enigma: a range of viewpoints from
the centre of crop circle studies
I. Title
130.941

ISBN 0–946551–75–8

Contents

List of colour plates

Note: *Those photos by others than Busty Taylor show the credit in the photo caption*

* *Colour POSTCARDS of these Plates are available from the Publishers at £2.00 for 8 cards (Inc.Post). Larger quantities by application.* # *19" × 27" Colour POSTERS £3.99 ea. (Inc. Post)*

Contributors

Michael Green, RIBA FSA, is a professional archaeologist and architectural historian with long experience in both disciplines. He took the initiative in calling together those who founded the Centre for Crop Circle Studies and is currently the Chairman of its Interim Council. He writes, lectures and broadcasts, not only on archaeological topics but on related matters which orthodox science is only slowly coming to recognise, including dowsing, of which he is himself an expert practitioner. He is preparing an extended study of the ancient mysteries in north-west Europe under the title, *The Celtic Zodiac.*

Professor Archie E. Roy, President of the Centre for Crop Circle Studies, is Honorary Senior Research Fellow in the Department of Physics and Astronomy at Glasgow University; a Fellow of the Royal Astronomical Society, the Royal Society of Edinburgh and the British Interplanetary Society; a Vice-President of the Society for Psychical Research; and a member of the International Astronomical Union and the Scottish Society for Psychical Research. Author of fourteen books, including six novels, he has also published over 70 scientific papers, edited journals and newspapers, lectured in many countries and addressed the Scientific Division of NATO.

Ralph Noyes entered the Civil Service in 1949 and served in the Air Ministry and subsequently the unified Ministry of Defence. He retired in 1977, leaving in the grade of Under-Secretary of State, in order to pursue a writing career. He has published a novel, *A Secret Property*, on the UFO problem, and writes, lectures and broadcasts on a range of topics which lie at the fringes of present understanding. He is currently the Hon. Secretary to the Society for Psychical Research and also the Hon. Secretary to the Centre for Crop Circle Studies, of which he is a founder member.

Hilary Evans, a member of the Council of the Society for Psychical Research and a co-founder of the Association for the Scientific Study of Anomalous Phenomena, is the author of many books dealing with remarkable but poorly-understood phenomena, including *Intrusions* (1982); *Visions, Apparitions, Alien Visitors* (1984); *Gods, Spirits, Cosmic Guardians* (1987); *The Evidence for UFOs* (1983) and *Alternate States of Consciousness* (1989). He is the editor of *Frontiers of Reality* (1989) and co-editor with John Spencer of *Phenomenon* (1988) and *UFOs, 1947–1987* (1987).

Since *The Flying Saucer Vision* was published in 1967 **John Michell** has written endlessly on many topics at the edge of present understanding, ranging from 'earth mysteries', leys and prehistoric science, through the meaning of number and measure in sacred buildings and ancient cosmology, to anomalous and curious phenomena in all their variety. His *New View over Atlantis* (1983) has been called "one of the great seminal books of our generation". He is a founder member of the Centre for Crop Circle Studies and editor of *The Cereologist*, a regular journal devoted exclusively to the crop circle enigma.

Bob Rickard has published *Fortean Times* since he founded it in 1973 to disseminate anomalous data. He has written books with John Michell (*Phenomena*, 1977, and *Living Wonders*, 1982) and with Richard Kelly (*Photographs of the Unknown*, 1980). He publishes special interest books under the *Fortean Tomes* imprint, and co-founded the Fortean Picture Library with Janet and Colin Bord to preserve illustrative material before it is irretrievably lost. He has a wide range of interests, finding almost any topic grist to his mill. A large part of Issue 53 of *Fortean Times (Winter, 1989/90)* was devoted to the crop circle enigma.

Dr. George Terence Meaden took his doctorate at Oxford University with research in low-temperature solid-state physics at both Oxford and the Atomic Energy Research Establishment, Harwell. Post-doctoral appointments at the Unversities of Oxford and Grenoble were followed by the tenured post of Associate Professor of Physics at Dalhousie University, Halifax, Canada. He founded the Tornado and Storm Research Organisation, with its international magazine, *The Journal of Meteorology, UK*, specialising in research on atmospheric vortices, tornadoes, whirlwinds, waterspouts and ball lightning. He has published extensively in physics and meteorology, and is the longest-standing researcher into the crop circle phenomenon. He has written *The Crop Circle Effect and its Mysteries* and is editor of *Circles from the Sky – The Crop Circle Mystery*

George Wingfield was educated at Eton College and Trinity College, Dublin, graduating in 1966 with an MA Honours degree in Natural Sciences. He worked briefly at the Royal Greenwich Observatory, Herstmonceux, on stellar spectra and the Earth's magnetism. He currently works for IBM UK Ltd in the field of Systems Engineering. He is a founder member of the Centre for Crop Circle Studies and has written, lectured and broadcast extensively on the crop circle phenomenon, both on radio and television. He relates these remarkable events to a wide range of other phenomena, including much of the data from ufology and paraphysics.

Richard G. Andrews is a founder member of the Centre for Crop Circles Studies, is a life-long Farmer and Agriculturalist with wide experience in Country Crafts, Forestry and Estate Managment. He has served as an area manager for Seed Breeders at Chester and a cereal crop inspector for N.I.A.B. To this deep professional understanding of the countryside he has, during the past twenty years, added the techniques of dowsing. Since 1985 he has been applying this expert knowledge and insights to systematic study of the crop circle formations. He has written, lectured and broadcast extensively on the Crop Circle Phenomenon on Radio and Television. He is also a member of the British Society of Dowsers.

John George Baillie-Hamilton Haddington, 13th Earl of Haddington, has inherited his father's keen interest in antiquities and life-long attachment to the study of ancient systems of belief and symbology. A frequent traveller to many of the remoter parts of the globe, he has long cultivated a keen amateur interest in the culture, ritual practices, systems of magic, and metaphysical beliefs of non-Western societies. He is a founder member of the Centre for Crop Circle Studies. Though living in Scotland, he has made many visits to southern England in recent years to study the crop circles at first hand.

F. C. Taylor — universally known as Busty Taylor — is a Wiltshire man, born and bred, with one of those knacks for mechanical gear of all kinds which his father encouraged from an early age. In 1967, just turned twenty-four, he found that he had a talent for teaching people to drive, and he now runs a thriving school of motoring. His private passions are flying and photography — two skills which have put him in the forefront of crop circle photography and given him an international reputation in this area. His talent for balancing an unwieldy camera at the top of a tall pole for ground photography of the circles is hardly less awe-inspiring than his ability to fly an aircraft with one hand and to take video pictures with the other. He has appeared many times on national and foreign television programes, and his still and moving pictures have enlivened many meetings and conferences. His presence will be felt throughout this book. It was a great pleasure to the Centre for Crop Circles Studies to welcome him as a founder member.

Lucy Pringle was educated in England, France and Switzerland and has travelled widely about the world, spending twelve years in Jamaica, where her elder son was born. At present working for a finance house, she is also the Hon. Treasurer and Hon. Membership Secretary to the Centre for Crop Circle Studies. She nevertheless finds time to pursue life-long interests in books, writing, art, gardening, horse riding, tennis, bridge, backgammon, people and lively conversation. In addition to all these she has recently begun to practise channelling.

Preface

M I C H A E L   G R E E N

The crop circle phenomenon is a wonder in the true sense of that rather over-worked word. Starting in a small way about ten years ago, the circle formations in the, mainly, corn fields of England have increased their numbers astoundingly in recent years and now exist in a complexity, size and beauty that is awe-inspiring. Their origins are utterly mysterious, but the formations clearly show a progression in terms of design, with individual occurrences often having extra features added during the course of the season. In short, it is almost impossible to resist the impression that the crop circles exhibit the action of an intelligence, operating through whatever physical processes may be in question. Associated with them are various strange phenomena, of which some of the most significant are apparently non-random high-frequency signals.

It was the attempt to confront these astonishing events that led to the genesis of this book, which explores on a wider basis and in greater depth than any previous study the possible nature, origins and purpose of the phenomenon. The book itself was the result of a seminal meeting of concerned investigators at Easter 1990. It was decided to set up an international organisation, the *Centre for Crop Circle Studies*, which would function as an open, impartial forum for research in this field. A learned society of this type was desperately needed since existing organisations were felt to be unsatisfactory for various reasons.

As will be immediately evident from its contents, this study incorporates assessments from most streams of thought on the subject to date, some of them mutually exclusive! It also brings together in a fast developing subject the most up-to-date records of the phenomenon in a wide spread of aerial photographs and measured drawings.

Where do we go from here? It is essential that the study of the crop circles in future is carried out in a planned, rational way, using scientific method at its best. With some notable exceptions, research has so far been carried out by dedicated amateurs for the most part, who have poured slender resources and precious time into monitoring the crop circles. A few simple circles each year could be coped with on this basis, but the size of the phenomenon and its geographical range now makes this impossible. The crop formations need to be found, and ideally this requires regular aerial surveillance on a national scale. Circle formations need to be accurately surveyed and their features recorded in a computerised data base whose information is regularly assessed and published. Ancillary soil, crop and atmospheric tests, not to mention a wide range of other on-site studies, some of which can at present only be guessed at, need to be systematically carried out. Little or nothing of this is being done, and what research is taking place is largely secretive and unpublished. There is a great need for a well-funded research organisation with proper equipment, access to laboratory facilities and the professional and administrative infrastructure which is required to underpin this level of research. The formation of the Centre for Crop Circle Studies is only a start in this direction.

The farming community has been understandably dismayed by the spread of the crop circle phenomenon and its side effects as regards trespassing and damage to property and crops. The farmers need to be taken fully into the confidence of the professional, authorised investigators, and a start in this direction has been made with the active collaboration of the National Farmers Union. It would be a disaster if investigations had to be halted due to hostility in the countryside.

Because the circles occur in a fragile medium (growing crops) and on private land, it is vital that research opportunities are made available when the circles first appear and conditions are at an optimum for their recording. If an analogy is needed, the phenomena are somewhat of the same character, and raise the same problems, as rare plants and animals in the countryside. After decades of public lobbying and parliamentary legislation some measure of protection is afforded to rare species. Could

such protection be made available for the crop circles? It may well be that some system of official registration of phenomena on a seasonal basis is required, together with a financial subvention to the farmers concerned on similar lines to that operated under the Ancient Monuments legislation for scheduled monuments. This would have the great advantage of being an inducement to farmers to report the phenomena promptly. In return they would be expected to facilitate scientific examination of crop circle formations on their land. During the open season the 'designated' phenomena would need to be patrolled by wardens to keep unauthorised visitors away.

All this postulates a level of public awareness and official concern that simply does not appear to exist at the present time. But the situation may change.

It is against a background of such possible sociopolitical developments that this book has been prepared. The crop circle phenomena are not just ordinary accidents of nature in the countryside, but may, indeed probably do, have serious implications for us all in terms of what may lie behind them.

Foreword

ARCHIE E. ROY

*W*e called them "the corn circles" to begin with. They looked like a minor quirk of nature, another of those little local difficulties which farmers patiently get used to. Few of us took much notice at the time. Those that did expected the problem — if problem wasn't too grand a word — to be solved in a month or two. But that was the summer of 1980. Our journey of exploration had only just begun.

More than ten years have now passed. The circles have multiplied and spread — at a rate which, in recent years, can only be called explosive. New shapes and patterns have appeared, many of remarkable beauty and elaboration. Other crops than corn have been visited. Increasingly strange events have been reported from the affected fields. What began as an oddity has grown to the size of "a riddle wrapped in a mystery inside an enigma". Those words of Winston Churchill's, spoken to the House of Commons in 1939 about an urgent problem in European diplomacy, apply with as much force to the puzzle which now confronts us in the cropfields.

Over this same decade since 1980 scientific hypotheses have been framed and scrapped. Other, stranger, guesses have multiplied as fast as the circles themselves. Several books have been written about them; and an international conference has been held, and its proceedings published. (See References.) Scores of television programmes have covered them. Hundreds of hours of flying time and foot-slogging have been spent in visiting them. Thousands of photographs have been taken. Reports and articles published in the local and national press have now passed well beyond counting. Yet the problem, far from being solved, continues to grow.

Each year brings fresh surprises. Reports reach us of new kinds of circle, new forms of circle-pattern, new locations in this country and abroad, new and weirder events at the circle sites. Whatever rash generalisation was last made is rapidly contradicted. The phenomenon begins to have the look of a large-scale jokester who is leading us by the nose. Even the most determined of those who have been seeking orthodox explanations, Dr. G. Terence Meaden, accepted in 1989[2] that "new facts appearing each year are susceptible of modifying the ideas we have put forward"; and that short of a massive research effort "decades may pass without much progress".

We have an enigma on our hands. It has some of the features of a good detective story — though a detective story which has since become an odyssey. The journey seems to be taking us towards strange shores. To quote Meaden again, this "arduous, complex study [is] one which will have far-reaching consequences in disciplines well removed from the one in which the investigation began".

This book has been put together because its contributors share that sense of excitement and expectation. Each of us feels that something more momentous than a simple hazard to the cultivation of crops is now in question. Even the most sceptical of us sees in the phenomenon at least a fascinating study of the human response to strange events; others expect an enlargement of our scientific understanding of the remarkable world we live in; others again have intimations of "something far more deeply interfused" which it would be foolish, even perhaps perilous, to ignore. What unites us is the belief that, after ten years of study, a great puzzle remains which deserves serious comment from a wide range of expertise, however remote some of it may seem from the 'simple' problem of a 'simple' disturbance to arable farming.

The media coverage of these strange events has made the public aware of them. It is entirely natural therefore that people should ask: "What is science doing about the crop circle mystery: what has science to say about it?" These questions, simplistic though they are, are the product of the public's faith in the ability of science to solve problems. They also stem from a misunderstanding of how science operates.

Science is the most spectacularly successful activity the human race has ever undertaken. Why it should have had its birth in the West at the time it did — many would put the date as 1687, the year of publication of Isaac Newton's *Principia* — has been discussed in innumerable essays. Whatever the cause or causes, the ingenious use by Newton of the test bed of the Solar System's planets and satellites to verify his celebrated law of gravitation and his three laws of motion led to ever-increasing progress in studying and understanding the marvellously varied phenomena of nature, both animate and inanimate. Great branches of science were developed by patient observation, hypothesis, prediction and carefully-planned experiment. Astronomy, dynamics, electricity and magnetism, heat, light and sound became the branches of the intellectual tree that used to be justly called Natural Philosophy and is now less accurately entitled Physics. But of course Physics itself was only one scientific discipline. Chemistry, Botany, Biology, Geology, Psychology and many other younger subjects were developed as the need arose, as phenomena were encountered hitherto unknown or unrecognised or neglected as irritatingly anomalous or of dubious reality and seemingly outside the province of science's application.

Such fringe phenomena are often embraced enthusiastically by non-scientists: they study the alleged phenomena, formulate theories to explain them and often feel aggrieved when the scientific establishment apparently treats their efforts with disdain, refusing to co-operate in research or even to recognise that here is a field worthy of attention. "Don't you realise" they cry, "that the whole history of scientific discovery is of the outsider being considered mad by the establishment and yet ultimately triumphing in the face of rejection and scorn to be finally accepted as a genius?"

This alleged process has even been cynically summarised in a set of three stages: (i) The man's mad; (ii) Oh look, how irritating; he won't go away. Let's just glance at his 'discovery' if only to show him where he went wrong; (iii) Of course, I always knew this was true!

While this can happen we should nevertheless remember the wise words of the sage Marx — Groucho, not Karl — who said: "They said Galileo was mad when he stated that the Earth went round the Sun, but it did. They said the Wright brothers were crazy when they claimed men could fly — but they did. They said my Uncle Wilbur was out of his mind — and he was as mad as a hatter!"

It is part of the strength of science that its practitioners demonstrate a seeming inertia in accepting strange new phenomena and theories to explain them, especially if these phenomena and theories have been brought to their notice by non-professionals and certainly so if these phenomena appear to clash with scientific laws that have had centuries of verification and utilisation in science and technology. This apparent inertia is in part due to caution, due in part to justifiable scepticism that a new discovery of importance can be made by someone who is scientifically untrained in a science that becomes increasingly specialised and esoteric year by year; it is also to a large degree the result of an ever-present knowledge that there are many 'respectable' research fields already available in the mainstream of scientific effort, which have a high probability of producing important new results. In other words use your available time cautiously and prudently. Additionally, research costs time and money and very few scientists are privately funded. They must therefore carry out their bread and butter science or fall foul of their paymasters.

If professional scientists do become engaged in a fringe area, it is often at their own expense and as a hobby. It also requires a certain courage. Their activity will be triggered mainly by curiosity, the driving force behind most of the fundamental and far-reaching discoveries that have shaped our scientific and technological society the way it is today. Newton, Faraday, Clerk- Maxwell, Rutherford, to name but a few, carried out long, painstaking researches in areas that promised no 'immediately-applicable' results. It can be argued that because their discoveries did lead to results of staggering importance and applications, it is a lesson that pure science — research conducted by scientists for no other reason than to advance knowledge — does pay off in totally unpredictable ways and is neglected at our peril in favour of immediately applicable research. As a case in point, the discovery of the hole in the ozone layer over the Antarctic would not have been made but for such ironically-termed 'blue sky' research, research under the constant threat of financial cut-backs.

Thus in the climate of today, it is not to be expected that funding and teams of scientists will be enlisted to study the crop circle enigma. Only individual scientists working in different areas who are curious about the phenomenon and entertain a suspicion that it may be of importance in ways we do not yet understand and who have time to spare, will play their part. They will not expect to find quick answers. They will want as many data about the crop circles as possible to be carefully collected and stored in a readily available data base. Among those data will be numbers, sizes, shapes, patterns of crop circles, where and when they have appeared. Photographs and measurements, ground- and air-based, will be important. In the absence of any convincing hypothesis, any associated data are relevant — meteorological, type of crop, geological, even the Moon's phase may be important, for all we know. Magnetic and radiation data should be logged when available; chemical analysis of crops and soil should not be dismissed. Instrumental data of strange sonic phenomena within and in the vicinity of some of the circles should be registered in the data base. The claims of dowsers to have detected anomalous phenomena in or near the circles should be carefully noted.

If people report strange experiences in circles or elsewhere, supposing them to be associated in some way with the crop circle phenomenon, their accounts should not be ignored or laughed at. In the absence of any satisfactory hypothesis, it is not scientific to make a priori judgements as to what is relevant and what is not.

When a hypothesis is put forward, it should be capable of being tested in a scientific manner. A 'hand of God' theory explaining the phenomena as due to the inscrutable purposes of the Almighty is by its very nature irrelevant to science. It may be correct but it is not scientific! A useful theory is one that not only embraces known data but suggests experiments to be carried out to test the hypothesis or to disprove it. It may be that the results of the experiments or fresh observations will suggest modifications to be made to the theory. New experiments or observational programmes will then be suggested. Suspicion may be cast on a theory if it has to be continually modified and loses its original pleasing simplicity under a grotesque and baroque growth of 'improvements'. A well-known case is the elaboration of Ptolemy's geocentric model of the world with epicycles superimposed upon epicycles in a desperate effort to 'save the phenomena'. The outcome of such a process is often a paradigm shift, a realisation that an entirely new perspective is needed, that to follow further the old theory is to continue a fruitless journey on a siding to nowhere.

But above all, the scientific edifice must rest on facts, data acquired, tested, found to be reliable. Many a beautiful theory, it has been said, has been slain by an ugly little fact. The best approach to a solution of the crop circle enigma will be the creation of an exhaustive data base capable of being made available to anyone with a serious interest in studying this strange new research field. It is for this reason that the Centre for Crop Circle Studies was created in the spring of 1990. In a real sense the present book is a first attempt by the Centre to provide an overview of the present state of play. Because it is the first such overview, taken at a time when no satisfactory body of theory yet exists, it is a broad view, a synoptic view that ranges far and wide in the hope that no relevant data have been overlooked. As our knowledge grows, future overviews will undoubtedly differ from this one: some factors will be found to be more important than others; new factors at present unsuspected will emerge. But it is hoped that the reader of the present book will experience that unique sense of tantalising intrigue the scientist gets when faced with a genuine and exciting mystery, the tingling sense of wonder that made Sherlock Holmes, quoting Shakespeare's Henry Vth, cry out joyfully: "The game's afoot!"

REFERENCES
1. Fuller, P. & Randles, J. *Mystery of the Circles* BUFORA 1986.
2. Meaden, G. T. *The Circles Effect and its Mysteries* Artetech 1989.
3. Delgado, P. & Andrew, C. *Circular Evidence* Bloomsbury 1989.
4. Fuller, P. & Randles, J. *Controversy of the Circles* BUFORA 1989.
5. Meaden, G. T. & Elsom, D. M. (Eds.) *Circles Research 1* Proceedings of the First International Conference on the Circles Effect held at Oxford, UK, June 1990. (Re-issued in hardback, with additional material, as *The Crop Circles Mystery* Artetech 1990).
6. Fuller, P. & Randles, J. *Crop Circles: A Mystery Solved* Robert Hale 1990.
Major review articles have also appeared in:-
Good, T. (Ed.) *The UFO Report 1990* Sidgwick & Jackson 1989.
Good, T. (Ed.) *The UFO Report 1991* Sidgwick & Jackson 1990.
The British periodicals, *Journal of Meteorology, UK, Weather* (the journal of the Royal Meteorological Society), *Country Life, Kindred Spirit, Flying Saucer Review, The Journal of Transient Aerial Phenomena (BUFORA), New Scientist* and *Fortean Times*.
The United States periodicals, *The MUFON UFO Journal, OMNI* and *TIME Magazine*.

Introduction

RALPH NOYES

In his Foreword Professor Roy describes the sense of wonder, the sense of a — great enigma, which grips us all in the presence of the crop circles and the ever-elaborating patterns they present. The enigma has four parts.

The first is a question of history. Are these things very new? Or very old? This is crucial to understanding them. If they have always been with us, the only puzzles are why we haven't noticed them before and why we are now doing so. If they are new, there is much to be explained.

The second enigma is one of 'mechanism'. How are the circles made? By magic — in which case there is nothing we can do except to await the magician's next whimsy? Or by *regular* forces which we can hope to identify, even if they remain obscure at present, and the operation of which we may come to predict even if not to control (as we have come to understand much about the factors which govern climate and weather and to make short-range predictions about them)?

Thirdly, whatever forces may be involved, are they operating 'blindly', 'mechanically', with no more 'purpose' than the force of gravity or the physical properties of matter which cause crystals to form (often of such beauty and elaboration that mystically inclined philosophers have tended to see 'intention' and 'design' in them)? Or is there an intelligent agency at work which is 'using' whatever forces may be involved for purposes of its own (as a man uses the properties of the world around him

— with or without much scientific understanding of them — to build a house, hoist a bucket of water out of a well, make a fire, chisel inscriptions on a piece of stone)?

Fourthly, if an intelligence is operating, is it conveying a 'message' — or merely entertaining itself (part of its entertainment lying, perhaps, in our sheer human bewilderment)?

These are the questions which this book addresses. Not long ago the third and fourth of them — those questions of 'purpose' and 'message' — would have seemed absurd to many of us. But the events of the last two or three years — dramatically so the events of 1990 — have put them inescapably on the agenda. You have only to glance at the Frontispiece to know that the burden of argument has now shifted from those of us who were fancifully talking about pattern and purpose a little while ago (and were being rebuked by trained scientists for doing so — very sensibly, it seemed) to those who are still fighting for a wholly mechanistic explanation. It is they who now seem to have their backs to the wall.

To those of us who have founded the *Centre for Crop Circle Studies* and launched this book it seems imperative to draw upon a far wider range of expertise than has so far been brought to bear, however speculative some of it may seem. Very probably, no single contributor is near to a solution (if 'solution' is the right word to be using in the context of a spectacular phenomenon of this magnitude and strangeness); quite possibly, every one of them offers important clues to our future understanding; and quite certainly none of them will feel wholly satisfied with what his fellow contributors have to say!

But this book is not a committee of enquiry which is compelled to reach agreement, it is an attempt to look from many different angles at a vastly puzzling set of events for which no explanation has been forthcoming after nearly eleven years of systematic study and a great deal of very *uns*ystematic fancy. We hope that it will provide a starting-point for an on-going series of further studies.

The sequence in which events have occurred since 1980 is not the least of the puzzles. It may help to put the succeeding articles in context if we begin with a brief history.

HOW DID IT START? HOW HAS IT CARRIED ON?

Westbury, 1980:
Mares' Nests and a White Horse

On 15th August 1980 the *Wiltshire Times* carried a report of three strange circular marks which had appeared in fields of oats near Westbury, Wiltshire, on a farm owned by a Mr. John Scull. They had turned up, said the newspaper, under the very gaze of the famous White Horse of Westbury. Each was about sixty feet in diameter. Nothing like them had been seen before. There was no ready explanation for them.

The picture printed by the paper showed the circles to have many of the features which most of these remarkable events have shown ever since: that sharp cut-off between the disturbed area and the rest of the field, the flattened swirling of the affected crops, the continued ripening of the crop long after its weird fate has overtaken it. You will find many pictures in this book which show these things.

It is to that *Wiltshire Times* report of 1980 that we can date the beginning of the extraordinary saga which has since ensued.

Very quickly on the scene were Ian Mrzyglod, editor of a small but influential magazine, *The PROBE Report*, (now sadly defunct but an invaluable source for historians on this subject up to 1983) and Dr. Terence Meaden, an atmospheric physicist who lives at Bradford-on-Avon, Wiltshire, edits the renowned Journal of Meteorology, is a senior member of the Tornado and Storm Research Organisation (TORRO, and has given much of his life to studying the stranger things which our atmosphere can do.

It was quickly established that the three events — singletons, as we would now call them — had formed on three widely different dates between May and late July. Meaden's view was that summer whirlwinds seemed the most likely explanation, the only oddities being that he hadn't seen this kind of ground-effect before and that a very *stationary* kind of whirlwind, with a very large and precise area of operation, had to be imagined.

That 'stationary' is important. Many of us have seen summer whirlwinds. Sometimes they stand still in the same place for a short while, but most of them are inclined to skitter about a field and to leave ragged damage with a good deal of scattered debris. A whirlwind able to operate with the precision of what looked like a gigantic biscuit-cutter was therefore a striking novelty.

And that word 'novelty' is also important. It is striking that an atmospheric physicist of Terence Meaden's experience had not seen anything of this kind before. His sense of surprise was shared by the local farmers.

Ian Mrzyglod, in *The PROBE Report*, put on record the interesting fact that the 'circles' were not circles at all: they were slightly elliptical or oval. His measured drawings were helpfully put on record by Meaden in the Journal of Meteorology and are reproduced here (Fig. 1). The same has been true of most crop circles we've seen since: it is one of the

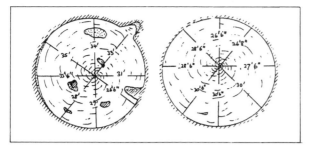

Figure 1. Measured drawings made by Ian Mrzyglod of two of the three 'circles' reported from Bratton, Wiltshire, in 1980. Note that they are far from perfect circles.

several reasons against hoax as a general explanation. Most of us can make circles in the hay if we want; few of us would bother to make ellipses.

Bratton in 1980 had given us a good start for what was to follow, though nobody could then have guessed at the elaborations which were to come.

Winchester, 1981: Down in the Punchbowl Something Stirred

A little to the east of Winchester and overlooked by the A.272 road is a famous punchbowl formation lying below Cheesefoot Head in the county of Hampshire. It is a well known beauty spot, fully open to public view from the surrounding area, much visited by tourists, and used for arable farming by the family which owns the land.

On 19th August 1981, three circles were found in the large field of grain which occupies most of the punchbowl. They were similar to the circles seen at Bratton the year before. There was the same sharp cut-off at the edge of each circle, the same clockwise swirl of the flattened grain, the same slight tendency towards the elliptical or oval.

But this time there was an interesting development. At Westbury the circles had been widely separated from each other, not only in time but place. This time they seemed to make a pattern.

They lay in a straight line, a large middle one of about sixty feet in diameter, flanked by two smaller ones, each of about twenty-five feet. There was every appearance that a single event had taken place even if it happened to have had three separate components.

The scientific problem had grown a little. If atmospheric physics was right, we now needed not just an unusually *stationary* whirlwind, but a whirlwind able to 'bounce' three times in the same field in quick succession, to be briefly stationary each time it came to earth, and to alter its diameter of operation from one bounce to the next.

Meaden somewhat elaborated his whirlwind model and began to relate his atmospheric vortex theory to peculiarities of the terrain — "to steep grass-covered hillsides having a kind of punchbowl or concave shape to them". His on-going tussle with the problem is recorded in many issues of the *Journal of Meteorology* from 1981 to date: they will one day be essential grist for the scientific historians of this subject.

To laymen there began to be the appearance that something was on the move and that it possessed features never before recorded by well-qualified observers.

The Coming of the Quintuplets: Does God play Dice?

1982 was a quiet year. Nothing was reported from Winchester, and we owe it to Mrzyglod that the few instances of singletons near Cley Hill in Wiltshire (quite near to Westbury) were placed on record and brought to Terence Meaden's attention. In a recent personal communication (1990) Meaden tells me that other occurrences were in fact reported to him for that year (see below), but nothing was placed on the public record at the time. Work undertaken later on by Paul Fuller on behalf of TORRO and the British UFO Research Association (BUFORA) also suggests that there could have been other events which went unrecorded at about this stage.

This patchiness in our knowledge is a great frustration to those who would like to have a fully documented account of the sequence of events. It is a matter which the *Centre for Crop Circle Studies* hopes some day to remedy. But it is relatively trivial in the light of what has since ensued — a matter for historians rather than for those currently grappling with the great enigma. What is beyond doubt is that 1983 brought new events which nobody had foreseen and which atmospheric physics had not predicted.

That three-in-line event of 1981 down in the punchbowl below Cheesefoot Head had seemed to one of my Fortean friends like the three on the face of one of those dice which emphasises the central pip by making it somewhat larger. He now curses himself for never having placed this whimsical thought on record. In 1983, and in almost the same place in the punchbowl field, a five turned up.

Figure 2 (though drawn from an event of a later year) shows what this astonishing occurrence looked like. (The measured diagram was made by Chris Wood of the *Daily Express*, many of whose excellent crop circle photographs have appeared in *Flying Saucer Review*).

Then it began to rain fives.

Fivesomes — though we soon came to call them quintuplets — turned up at Bratton below the Westbury White Horse; at the foot of the UFO-haunted Cley Hill near Warminster; and in a field just below the Ridgeway near Wantage in Oxfordshire. We continued to have quintuplets throughout the rest of the eighties (though they seem to have gone largely out of fashion in 1990!).

Quintuplets caught the imagination of the national media. Articles came thick and fast. Television producers began to take an interest. 1980 had seen the start of scientific attention to the crop circle enigma; 1983 was the year when the British public became aware that something extraordinary was going on.

Quintuplets not only stirred the public, they

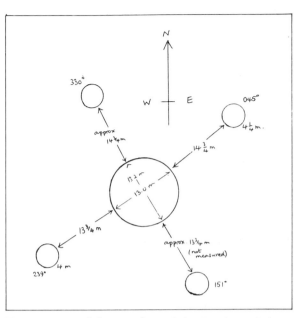

Figure 2. Measured diagram of a typical quintuplet made by Chris Wood and reproduced in Journal of Meteorology vol. 10, no. 97. Note the irregularities in dimensions and the non-alignments of the satellites — more the work of an 'artist' than an 'engineer' . . . and certainly not a 'space-craft'.

presented a serious problem for research. That 'threesome-bouncer' of 1981 had been tiresome enough for atmospheric physics to explain; the symmetrical fivesomes of 1983 were harder still. I must, again, refer the scientific historians to the listed issues of the *Journal of Meteorology* for an account of Terence Meaden's valiant attempts to take on board the tricks which the phenomenon was playing upon him.

There now entered upon the story another element for which we have needed to keep our eyes open ever since: the intervention of human jokesters. We had hardly recovered from the shock of the quintuplet found at Bratton below the Westbury White Horse when another turned up almost within spitting distance. Swift detective work ensued for which Ian Mrzyglod carries much of the credit, aided and abetted by the watchful editor of *Fortean Times*, Bob Rickard, whose article later in this book sets the crop circle phenomenon in the context of some strange echoes from myth and folklore.

Rickard, in true Fortean fashion, has a keen appetite for oddities but a sharp eye for fraud. Hoax had already crossed his mind as a general explanation for the circles. He made some shrewd observations to Mrzyglod. They were, as it happens, wrong in detail (nobody has yet been *right* about the circles for more than a short stretch of time!), but they pointed Mrzyglod in a fruitful direction. Within weeks the second quintuplet at Bratton was shown to be a hoax. The cheerful culprit, Francis Shepherd, gleefully displayed his rough techniques to the local Press. The Shepherd family had been paid by the *Daily Mirror* to 'duplicate' the first quintuplet, mainly in the hope of showing up the *Daily Express*, who had, to the irritation of the *Mirror*, scooped the real event.

The fact that 1983 produced not only those remarkable fivesomes but also a few singletons (all in Wessex) passed almost without comment. We were at the point of becoming blasé about mere single circles.

1984 and 1985: Multiplication and Division

The circles began to multiply. Researchers began to divide. And historians begin to despair.

From this point on it becomes impossible to be sure even about the number of events accurately *reported* and adequately logged in the files of serious researchers: separate collections of data were now beginning to be made by different groups of people and much of this information has never been published by those who hold it. Perhaps, one day, we shall find it all amalgamated and placed on record; this is certainly what the Centre for Crop Circle Studies would like to see. For the time being we have to make guesses.

It is even less easy to estimate the number of events which, though seen by farmers, went wholly unreported either to the Press or to any research group. We know from meticulous work undertaken by Paul Fuller, a professional statistician who is also a member of the Council of BUFORA, that some circles were certainly being kept quiet by the farmers who suffered them (anyway up to the date of Fuller's study in 1987[1]), perhaps because they seemed to be of no importance or perhaps for fear of sightseers.

So we don't really know at present how many circles actually came to the attention of research groups from 1984 onwards; nor do we know how many circles have gone unreported altogether before and since that date. And we can't even properly estimate the extent of our ignorance! These are facts to keep in mind throughout this book.

All circle research groups are approached from time to time by interested people who have a hunch about some grand pattern which they feel the distribution of the circles may reveal. "Just give us a complete read-out," they say. "Better still, give us a map." They will, alas, have to be patient a little longer.

Some attempt can, however, be made to piece together the likely tally of *reported* events in 1984 and 1985, even though the piecemeal information which exists has come out in bits and pieces, often in much later years, and even though some events have been claimed as hoaxes by those who wish to grind that particular axe.

Let us take stock to the end of 1985.

We had so far had a relatively few reports of some rather unusual patches of disturbance in arable crops in southern England. The main puzzles they presented were their striking precision (as compared with the untidy kinds of damage which the fields have always suffered from such things as wind, rain, birds, animals and human visitors); their surprising ability to form threesome and fivesome groupings; and the fact that they had come as a novelty even to well qualified observers.

But they hardly looked like a major problem for science. They seemed to be increasing a little from year to year, but only to the modest extent which might be expected from the fact that more people were now looking for them. They seemed to be clustering in Wessex, but this could probably be explained by the concentration in Wiltshire and Hampshire of the few people who were doing the serious field research. And their total numbers over these six summers was nothing much to write home about. Counting a quintuplet as five circles, we had had reports of something like eighty circles in all, an average of not much more than a dozen a year. Counting quintuplets as a single event, the average

was more like five or six events each summer. In the diagram of circle types in Fig. 3 the published records did not indicate that we had seen more than the singleton, the three-in-line and the quintuplet plus a few doublets of uncertain significance. (Doublets might, after all, have been formed by the sheer coincidence of the arrival on separate occasions of two singletons of different size). As far as the public knew, we were still at line one of Fig. 3.

Terence Meaden's search for an explanation in terms of a rarish kind of summer whirlwind seemed entirely reasonable even to the most mischievous of Fortean onlookers and despite some doubts expressed by other meteorologists (few or none of whom had actually bothered to look at a circle for themselves). Hints dropped by Meaden that he was in the process of developing his model passed most of us by. We merely picked up from J. Met. of March 1985 that there were some interesting theoretical problems to be solved, one of them being the question why all circles found so far were swirled clockwise.

It was an interesting question. Perhaps something read J. Met. and decided to write a Letter to the Editor — though one composed in sign language and delivered in several instalments.

Rims and Rings, Wheels within Wheels

Shockingly, abruptly, during the summer of 1986, the wheel began to turn.

And acquired a rim . . .

And spun the rim into the space around it to make a ring . . .

And showed itself capable of the anti-clockwise . . .

Perhaps we shall never know the true order in which these things happened; perhaps the sequence lies buried in somebody's records; perhaps the actual succession of events escaped attention altogether. What is beyond doubt, however, is that the phenomenon was suddenly on the move again.

At Headbourne Worthy, to the north-east of

Figure 3. A selection of the patterns reported up to the end of 1989. These are schematic only, and are not to scale, nor necessarily in sequence. For simplicity, the diagram does not attempt to show the many different combinations of clockwise and anti-clockwise swirling in the components of the more complex events. It is debatable whether the 'swathed' circle should be considered strictly as a crop circle.

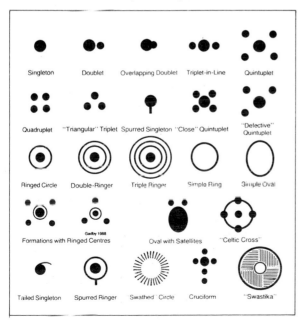

Winchester, a circle was found in August with — at last — an anticlockwise swirl. The event was multi-layered. Two things had evidently happened in quick succession. The first, found only by lifting up the top layer of the flattened grain, was an outward-going swirl in a vigorous anticlockwise spiral. Almost immediately there had been a 'change of mind'. The force had swirled back *inwards* and (again) anticlockwise, leaving the event with a mainly anticlockwise look to its visible, upper surface. Stranger than this 'doubling-back', however, was the final touch: a thin rim had been left at the very edge of the circle, though still confined within its circumference. Even the meticulous diagrams made by Terence Meaden and Colin Andrews (Fig. 4) do scant justice to this extraordinary occurrence.

During that same summer of 1986 *ringed* circles were reported — the earliest in June from those much frequented and closely observed areas of Bratton, Wiltshire (the site of those first 'simple'

Figure 4. Diagrams made by Terence Meaden and Colin Andrews of the complex 'rimmed' circle at Headbourne Worthy, Hampshire, in August 1986. Note striking differences in swirl between lower layer (left) and upper layer (right), and indications of a 'rim' in upper layer — powerful argument against hoax or other simplistic guesses.

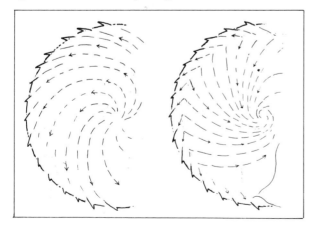

occurrences in 1980) and the punchbowl at Cheesefoot Head (host of the three-in-line of 1981). They are illustrated in several plates and figures in this book. They have been with us ever since. Setting aside the problem of the exact sequence of events, it is almost as though that rim at the edge of the Headbourne Worthy circle (and one or two other circles which have since, though rather rarely, been recorded) was the attempt of an experimental artist to break loose of the simple singleton in a still more dramatic manner than by making fivesomes.

But suspend your judgement for a while. Let us look for the least unlikely explanation we can find. Let us return to that 'stationary summer whirlwind' with which we began in 1980 and which had remained the model in J. Met. throughout these first seven years.

During its short history that summer whirlwind had proved versatile. It had shown itself able to bounce three times in a straight line while altering its diameter; to travel with a family of four, touching down with gentle precision in fivesome formation at the end of its brief life; to go anticlockwise when reminded of its duty to statistics; to make itself a rim; to cast a girdle round itself when it felt like doing so.

Some people began to wonder whether something else was casting girdles. Puck came up jocularly in private conversation (and gets his further look-in later in this book). Had something learned to ride the whirlwind? Was it really 'airs from heaven' which were making these things? Or were they blasts from some other place?

When, sometime later, anecdotes began to accumulate suggesting that the events of the 1980s had antecedents, one story told us was that country people (in Hampshire 40 years before) would never hand-reap circles found in the corn because they thought they were "uncanny and had some devilish origin". By the end of 1986 some people had begun to feel an uneasy prickle at the back of the neck.

In 1987 circles began to be found with *two* rings

around them. And the numbers found were growing. Belated reports from 1986 suggested (though with differing degrees of evidence) that at least one circle had sprouted a spur, and that a quintuplet had been found with a *ringed* centre.

The prickle at the back of the neck became, in some cases, an incipient shudder.

1987 to 1989: Phantasmagoria

A glance at Fig. 3 will show you the many new patterns which turned up to baffle us after 1986 and up to the end of 1989. And let it be noted that not one of them had been predicted — not by atmospheric physics, not by any of those drawn to more exotic speculations.

In a field to the south of Silbury Hill in Wiltshire, lying in the full gaze of the busy A4 road, a quintuplet was found on the morning of 15th July 1988. And then another on 26th July, intermingling with the first one at an angle of about 45°. And then a further three singletons in the same field about a week later. They added up to thirteen . . . But we were long past playing superstitious number-games! Plate 12 shows most of them.

Nothing much has ben reported from this field before, or from the area in which it lies — mysterious Silbury Hill, the largest man-made monument in Europe, whose purpose has never been discovered, together with its hinterland of other ancient sites. Why, some of us asked ourselves, have these things not been seen at Silbury until now if they are, as rational men would hope, a routine, even if a fairly rare, quirk of the atmosphere? (Now, in 1990, Terence Meaden informs me in a personal communication that his research group, Circles Effect Research — CERES — does in fact have traces of one-off occurrences in this area for the two preceding years. It is good to have this belated information; but it does little to diminish the impression that Silbury's rash of visitations in 1988 was virtually without predecessors).

In that same summer of 1988 a remarkable event occurred near Oadby in Leicestershire. It is better seen than heard — see that triangular array around a ringed centre in line 4 of Fig. 3.

Nothing like this had been reported before in circle history in this country; nothing like it has been seen since. Its nearest relation is an indentation in sun-baked earth in Australia, said to have happened in 1982, and far more closely resembling what ufologists would call a "UFO" nest than any gentle swirling in a modern English cornfield. Nonetheless, it came as a great relief to those who had been searching for instances outside over-haunted Wiltshire and Hampshire. And Meaden felt able to claim it as the partial fulfilment of a prediction he had made in the Journal of Meteorology in 1984. Partial only, it has to be added: nobody in 1984 was foreseeing *ringed* events: Meaden's forecast had been of a simple circle with three satellites. (It must also be said that the other forecasts made at the same time in the Journal of Meteorology from

Figure 5. Survey by Terence Meaden of a rare four-circle set from Leicestershire, June 1988 (not to scale). An aerial photograph of this circle system may be found in *The Circles Effect and its Mysteries*.

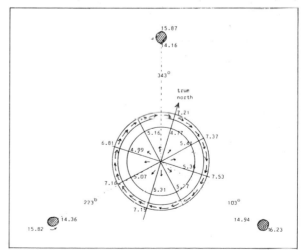

the standpoint of atmospheric physics have not yet been fulfilled.)

In the punchbowl field at Cheesefoot Head near Winchester, that already much-haunted site, there appeared in June 1988 not only a circle with two rings around it but, in the same month, and despite the angry surveillance of the farmer, an occurrence in which three singleton circles formed a triangular array — line 2 of Fig. 3. Something very similar was found a few days later about six miles to the southeast near Corhampton. (Plate 10.) It has not yet been seen again; there is only a very scanty trace of its having happened earlier. (In a personal communication of 1990 Terence Meaden tells me that CERES has reports of two similar events from 1982. Details have not yet been published. It is, again, welcome to have this information, even if only after the lapse of eight years. But it does not alter the impression that triangular arrays of singleton circles are a rare occurrence.)

Other ringed circles are reported from the summer of 1988; and the familiar quintuplets and singletons were also found. All of them, apart from that one-off event in Leicestershire, occurred in Wessex as far as we can now judge. And their numbers had greatly increased.

Valiant attempts — scientifically *necessary* attempts — have been made to dismiss that clustering in Wessex, together with the increase in numbers and the apparent elaboration of the patterns, as an 'accident of observation', the mere consequence of the fact that more of the researchers had been working — and with ever increasing keenness — in Hampshire and Wiltshire.

There is some truth in that 'clustering of observers'. George Wingfield (based in Somerset) had now joined Meaden, Colin Andrews, Pat Delgado, Busty Taylor and Richard Andrews. John Haddington, based in Scotland was sometimes able to join them. And there were one or two other friends and associates, notably Don Tuersley and Paul Fuller, who took part from time to time. But the total could be numbered on the fingers of two hands, and their eyes were on Wessex. It was a not unreasonable suggestion that the clustering of the phenomenon owed something to the clustering of these few individuals.

And yet . . . We were now in the eighth year of observation and the sixth year of media hype. The whole country had heard of circles. the number of newspaper articles and television snippets had passed beyond counting. Could it really be that many people outside Wessex had often seen these things and were merely keeping quiet?

Could it conceivably be the case, for example, that anybody — in Yorkshire or Nottinghamshire, say, or in Cumberland or Staffordshire or The Borders — could have glanced at his local hedge at something as remarkable as the 'Celtic Cross' (Plate 15) and line 4 of Fig. 3 and simply yawned, and gone away, and failed to mention it?

This beautiful event, pretty certainly the last of 1988, managed to combine two puzzles: it was not just a quintuplet, it was not just a ringed circle, it was a startling combination of the two. A problem for theoreticians, indeed . . . To laymen, seeking to follow the difficult technical argument presented from atmospheric physics, it was just possible to imagine a remarkable natural phenomenon which sometimes travelled as a fivesome, making quintuplets, and at other times went about with an outer sheath or two (as certain tornadoes are known to do), making ringed circles around the main disturbance. But it began to verge upon an act of faith to accept the notion of a fivesome circus which went about the place carrying its own circus ring.

Stranger still, a further look at the published record suggested that we had already had a hint from as far back as 1983, long before the ringed circles made their first appearance in 1986 that the phenomenon was toying not only with the idea of rings but also with the combination which produced the fully developed 'Celtic Cross' in 1988. A photograph of a quintuplet near Westbury, taken by Chris Wood of the *Daily Express* and published in *Flying Saucer Review*, shows the faintest of faint rings joining the four satellites. There is, again, that fanciful impression of an artist making a preliminary sketch but not returning to that particular canvas until five years later. In 1990, as we shall see below, this imagined artist has excelled himself with further startling elaborations of the 'Celtic Cross' (if that is what we should really be calling it), not to mention the other wonders which you will find in later plates.

As for numbers, there is no doubt about the increase in *reported* events in recent years. Terence Meaden, whose organisation, CERES, probably has the most complete database currently in existence, has kindly told me of his tally of 100 to 120 circles in the whole of the period from 1980 to 1987, followed by 112 for 1988, and 305 for 1989. At the time of writing (August 1990) the tally for the current year already exceeds 500. Later articles in this book will enable you to weigh up whether this is merely the consequence of the fact that more of us are now looking for these events or whether it reflects a real increase in occurrences.

The overwhelming majority of the 1989 events were found in Wessex, clustered in what have now become the three classical areas in southern England: Westbury/Warminster; the area within a ten-mile radius of Silbury Hill; and the haunted patch of country east of Winchester. You must, again, use your judgement about whether this reflects the concentration of serious researchers in Wessex or whether there is a 'Wessex Factor' which governs the distribution of these events.

In considering this, you must also remember that we had reports in 1989 (for virtually the first time with proper documentation) of perhaps a score or so of events from quite a large number of other English counties, most of them singletons and none of them showing the dramatic surprises which had turned up in Wessex.

In Wessex some totally new events occurred: 'Big Bertha', a ringed circle more than 100 feet across on Beckhampton Downs near Silbury Hill, the largest we had yet seen(photo, p. 82); a circle with a curlicue, 'The Tadpole' (Plate 24 and line 5 of Fig. 3), seen near Winchester shortly after some rash soul had said, "We shall soon have this thing by the tail"; three occurrences of what some observers have called 'The Cruciform' — see line 5 in Fig. 3; further occurrences in that very public field to the south of Silbury Hill in which a complex of thirteen had appeared in 1988, a field fully visible from the busy A4 road and frequently watched by police lest hoax should be in question; a great quantity of what some researchers have now come to call 'grapeshot', little circles of not more than ten feet across and sometimes smaller, but undoubtedly the genuine article and often giving the troubled field the look of a target riddled by giant shot-guns. By no means the least startling of the new events, however, even among that Barnum & Bailey Circus of 1989, was a mischievous circle which had the cheek to contradict a scientist within a few days of the publication of his book.

This impertinent event was a circle with a single ring around it, the kind of thing we were now quite used to. It turned up on the Longwood Estate in a field a little to the south-west of Cheesefoot Head at some time during the small hours of the morning of 18th June 1989. Its advent was accompanied by strange events (see George Wingfield's article later in this book). Equally strange was the new puzzle it presented for atmospheric physics.

Writing in *The Circles Effect and its Mysteries*, advance copies of which had become public by mid-June, Terence Meaden had noted from his carefully collected data that "Single rings around single circles always rotate in a sense opposite to that of the interior". This means that if the swirl in the centre of a ringed event goes clockwise, the ring is anticlockwise (and vice versa). This counter-rotation of ring and circle seemed to be necessary if

Meaden's atmospheric vortex, coupled with the surrounding sheaths which he had to postulate to account for the ringed events, was to act with all the necessary precision and not to tumble about while doing so. Meaden's generalisation sounded sensible to most of us.

But something else had perhaps read Meaden's book . . . We have noted before that the phenomenon seems to be among his most attentive readers. What was found on the morning of 18th June was a ringed circle in which both components rotated in the same direction.

This was not the sort of stuff which makes headline news. The newspapers did not report it. It is doubtful that any Fleet Street reporter would have expected his readers to be thrilled by this little oddity. But to those who were watching events more closely it sounded like the final nail in the coffin of any theory which depended solely upon an atmospheric vortex. But that final nail of 1989 had not yet been hammered home. It was almost the end of the season before the blow struck. It fell at Winterbourne Stoke, not far from Stonehenge in Wiltshire. It produced the event which illustrates the front cover of this book.

Atmospheric vortices often do great damage. Perhaps they sometimes touch the earth more gently, leaving no more than the prettiest of swirls. Perhaps they can clad themselves with a rotating sheath or two. But the essence of them is to be circular. What circular disturbance, we must ask ourselves, is able to make what looks like the symbolic figure of a swastika in a field of grain?

And what circular disturbance, however exotic its properties, can possibly explain the events depicted in the Frontispiece and illustrated in the plates 34 onwards?

ARE THEY VERY NEW? OR VERY OLD?

The strong appearance is of something which began to happen in 1980 and has since developed at an astonishing rate both in numbers and elaboration. About that development there can hardly be much doubt: if any of us had reservations up to the end of 1989, they have now been dispelled by the events of 1990. Something very new seems to be in train at this end of the twentieth century.

But it is not entirely without precedents. Later pages discuss the scanty evidence we have of a few occurrences before 1980; and Bob Rickard's article describes the strange — but also strangely elusive — links with a long history of myth and folklore. Moreover, the remarkable parallels with very ancient signs and symbols which are drawn by Michael Green and John Haddington in Part Three of the book suggest that we may be dealing with something which has haunted human consciousness from time immemorial.

Again we have a paradox, an enigma. The physical evidence — the evidence 'on the ground' — is of something which is far too recent to have been the cause of all our ancient myths and 'metaphysical imaginings'. Yet those myths and imaginings are as old as human history.

Was there once another era, long ago, when patterns were stamped into crop fields throughout the inhabited world by unknown forces? Did they inspire such reverence and awe that they came to be commemorated in the construction of stone circles, the forms of temples and burial places, the creation of myths and legends, the designs on the mosaic floors of sacred buildings, the formation of Buddhist mandalas? And if so, why did those forces cease to operate until very recently?

Or does that vast symbology of humankind come from some other source — the human mind itself, or the human mind informed by dreams and visions put into it from elsewhere? And have those dreams and visions now taken to stamping themselves upon the landscape in physical form? And if so, how and why?

We may soon have to choose between these alternatives if we are to make progress. For the moment the enigma remains. Only further research will point us in the right direction.

ARE THEY WORLD-WIDE?

For most of the past eleven years there has been an overwhelming impression of a phenomenon concentrated largely in Wiltshire and Hampshire, and clustering very markedly in three areas in those counties. Anecdotes existed of events elsewhere in Britain and in several countries around the world, but attempts made by most of us to validate these stories either failed to produce hard evidence in the form of photographs or drawings, or led us to incidents which were certainly *not* crop circles, strictly defined.

It is, for example, notable that those who were seeking events outside Wessex began to include in their tally at a very early stage ground-level disturbances, well documented in the literature of ufology, which had not occurred in crops, exhibited none of the delicate precision of the crop circle events, and almost invariably lacked the complications of pattern with which we have become familiar in the cropfields.

Terence Meaden, for example, writing in the Journal of Meteorology in 1983 (vol. 8/no. 75), saw little difficulty in embracing an event reported from Tully in Australia in 1966 in which reeds in a swampy lagoon had been violently uprooted and widely scattered, leaving a patch of disturbance which some ufologists described as "a UFO nest". A near-witness to the disturbance had in fact reported an unidentified aerial object at about the same time. Meaden's comment, under the heading "A Mystery No Longer", was that the reported "bluish-grey spaceship" could well have been "a whirlwind rising and then literally 'disappearing into thin air' as it moved off . . .".

Many hundreds of other disturbances at ground level, supported by photographs and drawings, rest in the annals of ufology from the last forty-seven years and from virtually all countries for which information exists. They have been the subject of much fervent debate. The diminishing band of those who believe that we are being visited by extraterrestrial life-forms claim these disturbances as 'UFO nests' or 'UFO landing traces', and they use the acronym UFO (unidentified flying object) as though it were a noun with the meaning 'extraterrestrial space-craft'. (The same band of enthusiasts quickly identified the quintuplet occurrences in the Wessex cropfields in 1983 as the latest evidence for their point of view, much to the amusement of the silly-season Press and the rage of more sobre researchers). Most ufologists, anyway in recent years, have simply suspended their judgement about the cause of these many peculiar markings, and many of them would welcome the kind of meteorological explanation for which Meaden has been seeking.

But a 'UFO nest' is one thing and a crop circle is quite another. Look at the many pictures in this book; examine Figs. 3 and Frontispiece again; recall that crop circles occur almost invariably in *crops* (tidily avoiding field boundaries); and then ask yourself whether these events can possibly be placed in the same category as such things as the following, all drawn from the literature of ufology: a circular mark gouged to a depth of several inches in *rocky*, sun-baked ground; a circular, saucer-shaped depression in soft earth, many feet in diameter and a foot or so deep at its deepest point, *lacking any indication of 'swirl'*; a large circular patch in an arable field *from which the crops have totally disappeared* without other damage occurring; a large circular *scorch-mark* in bare earth. And remember that in almost none of the many hundreds of comparable cases which could be cited has there been anything approaching the more elaborate patterns depicted in Figs. 3 and Frontispiece.

In *The Circles Effect and its Mysteries* Terence Meaden provides two maps (pp. 106 and 107) which purport to show a wide incidence of crop circle occurrences in England, and a world-wide scatter of 'circles-effect vortices'. But the data on which these maps depend has not yet been published. Until we know what kinds of event have been included it seems to your editor entirely premature to conclude that the crop circles we now know so well from the Wessex cropfields are a world-wide phenomenon.

But they may be becoming so . . .! One small singleton, supported by a photograph which places the event fairly clearly in the crop circle category, has reached us from the United States in 1990 (associated, as it happens, with an on-going series of strange UFO events in Florida). In December 1989 a group of large singletons was reported from an arable farm in Australia, possessing all the necessary characteristics of precision and swirl and differing markedly in these respects from the many earlier 'UFO nests' and 'landing-traces' which Australian UFO researchers have reported for many years past. It is also beyond doubt — because the photographs and information have been *published* — that many other counties in England and at least one in Scotland were 'visited' by crop circles, strictly defined, during 1989. Before that, we had merely had the one fully documented case in Leicestershire mentioned above. In 1990 there is every indication at the time of going to press that the phenomenon is occurring country-wide, though Wessex remains the focus for most of the more spectacular events.

To the question "Are they world-wide?" the answer must for the moment be (as a British Prime Minister once put it), "Wait and see".

HAVE WE SEEN ONE FORMING?

Well, we tried to . . . In June 1989 an eight-day operation was mounted by Colin Andrews on a hillside overlooking that much haunted field in the punchbowl at Cheesefoot Head. About sixty of us took part, watching for twenty-four hours a day in three eight-hour shifts and using a great deal of expensive equipment. The operation was called *White Crow*. An account of it, together with a description of its strange aftermath, is given in George Wingfield's article. Suffice it to say here that we were clearly pointing our instruments and our attention in the wrong direction — or something decided to teach us a lesson. For the whole of those eight days not only did we fail to detect anything in the field we were watching, but no circles were reported from anywhere in the country, though we had already had ninety or so in Wessex up to the start of the operation. As we were packing up to go . . . But read what Wingfield has to tell you. Operation *White Crow* was, from one point of view, a dismal failure; from another, it had the appearance of a very close encounter.

Other — unplanned — close encounters have been reported. They remain very much debated; people of different views have read into them whatever suits their immediate purposes. They have been taken as evidence for UFO visitation, poltergeist manifestation, the flickering of 'earth energies', the side-effects of an atmospheric vortex.

Examined closely, the few narratives we have of the supposed witnessing of crop circles in the act of forming are a strange collection of very different kinds of experience — ranging from the upward spiralling of an evening whirlwind in 1983, when whirlwinds were the leading guess from meteorology, to the downward descent of some vast luminous object near Margate in 1989 in the small hours of the morning, when Terence Meaden had developed his theory of a plasma vortex with electrical and electromagnetic properties (and something perhaps decided to give him some support for it — it had rarely done so before).

In between, we were given accounts of daylight sightings of misty cones of something vaporous rising (or descending?) at ground level; and of the sweep of some invisible force in a field of grain which then abruptly pivoted about an invisible centre to make a circle. Most recently, we have had an account from Scotland in which the witness speaks (in one version) of a mysterious darkening of the dawn sky and the falling silent of the dawn chorus of wild birds before the circles formed before his eyes in rustling barley which laid itself flat in the still and peaceful morning air.

Material has also been invoked from the literature of ufology: in a famous account that veteran ufologist, Arthur Shuttlewood, reported that he and a party of friends, walking near UFO-haunted Warminster in Wiltshire, saw *grass* (not crops) laying itself flat in a clockwise spiral, "just like the opening of a lady's fan", in the absence of any visible or tangible agency. And we have another comparable report from Shuttlewood in which only the segment of a circle seems to have been formed, again in the presence of some invisible force.

It seems to your editor that markedly different things have been seen on different occasions — or that we are dealing with a Protean something which adapts its performance either according to its own whim or to suit (or tease) its human observers. I believe we are still far from a decisive sighting. We need well-mounted and carefully planned surveillance operations in which we are prepared to wait and watch for a long time, preferably well away from media attention, and with the aim of gaining knowledge rather than swift publicity.

HOAX?

If patriotism is the last refuge of a scoundrel, hoax is the last refuge of those who cannot bear to face uncomfortable facts. Hoaxes we have indeed had — sensationally so at the ill-fated *Blackbird* operation mounted by Colin Andrews and Pat Delgado in July and August 1990 (see Epilogue). But that notorious fraud, perpertrated for obscure though undoubtedly mischievous purposes, was very quickly detected as such by its unfortunate victims. As for the general run of occurrences, Terence Meaden and other experienced observers have personally surveyed over 1000 crop circles; they know a hoax when they see one.

But for those who distrust the 'appeal to authority' and still cherish the thought that hoax may explain it all or most of it, the following questions need answering.

What pantechnicon of skilful technicians has succeeded for eleven years in rushing about Wessex and, latterly, other parts of the country, not to mention the wider world, without ever being detected, even in the most public areas? (Remember those thirteen circles which formed on three separate occasions in 1988 in the full gaze of the much frequented A4 road). What techniques have enabled them to produce the patterns depicted in Fig. 3 and more particularly those very large, complex and much elaborated patterns of the latter part of the 1990 season? Why have so many of their efforts been directed to remote and hidden parts of farmland, where the event may never be reported? Why have they tended to hoax ellipses rather than simple circles? What is their motive? (If Richard Branson is behind it all, he has waited inordinately long to tell us what he is trying to make us buy.)

Hoax, as a general theory, can be consigned to the dustbin of 'explanationism', together with hedgehogs, helicopters, funguses and all such other hideaways from the marvellous. But we must now be on guard for those who, for whatever reason, wish to muddy the record by crude practical jokes.

1990

It would be wrong to say that 1990 has passed beyond belief. Belief doesn't come into it. The circles are *there*, tangibly, visibly, measurably. They are there for all to see. There can be no doubt about their physical, their palpable, existence. We don't have to *believe* in them, we merely have to observe them — and to puzzle our wits about them.

But it now requires an act of faith to suppose that anything short of some revolutionary advance in our understanding of the world can possibly explain them. They are no longer merely 'circles', some of them have become intricate designs of great force and beauty. Perhaps even the word 'explain' is now the wrong one to be using if by 'explain' we simply mean 'explain away' in terms of current scientific paradigms. Some larger conception now seems imperative.

At the time at which this Introduction is being written we have already had well over four hundred circles, the preponderance of them in 'haunted' Wessex, but with 'outbreaks' in many other counties. Patterns have been seen which we could hardly have dreamed of, even by the most fanciful elaboration of all the phantasmagoria which is well documented from 1989.

Not one of the astonishing new events of this current season has ever been predicted — not by the hardest-headed of scientific hypotheses, not by the wildest of the many other fancies which have been on offer. Whatever agency is making these things — and you must take your pick from the wide spectrum which runs from 'blind natural force' to 'non-human intelligence' — it is running so far ahead of us that we can only stumble along behind it with an awkward, shambling and sometimes comical gait.

But enough is now known from 1990 to give further collateral to a fanciful thought which has been mentioned several times in this Introduction.

A *development* is in train.

It shows every sign of 'purpose' (whatever 'purpose' may mean).

THIS BOOK AND WHAT IT TRIES TO DO

I hope that enough has been said in this Introduction to make clear that no single mind, not even the mind of that dedicated scientist, Terence Meaden, yet seems near to solving our riddle. Meaden himself says in his article that the phenomenon may be capable of generating hundreds of patterns which we have not yet seen and which cannot at present be predicted. No apology is needed in 1990 for the decision by the editor and publisher of this book to invoke not only a summary of Meaden's latest thinking but also a wide range of other views.

I will also myself, as editor, exercise an editor's licence — by no means to express opinions (which, in editors, is always a doubtful practice), but merely to stress once more an overwhelming impression which the *facts* appear to force upon us.

The facts — the sheer brute history of this subject — suggest that we have an agency at work which exihibits a degree of skill, an agency which makes a preliminary sketch, pauses a while to take stock of its handiwork, and then goes on to complete the polished version. An agency which, after a while, grows bored with what it is doing . . . And doesn't do it again, except perhaps to keep its hand in . . . And then stretches its imagination further.

Appearance is, of course, one thing, actuality may be another. We must be on our guard against seeing patterns where none exist. The story of 'The Wessex Corridor' and 'The "W" factor', given later, is an entertaining tale to caution us against idle fancies; Hilary Evans is right to remind us of the human faculty for making mysteries out of mole-hills; and we must never forget that silly-season flurry of 1983, when quintuplets became the landing marks of our Brothers from Above.

And yet . . .

Glance at the cover of this book. Study that 'swastika', that very *un*-round occurrence, that most *un*-vortical event. Give it whatever name you will. Then study what seems to be the first rough sketch of it a few weeks earlier in a nearby field (Plate 25). Was something *practising* on that earlier occasion? Did it give us the 'completed version' — the version which might be offered to galleries or to eccentric millionaires — a short while later in Busty Taylor's remarkable photograph which graces this book?

Consider the 'Celtic Cross' of 1988 (Plate 15). Remember what seemed to be the first faint hint of it in 1983. Then closely examine the 'Celtic Cross Elaborated', which appeared in May 1990 (Plate 28). And then the 'Celtic Cross Exaggerated' of June 1990. Is this a mere accident of the sequence in which events have become known to us? Or has something been perfecting its techniques as the years have passed?

Consider that *'rimmed'* circle of 1986 (Fig. 4 above). And then its *ringed* successors . . . And its *double-ringed* successors . . . And its treble-ringed successors . . . And its successors which have, in 1990, cast no fewer than *four* rings around them . . . Are we to blame the hard-pressed, over-worked observers for having inadvertently created that strong appearance of 'designed development'? Or are we, instead, to guess at some other factor, some other agency? Did something find it amusing to put a ring round its singleton handiwork in 1986 (bursting beyond that mere *rim*), and then to make two, three and even four rings around itself?

Consider the dimensions of those first singletons of the early nineteen-eighties; some of them reached sixty feet across but most were smaller. Then recall 'Big Bertha' of 1989 with its diameter of well over a hundred feet, not including that determined (if somewhat shaky) ring around it (photo, p. 82). Then glance at the *Epilogue*, where you will find an event which is close to three hundred feet in diameter. Is it merely we poor humans who are creating the appearance of this extraordinary elaboration by our failure to look over hedges before 1980?

Consider . . . But this Introduction has already tried your patience far enough.

It is against this background of mounting wonder that we have felt it imperative to include in this book not only the scientific arguments presented by Terence Meaden and George Wingfield but also material drawn from many other fields: the remarkable parallels which Michael Green draws with ancient metaphysical symbols, based on his experience as an archaeologist; John Haddington's insights drawn from systems of philosophy; Richard Andrews' perception, as an experienced dowser, that the land itself is vibrant with invisible energies; Bob Rickard's ingenious links with folklore; John Michell's Fortean and Puckish insights; Hilary Evans' remarkable observations on the psycho-social — perhaps even psycho-physical! — factors which may be at work.

If you share the perplexities which this book exposes, we also hope that you will share its sense of excitement. Write to us with your views — care of the publisher of this book, or care of the editor of *The Cereologist*, the Journal for Crop Circle Studies. If you want to take part more actively, join the Centre for Crop Circle Studies. (The necessary addresses wil be found elsewhere in this book).

Above all, keep your sense of wonder in these strange occurrences of the late-twentieth century. They may possibly mean more than any of us can yet divine.

REFERENCES

1. Fuller, C.P. A sample survey of the incidence of geometrically-shaped crop damage. BUFORA/TORRO 1988

Sources My main source in compiling the history of the cropfield events have been many issues of the *Journal of Meteorology* which have dealt with the subject since Vol.6/no.57 of 1981; the books and journals mentioned in Professor Roy's Foreword; and the many personal communications which I have had by courtesy of *Country Life* and from field researchers, particularly Terence Meaden and George Wingfield. But I alone am responsible for all errors and omissions.

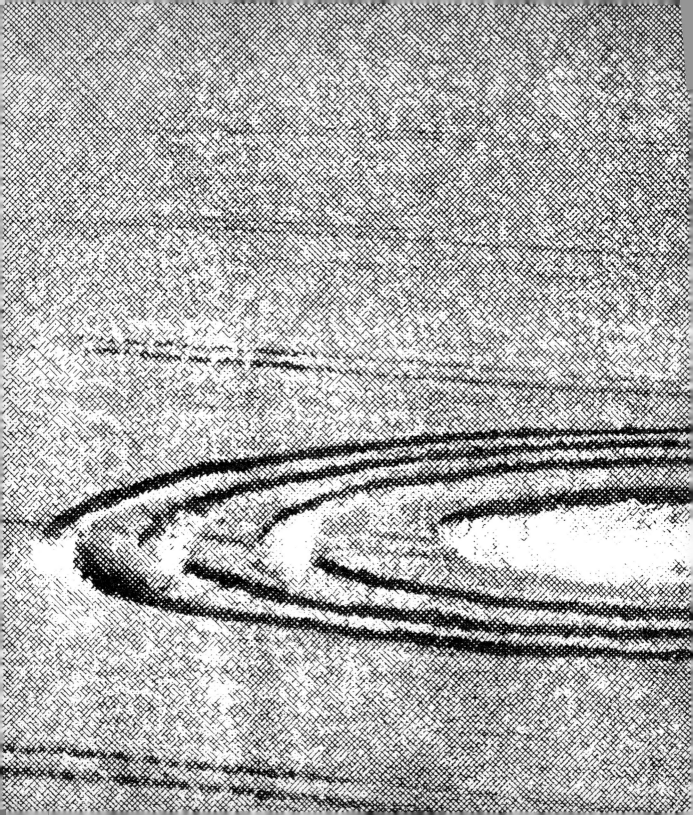

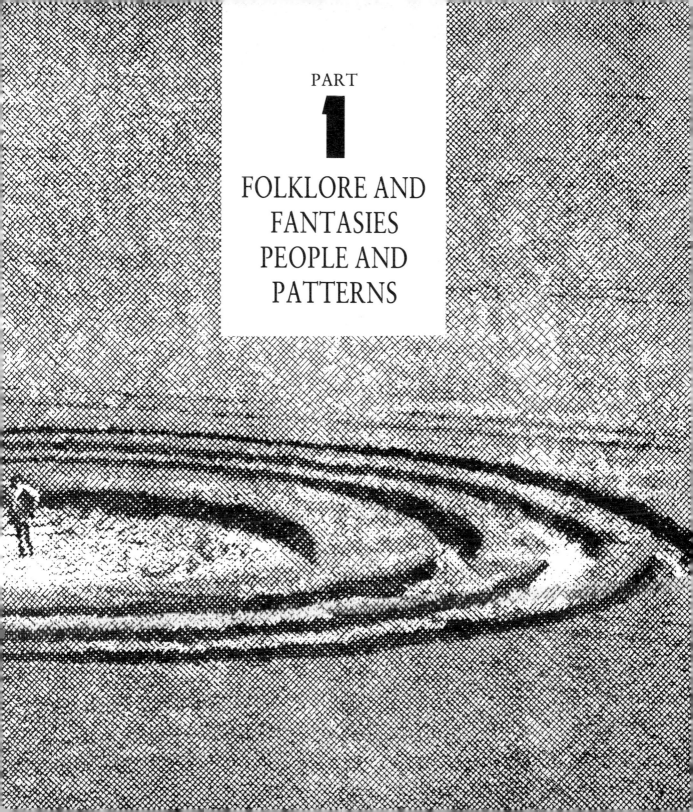

PART
1
FOLKLORE AND FANTASIES PEOPLE AND PATTERNS

PATTERNS

Do people make patterns? Do patterns make people?

Between ourselves and the world around us there is a more complex interplay than we used to think.

In the days of the great Victorian anthropologists — J. G. Frazer, in *The Golden Bough*, was their belated and last exemplar — the traffic was seen as wholly in one direction. Benighted savages, awed by the great forces of Nature which they could neither control nor understand, had as we then saw it: taken refuge in foolish superstition and fruitless magic. Latter-day gentlemen of suitable social class and adequate learning could afford some good-natured loftiness about these primitive imaginings. Technology had conquered much; science stood near to a final understanding of the mindless forces around us; our species had nearly triumphed. It was not long since Lord Kelvin had urged a sharp reduction in the intake of student physicists to Imperial College, London, on the grounds that little now remained to be done except to tidy up some loose ends at the edge of knowledge.

But wheels turn, and they tend to come full circle. In our own times, the mysteries of physics have increased instead of diminishing. "I hope," said that great physicist, Richard Feynman, in his *QED: The Strange Theory of Light and Matter* [Penguin Books, London, 1985], "that you can accept Nature as She is — absurd". And he reflects the temper of the age in giving back to Nature (even if perhaps in fancy) that soubriquet of the Great Mother, "She" — with a capital initial letter.

Magic and (as some would see it) 'superstition' are once more back in vogue. Cults abound, many of them as arrogant and foolish in their pretensions as the least perceptive of the more blinkered of nineteenth century scientists. The traffic has again become one-way — but in the opposite direction. The self-appointed magi, each with his own hot-line to the invisible Powers which favour him (all others being corrupt or evil rivals), seek to exert control from Man to Nature and expect to gain it. We stand at risk of the emergence of some new terrible faith (when the sects have fought it out and burned a heretic or two). It is hardly to be wondered at that scientists of the dogged determination and humane values of Dr. Terence Meaden are prepared to carry their scientific speculations to great lengths in opposition to the dangerous and undisciplined dogmatisms which they see springing up around us.

But there seems to many of us to be a middle way between 'magic' and 'mechanism', between the rival faiths that 'all is material' and 'all is spiritual'.

More than a century of laboured gathering of facts in psychical research and related fields puts it, for many of us, quite beyond doubt that the traffic between Man and Nature is a two-way process — and not merely in the trivial sense that muscles move matter. In circumstances which we are yet far from understanding (but which undoubtedly occur) human will interacts with the way the world works — and the world sometimes plays tricks upon us in a manner which lies far beyond the grasp of current paradigms.

Momentous truths lie buried in the mass of strange material from which these insights spring. And, alas, 'buried' is the operative word. The facts are elusive and sometimes whimsical; they do not occur to order; they come and go abruptly, like the lightning; and they are muddied and muddled by the mischievous intervention of human hoaxers and the gullible yearnings of those who seek instantaneous illumination or instantaneous power.

In the first article in this part of the book HILARY EVANS draws our attention, very rightly, to these human gullibilities — to the all-too-ready tendency to see patterns where none exist, even in our dealings with so tangible, so *undeniable*, a phenomenon as the remarkable markings in our fields of crops. But he also examines the possibility that in some strange way the patterns which we can establish beyond doubt owe something to an interaction between the 'blind' forces of Nature and deeply hidden faculties and forces of the human imagination. Are we witnessing in the crop circle phenomenon something like psychokinesis on a scale which only such mavericks as Charles Fort and a few others have hitherto dared to contemplate?

In *Clutching at Straws* ROBERT J. M. RICKARD (a Fortean to his fingertips) relates what is now happening in our crop-fields to myths and rituals of very great antiquity. We again see the possibility of a creative interaction between Man and the Great Mother which our forebears instinctively perceived under the modes of magic but which we, at last — nearing the end of the twelfth millenium since we emerged from our sunless caverns at the passing of the last Ice Age — may now be on the verge of integrating into the great enterprise of the last three centuries of hard-headed scientific endeavour.

What Mean these Marks ? asks JOHN MICHELL at the conclusion of this part. And 'meaning' will be as much a preoccupation of this book as the nearer-to-earth question of what forces — what physical goings-on — succeed in making these extraordinary patterns we have witnessed with increasing elaboration during these past eleven years.

Do men make patterns or do patterns make men? You will find in this part of the book some indication that the question is mistaken. The answer may be that we and the world belong to a single pattern.

The crop circle paradox

Anomaly-fact, anomaly-cluster, anomaly-image and anomaly-spill

H I L A R Y   E V A N S

FROM ANOMALY TO MACRO-ANOMALY

The manner in which the crop circle phenomenon is manifesting is bizarre sufficiently so to encourage many to look for correspondingly bizarre explanations. So, underlying the anomaly itself, they discern — or think they discern — a macro-anomaly.

Without being obliged to take seriously the more facile hypotheses — extraterrestrial spacecraft, ley lines, etc. — those who interest themselves in the cultural dynamics of rumour, myth and fantasy are finding that the crop circle phenomenon is generating a rich harvest of grist for their mill. So much so, that it does not seem ridiculous to ask whether, beneath the particular manifestations, some more general process — benign or sinister or simply the inexorable working of cosmic destiny — may be at work? Is it really too outrageous to contemplate some such hypothesis as this:-

From time to time a collective cultural impulse is generated by a community, sufficiently powerful to cause a wave of anomalous happenings to occur.

These happenings, because they transcend consensus ideas of the limitations of 'reality', force the community to open more widely its collective mind so as to admit as possibilities phenomena which were hitherto considered impossible. It may even be inferred that it was for the purpose of bringing about this wider scope of the possible that the original impulse was generated.

Hypotheses of this kind have been proposed periodically in the past, and come in many forms. The most notable variants, of course, are those which propose that the impulse which extends our frontiers of perceived reality emanates from some *external* source, subtly introduced by this or that 'them' into our (your and my, among others) 'group mind' or whatever. Jacques Vallee's 'control system' hypothesis[1] is perhaps the most acceptable version of this myth: he proposes that some extra-human power is subjecting the human species to a process of education, in the form of UFOs and other paranormal phenomena: crop circles would no doubt be just another such manifestation, designed to set us all thinking — so that even a book like this can be seen as an educational exercise whereby we are all, we the writers and you the reader, stretching our intellectual grasp . . .

Among other frameworks on offer, those in which such ideas might find not-too-uncomfortable lodging are perhaps those of Jung[2] and Sheldrake[3].

Such hypotheses have been implied, if not formally proposed, in respect of other anomalies, long before the crop circles came to widespread attention. The writings of John Keel[4] are perhaps the most obvious example: it is probably true to say that no one researcher has done more to rattle the conventional approach to the study of anomalous phenomena. It remains a matter for argument whether this has been ultimately to the benefit of anomaly research. Insofar as Keel has encouraged serious and thoughtful researchers to extend their notions of the possible, he can have done nothing but good; but insofar as he has encouraged flightier minds to espouse dubious notions for which the evidence is less than adequate, he may have done more harm than good.

Before we go any farther, I should in all honesty say that personally, while I am ready to entertain such a hypothesis, I am not yet convinced that we need it. Along with conspiracy theories, control-system theories, ancient wisdom theories and other such, I see these macro-scenarios as exercises in mythmaking, enjoyable enough as an armchair pursuit, but not serving more productive purposes.

At the same time, I feel obliged to recognise that my reluctance may stem from an unspoken fear that such a view threatens all the carefully assembled notions which piece together to form the structure of 'my' world-picture: maybe it is precisely to shake the complacency of stick-in-the-mud folk like me that the crop circles occur: this, in other words, is what the frontier-extending hypothesis is all about!

And I certainly recognise the obligation of any satisfactory hypothesis to offer a plausible explanation for *why* these anomalies should present us with such a challenge. In the case of the crop circles, why are they appearing *now* in increasing numbers and complexity? why so much more prevalently here in England than anywhere else? why do their manifestations so often display a mind-boggling synchronicity? and why should they seem to present such an appearance of intelligent direction?

Why should what is seemingly a straightforward natural puzzle, seemingly solvable in straightforward natural terms, display such devious and artificial characteristics? Or, if they are not devious and artificial, why should we think them so?

And (clearly not an unrelated question) why have the crop circles — like some, but not all other anomalies — generated such widespread and often highly colourful popular response?

ANOMALY-FACT AND ANOMALY-SPILL

In considering each of the classic anomalies of the past, it is helpful to draw a distinction between, on the one hand, the primary anomaly — the anomaly-fact, the UFO, the otherworldly vision, or whatever; and on the other, what we may label the anomaly-spill — the cultural artefact which is its parasite (though confusingly often bearing the same name).

Thus we need to distinguish between the 'fact' (such as it is) of witchcraft and the 'spill' of the witch mania; between the 'fact' of 'phantom airships', and the 'spill' of airship scare they inspired between the fact' of UFOs and the 'spill' which takes the form either of the 'science' of ufology or of the 'religion' of saucer cultism to which they gave birth; between the 'fact' of 'UFO' abductions and the "spill" of the abduction mania currently running riot in the United States.

The distinction can be seen most clearly cut in the case of religious visions, where the primary experience — Bernadette's private encounter with the Virgin — leads to the secondary experience, that of the countless pilgrims who participate vicariously and extremely publicly in 'the Lourdes experience'.[5]

EFFECTS WITHOUT A CAUSE?

Anomalies fall into two more-or-less clearly-defined categories:

those where the existence of the anomaly fact is not in doubt; and

those where it is.

One of the most puzzling (but also one of the most revealing) aspects of anomalies is this: that *whether or not an anomaly is known to exist in fact, it is equally capable of generating anomaly-spill.*

In a good many cases — for example, the pre-World War One airship scare in Britain — while testimony is abundant, physical evidence is meagre to the point of non-existence.[6] Similarly, the lively interest currently being taken in alien abductions largely consists of a disagreement as to whether any physical event is occurring or whether the claimed experiences are no more than psychosocial fabrications lacking any correlation in the physical world[7]

However, in the case of our crop circles, the existence — visible, tangible and photographable with the crudest instamatic — is manifest. Which confronts us with the next paradox.

The crop circles appear to be much the same kind of natural anomaly as we find catalogued in volume after volume of William Corliss's wonderful Sourcebooks.[8] We would suppose, therefore, that in the normal course of events they would undergo the same fate as most of the anomalies he lists: first to be reported by an observer, then perhaps discussed in the correspondence columns for an issue or two of some learned journal; then catalogued by a Fort[9] or a Corliss; and thereafter left to rest, to be a momentary source of wonder for the occasional reader, but exciting no widespread public or scientific interest.

Once in a while, however, a primary anomaly will generate anomaly-spill. It is unlikely that this will occur if the anomaly is one-of-a-kind: almost always, anomaly-spill occurs only after the anomaly has recurred a number of times.

But this very fact requires us to face up to yet another paradox . . .

FROM 'ANOMALY' TO 'ANOMALY-CLUSTER'

From the moment when, for whatever reason, public attention is focused on an anomaly, it is likely that a snowball effect will occur. What happens is that other events, which may or may not be related, are gathered under the same umbrella. Ball-lightning is just one example where it is evident that the label is being incorrectly applied to a number of disparate phenomena.[10]

We may describe the resulting collection as an 'anomaly cluster'. It is rare that an anomaly becomes the focus of widespread interest until a cluster has been created from the one-off events. The process is well exemplified in the case of the 'bedroom visitor' experiences studied by Hufford, who found that by identifying and labelling his phenomenon, he caused witnesses to appear who, more often than not, would tell him that until they read or heard his ideas, they had not known what to make of their experience.[11] I expect something of the sort to occur in the case of street light interference currently being studied by SLIDE:[12] time and time again a respondent will tell us they thought their experience was unique until they heard through SLIDE that others too have known such experiences.

But while the material which composes the anomaly-cluster may not always be homogeneous, it may prove difficult to sort out the genuine from the spurious. Indeed, it may not be a case of spurious, so much as a 'different kind of genuine' which has got mixed up with the rest. Unless researchers are on their guard, they may end up treating as alike, phenomena which are only superficially similar. Clearly this is what has happened with the UFO phenomenon, which is surely a number of separate phenomena lumped together by people who failed to see the necessity of sorting out one from t'other — or who, for reasons perhaps not even admitted to themselves, did not wish to do so.

'ANOMALY-FACT' AND 'ANOMALY-IMAGE'

Even an anomaly whose existence is not established as fact can be recurrent: and it may help our overall comprehension of the problem to see how this paradox can occur. The sabbats of the witches in the 16th/17th centuries is one notorious example, while in our own time once again the UFO demonstrates the same process revealingly.

What has happened with the UFOs is that the anomaly-fact — some genuinely puzzling observations — generated a pseudo-anomaly, which we may conveniently label the 'anomaly-image'. It came to be believed that these puzzling observations were caused not, as might reasonably have been supposed, by existing phenomena observed under unusual conditions, but by a specific phenomenon existing in its own right, which was labelled 'UFO', thereby leading to a forty-year breakdown of communication between those who use the term 'unidentified flying object' to mean no more than it says, and those who use it to refer to a specific hypothesis (usually that of extraterrestrial spacecraft).

And as we are all sadly aware, the public concept of UFOs usually relates to the anomaly-image rather than to any anomaly-fact.

We may reasonably suppose that in any instance where the anomaly-image differs from the anomaly itself (which is probably virtually every instance) the difference results from a cultural process.

From which we may reasonably take one step further, and infer that the same cultural process which modifies anomaly-fact to anomaly-image is also that which generates the anomaly-spill.

But it may be more meaningful if we put it the other way about, and see the process of replacing anomaly-fact with anomaly-image as the first, and probably necessary, step in the generation of anomaly-spill.

That is to say, in terms of the macro-process which is supposed to be occurring, *the bringing about of the anomaly-spill is the true purpose of the process, and the transformation of anomaly-fact to anomaly-image no more than a means to that end.*

To summarise:

1. an anomalous event occurs — the anomaly-fact

2. the anomaly recurs, and/or other anomalous occurrences are lumped with it, and an anomaly cluster is created

3. the anomaly cluster is given a label and a definition, usually sufficiently loose to allow for a variety of interpretation within a limited range: by this means the anomaly-fact is replaced, in general awareness, by an anomaly-image

4. the anomaly-image attracts all kinds of cultural response which together form the anomaly-spill.

The psychological and sociological dynamics are not necessarily difficult to discern. For example, psychology offers viable explanations as to why a Bernadette might have her encounter with the Virgin, irrespective of whether any physical event occurred.[13] In turn, sociology offers explanations as to why millions of pilgrims should respond to Bernadette's primary experience by creating, by their own efforts, the secondary anomaly-spill.[5]

Generally such explanations are on the lines of 'an idea whose time has come', and it is not usually a problem to identify the specific sociological factors operating, either singly or more usually synergistically, in any particular instance. Thus the transformation of anomalous aerial phenomena into the anomaly-image of 'UFOs-as-vehicles-of-extraterrestrial-visitation', and the consequent emergence of cults taking this concept as the basis for their beliefs, can be accounted for easily enough by reference to the decline of religion, the coming of the space age, dissatisfaction with terrestrial leaders, etc.

I don't doubt that at this very moment, the behavioural scientists are getting to work on the crop circles, identifying cultural motivations within the collective unconscious and charting the dynamics of their emergence as authorised myth. Good luck to them.

HOW CROP CIRCLES FIT THE PATTERN

Our present outbreak of crop circles seems to be conforming neatly enough to the pattern outlined above:

The anomaly-fact: the circles themselves, presenting a particularly puzzling phenomenon for which science is not immediately able to provide a plausible answer.

The anomaly cluster: all kinds of circular traces and contingent events are added, rightly or wrongly, to bulk out the phenomenon.

The anomaly-image: following on suggestions that the circles might be created by UFOs, positioned along ley-lines, and so on, the matter is allowed to get out of hand — out of the hands, that is, of the scientists, and into those of the supernaturalists who exploit the phenomenon because its very physical reality offers a welcome confirmation for ideas which all too often lack any physical evidence.

The anomaly-spill: fuelled by those who visit the circles armed with their own private insights (perhaps supported by private gadgetry of the 'black-box' type whose undeclared function is to exteriorise the subjective response as some kind of measurable effect), enabling them to report vibrations and mysterious forces of the earth-mystery kind with which our environmentally-caring generation is only too eager to identify.

Such an interpretation would seem to settle the matter. But before we classify the crop circles as simply another example of sociocultural opportunism, transforming a scientific puzzle into a supernatural mystery, we should face the fact that there is a further dimension of anomaly to the crop circle phenomenon which, if we are to be honest, we should take into account.

HOW ANOMALOUS ARE THE CIRCLES?

So far, you may feel, it has been downhill all the way — we have disentangled the true anomaly-fact from the extraneous and gratuitous anomaly-image, and pruned away the anomaly-spill which had all but hidden it from sight with the luxuriance of its parasitical growth.

But it would be presumptuous of us to suppose that those who construct the image and participate in the spillage are idiots and loonies, motivated by wishful thinking and prejudgment. It is not by chance that some anomaly-facts are transformed into anomaly-images and generate anomaly-spill while others rest in oblivion.

The question must be asked: why are crop circles one such instance?

Consider a parallel, the Egryn Lights, the dramatic feature of the Welsh religious revival of 1904–5. Anomalous lights were reported on several occasions by competent observers in anomalous circumstances, acting seemingly intelligently in association with participants in the revival.

As the McClures have shown,[14] anomalous lights had been reported in the district long before the revival; and as Devereux et al have shown,[15] there may be natural geophysical forces in the district conducive to the physical generation of such lights.

Here again, the easy comment is to say that the 'true believers' (no doubt subconsciously) exploited the lights for their own purposes. But the fact remains that if the testimony can be accepted (and much of it came from persons who seem to have been impartial to the point of scepticism), the primary anomaly — the lights — was physically real; and no less real was the behaviour which seemed to imply interaction with the human goings-on of the religious revival.

The question must be asked: can we attribute this seeming synchronicity to wishful thinking, and so be allowed to stick with our comfortable physical-trigger-plus-psychosocial-process explanation?

Or should we bite the bullet, accept the testimony, and entertain the possibility that something more than synchronicity and wishful thinking may have been involved, and that some kind of cause-and-effect was occurring?

This would involve envisaging some such scenario as this: that the emotional circumstances of the religious revival caused, or at least enabled, the anomalous lights (which already existed, at least potentially) to manifest at that time and in that place.

That would be tantamount to hypothesising that the mental, or spiritual, or psychic forces unloosed by the revival unloosed, in their turn, physical forces which interacted with physical phenomena which needed such mental/spiritual/psychic energising to manifest.

That such processes may occur is not as farfetched as may appear. The 'street-lamp-interference' phenomenon already referred to is just one example of a situation in which certain individuals under certain circumstances seem able to exert some degree of physical effect on the physical environment. 'Poltergeists' seem to be another example, and laboratory psychokinesis seems to have been sufficiently often reported by competent observers that we should consider seriously the possibility that it occurs.

It will be objected that these relatively small-scale incidents are quantitatively in quite a different class from crop circles; even those of us who are prepared to accept the possibility that some people can influence, say, a random number generator, will shrink from the suggestion that the same process could result in anything so massive as the crop circles, to produce which, as Meaden has calculated, very large forces are required.

However, this objection can be countered. The person whose emotional state causes a street lamp to go off is, presumably, acting on some component of the switching mechanism, whose sensitivity is such that it can be activated by a miniscule force.

But there is no limit to the size of an event that may be unleashed by the manipulation of a switch. Presumably the turbines of Niagara are operated by an electric switch requiring no greater degree of physical force than that of a desk lamp: if the one is vulnerable to mental force, why not the other?

Here, I suggest, are lines upon which research might reasonably proceed.

The questions raised by the circles fall into two categories:

those which are proper to the anomaly-fact, and those which result from the anomaly-spillage.

Once this is recognised, we see that some are the domain of the physical investigator, others the province of the behavioural scientist.

Until we have explored the 'ground-level' dynamics which may be involved, whether physical or psychosocial, it would be premature for us to entertain the macro-hypothesis that some deeper, wider process may underlie the phenonemon. It may be so: but at this stage of our ignorance, such speculation is no more than game-playing.

But then, since whoever/whatever is responsible for the crop circles shows every sign of playing games with us, haven't we every justification for indulging in a little game-playing of our own? (Based on an article published in *Fortean Times*, Issue no.53.)

REFERENCES
1. Jacques Vallee, *Messengers of Deception*, And/Or Press, Berkeley, 1979.
2. C. G. Jung, *Flying Saucers, a Modern Myth of Things Seen in the Skies*, Routledge, 1958; and other writings.
3. Rupert Sheldrake, *A New Science of Life*, Blond & Briggs, London, 1981.
4. John Keel, *UFOs: Operation Trojan Horse*, Souvenir, London, 1970; and many other writings.
5. Kevin McClure, *The Evidence for Visions of the Virgin Mary*, Aquarian, Wellingborough, 1983.
6. Nigel Watson, "Before the Flying Saucers came" in Evans & Spencer, *UFOs 1947–1987*, Fortean Times, London, 1987: a more comprehensive study awaits publication.
7. for example: "UFO Abductions", a forum, in *Journal of UFO Studies*, J. Allen Hynek Center for UFO Studies, Chicago, 1989.
8. William Corliss, *Sourcebook Project* (many volumes, and more to come), Baltimore.
9. Charles Fort, *Collected Works*, Holt, New York, 1941.
10. C. Maxwell Cade & Delphine Davis, *The Taming of the Thunderbolts*, Aberlard-Schuman, London, 1969.
11. David J. Hufford, *The Terror that comes in the Night*, University of Pennsylvania Press, Philadelphia, 1982.
12. *Slidings*, bulletin of the SLIDE project, compiled by Hilary Evans.
13. Hilary Evans, *Gods, Spirits, Cosmic Guardians*, Aquarian, Wellingborough, 1987.
14. Kevin & Sue McClure, *Stars and Rumours of Stars*, private, circa 1980.
15. Paul Devereux, *Earthlights*, Turnstone, Wellingborough, 1982.

Corridors & W's, Funguses & Fantasies

RALPH NOYES

Whether or not the crop circles are an "anomaly fact", as Hilary Evans calls it — meaning that they lie so far outside our present understanding that a radical re-think of some very basic ideas about Nature is going to be needed to accommodate them — they've certainly had their share of what he describes as "anomaly-cluster" and "anomaly-spill".

To take cluster first, many observers have tended to assimilate the crop circles to a number of other things which may — or may not — be related.

Nuts-and-bolts UFO buffs lumped them in immediately, of course, with nuts-and-bolts craft from other planets. Those quintuplets, for example . . . What could they possibly be but the body and four pods of a descending vehicle? Other patterns have proved trickier, but there is almost no limit to the ingenuity of faith and hope. Even when the 'landing traces' lie directly below overhead power-lines, can we not assume that the technology of our brothers from Out There is so far in advance of ours that dematerialisation and rematerialisation are minor technical tricks?

This kind of 'anomaly-clustering' of circles and UFOs perhaps adds to the climate of excitement which Hilary Evans suspects may 'fuel' the growth and elaboration of unusual (though basically 'natural') events, just as the religious fervour in Wales may have 'fuelled' that oubreak of 'lights in the sky' at Egryn.

But a rather more troublesome kind of anomaly-clustering also seems to have taken place, one which has possibly confused the record for crop circle researchers. So anxious have some observers been to argue that the circles are nothing new and far from concentrated in Wessex that they have tended to drag in to their tally of events many other kinds of strange ground-markings which have been found from time to time in many countries and for a long time past.

Such markings have often been claimed by UFO buffs of the nuts-and-bolts school as 'landing traces' of extraterrestrial craft — to the doubt of most of us. But about the existence and strangeness of such marks there is no question at all: many have been recorded in William R. Corliss's *Catalogs of Anomalies* and in such careful surveys as that conducted in Australia for the period 1868 to 1980 by Keith Basterfield in his *Close Encounters of an Australian Kind* (New Zealand, 1981). It is something of an irony that some of those faced with the major anomaly of an apparently rapidly increasing outbreak of ever-elaborating crop circles, heavily concentrated in Wessex, should have turned to 'rounding out' their records by dragging in what many of us have hitherto called — whether with faith or contempt — 'UFO nests'. Until full records of crop circle events have been published (see Introduction for the editor's lament at the secrecy and hoarding of data which marks this subject) we shall not be able to confirm or dispel our suspicions that all sorts of events which are certainly *not* crop circles, properly defined, have been prayed in aid of contentious statements about the distribution of these occurences in time and place. Many researchers will certainly be aware that anecdotes are told them from time to time of alleged crop circles for which nothing approaching the meticulous details we have for Wessex can be provided.

But perhaps this kind of 'anomaly-clustering', too, adds something to the climate of fervour which helps to engender 'anomaly-spill'. And 'spilled' the crop circle anomaly most certainly has! As though the facts themselves were not enough to be going on with, eddies and flurries of strange ideas have surrounded the subject fron an early stage. 'The Wessex Corridor', for example . . .

You will remember that the first crop circles we ever heard of turned up near Westbury, Wiltshire, in 1980. The next lot were picked up in 1981 near Winchester. In 1982 they returned again to near Warminster.

If you join Winchester to Westbury/Warminster you get a suggestive line which points south-east. Or perhaps north-west, of course . . . But south-east is more interesting: with a bit of juggling, the right kind of map and an awakened spirit you end remarkably close to the Great Pyramid at Giza. A fanciful thought, perhaps; but strange new phenomena demand bold new thinking. Sceptics jeered, of course; but then they always do.

In 1983 we again had circles at Westbury and Winchester, both once more in Wessex. This was beginning to look exciting.

In 1984 a quintuplet turned up at Alfriston in Sussex. Sussex was a bit of a let-down for those who were beginning to pin their faith to Wessex. But wait . . . If you project that south-east line, it passes very close to Alfriston before plunging into the English Channel and charging on towards Egypt. The line had perhaps to be broadened a bit, but the evidence for at least a Corridor was growing. As it obviously began in Wessex, 'The Wessex Corridor' seemed a good name for it.

Thrilling new evidence for The Wessex Corridor turned up in 1985. A quintuplet was found near Findon, also in Sussex but distinctly in that south-easterly direction. Other events in Wessex in 1985 lay clearly within the Corridor. A grand hypothesis was taking shape.

Some rotter then pointed out that there had been a circle at Wantage as far back as 1983. Wantage is in Oxfordshire. The 'Corridorians' were somewhat nonplussed. Perhaps that south-easterly something should be renamed 'The Wessex-and-Neighbouring-Counties-Geomantic-Highway'? (After all, government departments do this kind of thing simply for administrative convenience).

Others felt that perhaps we should now be thinking of A Wessex Triangle, its base-line being Warminster-Winchester and its apex Wantage. Scholarly attempts were made to establish whether Wessex, at its Anglo-Saxon peak, had included not only Wantage but also those tiresome bits of Sussex.

But a rival hypothesis was forming. Somebody noticed that the circles seemed to have a quirky interest in the letter 'W'. We had, after all, found them mainly near Westbury, Warminster, Winchester and Wantage. They were cropping up in Wiltshire and Wessex. The Sussex events were awkward until somebody spotted that Findon was very close to Worthing. Later events have proved to be too far north to accommodate the Wessex Triangle; and places not beginning with a 'W' have now had circular visitations. It may well be, however, that somebody is still secretly working in a back room on a multi-sided Wessex polygon and that others are searching the British Library for older place-names which will re-instate the 'W' hypothesis.

But we should not mock such things. Stretching the imagination is always a useful exercise, and the people who do it are usually better company than those whose concern is solely with counting costs and saving candle-ends. Perhaps we should reserve our spleen for those whose purpose seems to be to diminish the imagination rather than to widen it: the folk who instantly dismiss all circles as the work of funguses, for example, or hedgehogs, hoax and helicopters, and who have either never seen a circle at all or were so frightened by it when they did that they at once slapped the blinkers across their sense of wonder.

Arguing with these 'rationalists' is useless, as any serious researcher knows. The best response is good humoured wit. The national magazine, *Country Life*, which deserves a lasting place in scientific history for the serious cover it has given the crop circle phenomenon and the great number of ensuing letters which it has kindly channelled to researchers, has, from time to time, printed in its correspondence columns letters of great charm which far more effectively burst the bubbles of 'instantaneous explanationism' than any more sobre arguments could hope to do. Here are two of them.

A BLAST OF HOT AIR

Allegedly from the founder of the Fun Balloon Experimental Company

WE did enjoy Ralph Noyes's "Going Round in Circles" because *we* are, and will continue to be, responsible for most of the beaten-down corn described.

I am a redundant aeronautical engineer, British to the core, and with old colleagues formed some years ago The Fun Balloon Experimental Company, as yet unregistered, for "ladies and gentlemen who like to do things differently".

We meet once a month, at a friend's considerable estate and frolic on foggy nights in balloons (two to a basket) which, because of the materials used throughout, give no radar bounce. We are, in any event, a *low*-level team, and are no danger to other fliers.

As I have pointed out, we stick to foggy nights for cover, and the usual drill is for couples to go off for a low-altitude evening drifting in complete peace.

Culmination of our unusual hobby usually takes this form: we descend into cornfields, because we know we won't burst, and releasing gas, allow the balloon partly to deflate over our roofed baskets. Once this has been achieved we sit snug in our cabins concocting Anglo-Saxon tales as we pop a bottle.

So the crop marks to which you refer are mostly our doing. In fact, the central circle and its two outliers in the same field can be accounted for quite easily. On this occasion a wind got up, the fog suddenly lifted, the temperature changed, and the balloon rose from its alighting spot and twice allowed the basket to touch the ground, like a pendulum. The "corridors" in the corn resulted from hanging ballast bags being dragged.

As COUNTRY LIFE seems to be infatuated with the subject, we will, on seeing our letter printed, consider agreeing to a reduced subscription to this company for genuine COUNTRY LIFE readers. All we ask is that members are generally slim, for obvious weight reasons, and that they are non-smokers, partly because discarded cigarette ends might set fire to one of our landing spots in dry weather. But the initiation ceremony for membership of the Fun Ballon Experimental Company is extremely tough and lasts a week at the Hall. Grand meals are served, however, and all the tests are humane and bearable, provided one has a *high* sense of humour.—ROBIN VERNON-SPRAKE, *Dingle Cottage, Cold Blow Lane, Burgh Heath, Surrey.*

CIRCULAR COMPLEXITY

From Mr Richard Shaw

MR MACARA's letter (March 8) makes a notable contribution towards solving the mystery of the crop circles. But, although he correctly lays the blame on a fungus in the soil, he has not said precisely what this strange fungus is.

The reason why botanists have claimed to be baffled is wrapped in official mystery, but it may be significant that, when signals from the Voyager spacecraft were interrupted for a time, one theory was that its aerials had become coated with jelly-like spores. It is believed that these spores, borne on the solar wind from some extra-terrestrial source, could well be those of the fungus mentioned by your correspondent.

Circumstantial confirmation of this theory is provided by the fact that, on reaching earth, the spores spread in circles. Could this be evidence of alien intelligence?

Less widely known, is the mechanism by which the crops are flattened to the ground. The flattening of the crops in circles is caused, quite simply, by pigs who follow the scent of the fungi, which resembles that of truffles.

One objection to this explanation, which may be raised by sceptics, is that pigs could not enter and leave a crop without making tracks. Improbable as it may sound, the simple answer is that they fly over the crop after eating magic mushrooms.—RICHARD SHAW, *Woodlands, 14 Castle Close, Totternhoe, Dunstable, Bedfordshire.*

It is to a further, gentle blast against 'explanationism' that we now turn in John Michell's article.

What mean these marks?

JOHN MICHELL

In one exraordinary sentence, Delgado and Andrews[1] enumerate the twenty-one qualities which, they say, must be attributed to the unidentified agency responsible for crop circles. It is "a silent, short-duration, strong, contra-rotative, damage-free flattening, swirling, whorl- and vein-forming, swathing, stem-bending, horizontal-growth-inducing, non-growth interfering, straight-path-forming, plant-extracting, total darkness operating, gap-seeking, superimposing, circle-grouping, weather condition free, extraneous marks free, topographically conditionless, worldwide operative force".

To these attributes they might well have added a twenty-second: "un-pin-downableness", for the phenomenon constantly transcends, not merely every explanation, but even the definitions which are applied to it. Several items in the above list have since been disproved or disputed. The formation of crop circles is not always silent; sometimes it is accompanied by the humming or chirping sound which has also been heard later at established sites. Nor is total darkness an invariable conditon, for circles have appeared at dusk and early dawn. They are far from "topographically conditionless". Meaden sees them as linked to terrain; others notice an apparent attraction to the vicinities of ancient sacred sites, such as Avebury, Silbury Hill and Wessex tumuli and everyone agrees that they 'cluster' very markedly. Finally in 1989 the belief that rings around a ringed circle are bound to be "contra-rotative" was contradicted with dramatic emphasis.

This contradiction took the form of a cruel joke, perpetrated at the expense of the most professional of the cereologists, Dr. Terence Meaden. In his book, *The Circles Effect and its Mysteries*,[2] Meaden postulated that an unknown meteorological cause, an electro-magnetic plasma vortex, is responsible for the crop marks. As evidence for this, he pointed out that in every case of a circle with one or more outer rings, the circles and ring were swirled alternately in different directions. This seemed necessary for the stability of a plasma vortex. Yet within days of the book's appearance, on the morning of 18 June 1989, a new type of circle was found at Cheesefoot Head near Winchester. It almost seemed intended to discredit Meaden's generalisation for around the circle was a ring, and both ring and circle were swirled in the same direction.

This typifies a repeated characteristic of the crop circles which several experienced observers have remarked upon: their apparent responsiveness to human ideas projected upon them. As in the above case, the response may take a mischievous form, as though the phenomenon delights in confounding its investigators and upsetting their theories. More than once, the scientists have had to abandon hypotheses when their enunciation was immediately followed by evidence which refuted them. Meaden and his colleagues are not the only sufferers from this effect. In 1988 the extraterrestrialists — those who think in terms of alien space-craft — were

45

confronted with a crop circle which appeared immediately below a stretch of electric power cables, thus precluding the possibility of a landing from above, and there have been several such cases since.

The effect also has a positive side, a tendency to fulfil wishes. Busty Taylor, one of the pioneer cereologists and aerial photographer, gives an example of this. One evening in 1986, while flying home from a day's circle-spotting, he remarked that he would like to see a crop circle which combined in one formation everything seen so far — satellites and rings together, surrounding a central circle. He says the words, "Celtic Cross", were in his mind. Not much more than twenty-four hours later, as he flew over the spot where he had made the wish, he looked down and, as he said, nearly fell out of his aeroplane at the sight of the formation below him — an outer ring passing through four small circles with a larger disc in the middle, the pattern which was immediately christened the "Celtic Cross". Two years later it was well and truly put together at Charity Down (Plate 15), and there have been many elaborations in 1990.

Many such anecdotes, strongly suggesting the responsiveness of the crop circle agency to the minds of the investigators, are current among cereologists. This was one of the reasons which led the authors of Circular Evidence to conclude that "the circles are created by an unknown field force manipulated by an unknown intelligence". The argument for an intelligent purpose behind crop circles, whether human or non-human, is strengthened by several other features of the phenomenon: the strong clustering around three areas in Wessex, for example, and the marked association with ancient sites. The impression grows that something is being deliberately pointed out. It is something which seems to have become urgent around 1980, though with traces from before that date. Its symbols have been repeated with growing emphasis and elaboration ever since.

Observations of this sort are not welcomed by orthodox scientists, who are debarred by the rules of their game from considering the possibility of unknown intelligences. Thus the meteorologists have attempted to explain away the concentrations in Wessex and near ancient sites by suggesting that they are mere freaks of observation, though the arguments for this view have grown less and less convincing with the passing years.

The peculiar distinction of Wiltshire is that it contains Stonehenge, Avebury, Silbury Hill and one of the greatest concentrations of prehistoric stones and earthworks in Europe. Wiltshire is also distinguished as a centre of UFO activity. During the 1960s and 1970s UFO-spotters from all over the country held regular night vigils at Warminster in south-west Wiltshire. Every year strange aerial lights were reported, and many of the weird events which took place at the same time are described in the writings of Arthur Shuttlewood. In two of his books, The Warminster Mystery[3] and The Flying Saucerers[4] are some very early references to the modern crop circle phenomenon. Together with the American radio journalist, Bryce Bond, Shuttlewood witnessed the formation of several circles. One of them, which appeared in a field of grass, was observed by a party of ufologists. A high-pitched hum was heard, and the grass was swiftly laid down in a spiral form. "It was", said Shuttlewood memorably, "just like the opening of a lady's fan".

In this series of incidents, as with UFO and crop circles phenomena generally, there is a strong feeling of interplay between the effects and their observers. At Warminster in the mid-1960s mysterious lights were seen in the sky. They were seen also in many parts of Britain, but Warminster was the home of Arthur Shuttlewood, a local journalist, and the public meeting which he called at the town hall to announce the UFO sightings laid the foundations of Warminster's reputation. Those who wanted to see UFOs flocked to Wiltshire and many of them saw mysterious lights, sometimes followed by strange psychic experiences. As the excitement grew the phenomenon increased accordingly, developed new ramifications and eventually took the form of crop circles.

The connection between UFO phenomena and crop circles is acknowledged by cereologists of all schools and persuasions. It is well illustrated at Warminster, where Cley Hill, an oddly shaped chalk knoll towering above flat meadows to the west of the town, has been a notable UFO centre. Unidentified lights have often been seen over and around it by night, especially during Arthur Shuttlewood's era. Then, in 1982 and for several years afterwards, when the UFO excitement was largely past, crop circles appeared in the fields below Cley Hill. Terence Meaden identified Cley Hill as the kind of feature which would generate plasma vortices. Yet no one had observed circles here before the 1980s, and as soon as Meaden drew attention to them, in 1986, the circles withdrew from Cley Hill and began to infest the Avebury area.

A remarkable and disturbing effect of the UFO phenomenon is its tendency to 'home in' on its researchers. This effect was described by John Keel, the most interesting of writers on UFOs and modern mysteries, in his book, *Operation Trojan Horse*.[5] As background reading for students of crop circles this book is of great value, for it gives warning of the strange ideas and experiences which force their way into the lives of all who inquire into such subjects. Delgado and Andrews confirm this in *Circular Evidence*. Like many other cereologists, and like Keel, Shuttlewood and ufologists before them, they admit that their lives, minds and outlooks have been radically changed by their investigations. On one level the change is philosophical; after honest appraisal of ufology and crop circle data it is impossible to maintain the rationalistic world-view on which modern science and education are founded. One is led into unfamiliar channels of thought, which point away from structured theories and hard-and-fast beliefs towards a more mystical view

of reality and, eventually, towards the greater mysteries of divinity and the living universe.

At the beginning of this process, the researcher is liable to be plagued by weird events, such as are commonly associated with poltergeist hauntings. When Keel began his professional UFO studies in 1966, he was immediately caught up in a world of strange lights, sounds and smells, spirit messages, unearthly beings and ominous coincidences. He felt at first that he was losing his sanity. Among the UFO contactees he studied, some had indeed been driven mad, others had become, at least for a time, inspired prophets, and in extreme cases the UFO messages had caused their recipients to found cults and millennial movements which often led to the destruction of themselves and their followers.

John Keel's original purpose was to make a systematic, scientific study of the UFO phenomenon and thus to discover what lay behind it. In the same spirit of rational inquiry Delgado and Andrews, together with Terence Meaden and a few other brave colleagues, embarked on their crop circles studies. Meaden so far has held strictly to the scientific line, and his own personal experiences, if any, have not been published. Delgado and Andrews, however, have honestly reported the peculiarities — inexplicable events and encounters, the malfunctioning of instruments etc., — which have dogged their researches. These experiences have not been confined to their fieldwork, but have sometimes followed them home. For several weeks in 1986, after Colin Andrews had brought back a soil sample from a crop circle site near Wantage, he and his houschold were constantly disturbed by a series of accidents and upheavals, typical of poltergeist activities. His wife said she felt a malign presence in the house, somehow connected with the circles. One cannot help recalling the disturbing anecdotes given by Don Robins in the opening pages of his *Secret Language of Stone*.[6] A BBC television crew also reported malfunctioning of equipment when filming in a circle in 1989.

In the early days of ufology, many researchers were confident that the mystery would soon be resolved, either through scientific studies or by some revelation from outer space. Others believed that governments knew all about UFOs but were keeping their information secret. The most unpopular view was that no one had the slightest idea of what was going on, that there were no conspiracies, no cover-ups, and that, even in this modern age of scientific triumphalism, humanity was destined to inhabit and to be reconciled to a world of mystery. That, however, seems to be the truth of the matter, implying a world-view which is quite different from the picture presented by modern science.

In his last and most prophetic work, his book on Flying Saucers published in 1959, C. G. Jung identified the strange lights or objects seen in the sky as portents of great changes impending in the collective psyche.[7] Such things, he warned, must be expected as the Age of Pisces gave way to that of Aquarius. In seeing UFOs both as portents and as active agents of the due changes, Jung was certainly ahead of his time. He expected neither thanks nor understanding from his scholarly contemporaries, nor did he receive any. Even his followers were embarrassed by his prophecies, and his words made scarcely any impression on the UFO fraternity. For many years ufology continued to reflect the narrow obsessions of an age in which scientific materialism was the dominant orthodoxy. This allowed, on the one hand, conventional scientific investigations which finally achieved nothing and, on the other, fantasies, superstitions and cultism. Jung's approach to the UFO phenomenon, through its meaning rather than its 'mechanism', was generally ignored; instead, the field of ufology became a battleground between rival theory-mongers, most of whom took as mechanistic a view of the phenomenon as any conventional scientist might have done.

After all our experiences throughout the post-War period, how sad it would be if cereology were to re-enact the history of ufology, losing sight of the phenomenon and degenerating into a state of petty-minded sectarianism. This, unfortunately, has already begun to happen. Sneers and name-calling have disfigured several recent publications on crop circles and, almost incredibly, rival cereologists have had recourse to solicitors and threats of legal action.

Since there is no dispute about the data of crop circles, and since no one knows the answer to the mystery, there are no good grounds for rancour and vindictiveness among researchers. A reason, however, exists, and it is a bad reason, based on a primitive and fallacious approach to the subject. Instead of following Jung's example and contemplating the significance of the phenomenon, cereologists have devoted their efforts largely to seeking a physical agency behind it. It is as if the guests at Belshazzar's feast, when the moving finger traced out a message of doom upon the wall, had been more interested in the mechanics of the communication than with what it said.

This tendency to concentrate on the mechanism rather than the message is typical of the present times, when the ability to issue explanations and firm opinions is the distinguishing mark of experts and pundits in every field. The convention of televised debates, for example, is to pit two people of opposite opinions, one against the other, a process which engenders more sound than light and is by no means conducive to the establishment of any truth. Civilized discussions, where the object is to resolve a problem rather than to sound clever and original, are not conducted in this way, nor is this method appropriate to cereology. In this debate the interests of all parties are the same: to acquire some means of understanding these amazing happenings which are, so far, quite inexplicable. This is best done by sharing observations rather than by commitment to any particular theory.

Understanding a phenomenon is not necessarily the same as explaining it scientifically. Many aspects of nature and human nature have not been

Plate 1. In a dry spring as in 1988 you find all sorts of markings coming through the crop. As in this photo the round ones are the outlines of prehistoric burial mounds now flattened, these show up very well in the spring crop. The other lines are ancient pathways and boundary ditches. The photograph was taken at Longstock Downs.

Plate 2. Some other prehistoric ground markings were found at Silbury Hill. In this photograph you see that the six small 'grapeshot' crop circles have appeared to line up with the ancient markings. I wonder why?

Plate 3. Circles appear in all manner of crops, but perhaps the most beautiful are in oil-seed rape. It has very brittle stalks but they are not broken by the energy, but bent as though steam heated. The aerial photograph was taken at South Wonston two days after the event in May 1987.

Plate 4. A large circle formed in wheat at Chilcomb in 1987, with particularly beautiful spiralling splays, and a fairly precise centre. In one of the photographs taken at this site two black darts appeared on the print. Analysis has proven that both objects were in front of the lens at the moment of exposure. What they are we do not know.

Plate 5. This well proportioned quintuplet was found at Beckhampton in 1987, and measured over two hundred feet across.

Plate 6. The first double-ringer appeared at Bratton in 1987 on August 8. The photograph shown was taken from the end of my 20 foot pole, which I have now managed to get up to 37 feet.

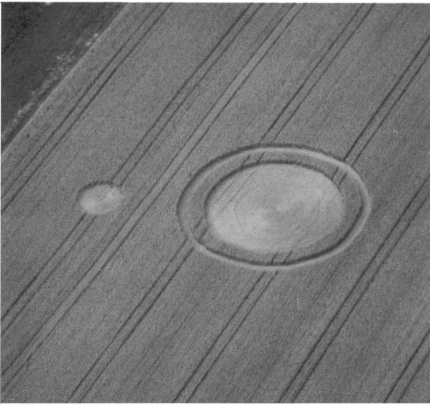

Plate 7. In 1987 at Winterbourne Stoke I discovered a new circle site. This was a circle and ring with three small satellites. From the air the twenty-five metre centre circle shone brilliantly in the sunshine, and this made a very impressive sight. I entered the field some two hours later and was immediately impressed by its beauty and complexity.

Plate 8. Cheesefoot Head east of Winchester is a favourite area for circles. It also has a number of ancient sites, this nice double-ringer appeared there in 1988 in a field of barley. It was acccompanied by five smaller satellites and shown on BBC t.v. documentary called "Running Rings around Arthur". (My pole technique was demonstrated on this programme.)

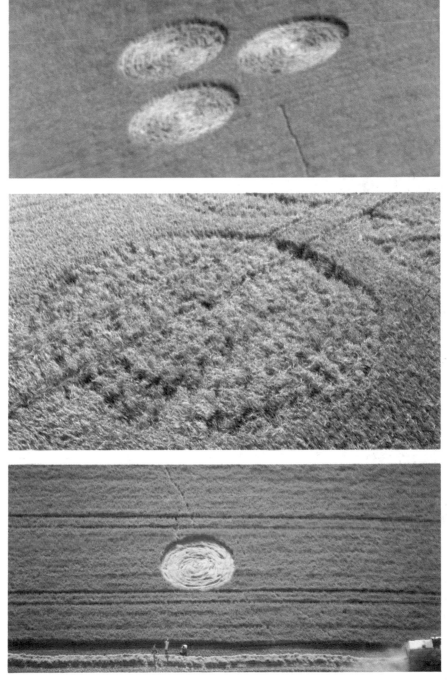

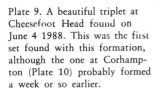

Plate 9. A beautiful triplet at Cheesefoot Head found on June 4 1988. This was the first set found with this formation, although the one at Corhampton (Plate 10) probably formed a week or so earlier.

Plate 10. This triangular set was found at Corhampton on June 8 1988 in barley. The vigorous grain has tried to regain a vertical position, but notice how it has formed a rippled set of seven concentric circles and 48 radials.

Plate 11. A barley singlet near Amesbury at harvesting time in 1989. This set was found very close to Boscombe experimental airfield.

Plate 12. Silbury Hill, the largest prehistoric man-made hill in Europe, is part of the giant Avebury complex, one of the most important sacred sites of the ancient world. From 1988 onwards it attracted multiple quintuplets, the ones shown here are on the south side. A double event occurred in this field over the space of a few days.

Plate 13. The first circle appeared on the night of July 14/15 1988. This was possibly witnessed by a lady called Mary Freeman who was driving down the Avebury avenue late at night when she saw a bright light in the Silbury area. The circles were found the next day.

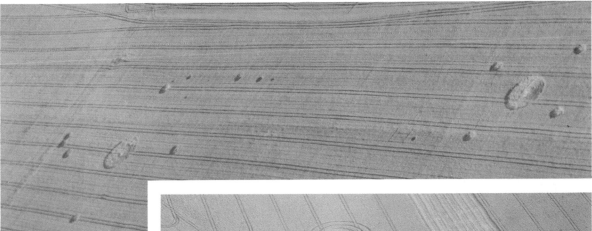

Plate 14. Large quintuplet sets with contemporary satellites in wheat on the north side of Silbury Hill in July 1989. This field had 28 circles in total, and they appeared over a three week period.

Plate 15. The Charity Down single-ringer with joined satellites was one of the first true Celtic designs to appear. Found late, at the end of August 1988, this circle appeared two hundred metres south of my 1985 quintuplet set which had a very thin ring through three of its satellites. Is it possible that we had a malfunction in 1985, but managed to get it right in 1988?

Plate 16. This is a ground level shot of one of the satellites with the intersecting ring. The satellite is clockwise in rotation and the ring itself is also clockwise.

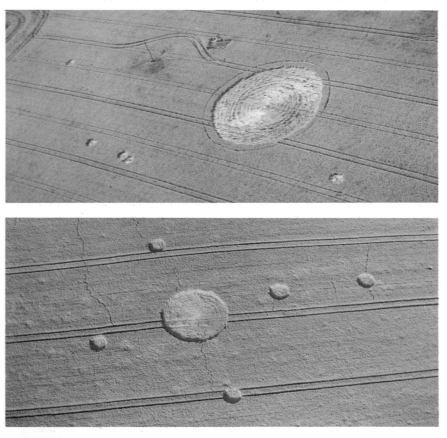

Plate 17. In late 1989, the ringed circles are now starting to get very fine rings. You see from the photograph how close it is to the main circle; the photograph was taken at West Overton, two miles east of Silbury Hill. This circle was accompanied by a further seven satellites in the surrounding area.

Plate 18. An exciting new 'crucifix' formation turned up in 1989. The first one was at Warminster and a few days later a second one appeared at Cherhill, east of Calne. This one was eighty-five metres in length and was accompanied by other satellites in the field. From the air this was a truly impressive sight which was seen on television all over the world.

Plate 19. A triple-ringer at Cheesefoot Head in immature wheat in 1990. You will note that the rings have been flattened and that they match up with the tramlines; as you see from the photograph the stalks have taken up a radial spoke effect.

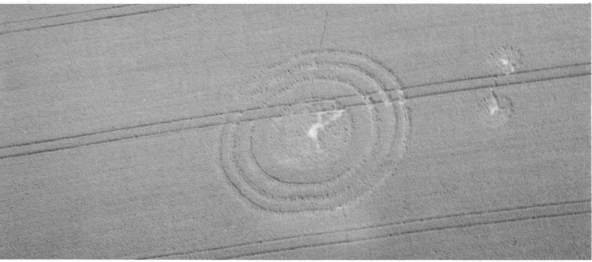

explained by science, and the gaps are filled by myths and traditional beliefs. Crop circles are peculiarly disturbing because they have no explanation, either scientific or traditional. Due to their novelty they have attracted no body of folklore, though the incident of the Mowing Devil in 1678 (p. 63) suggests that any circles of swirled corn or grass discovered in earlier times would have been attributed to supernatural forces. The folklore of fairy rings may here be relevant. It is normally supposed that the reference is to those dark rings of grass which appear in the meadows and are known to be caused by a fungus. Yet in many local tales, the details of supernatural music, lights and dancers in a ring of crushed grass are suggestive of modern crop circle phenomena.

The famous old English ring-dancer was Robin Goodfellow, Shakespeare's Puck, a mischievous imp who delighted in pranks, upsetting and amusing the good countryfolk. A noted feature of crop circles is the impish sense of humour which appears to be associated with them. This is certainly a mark of Robin Goodfellow, and thus the traditionalist view of crop circles would be that an old rustic spirit has awoken and is up to his tricks again in the cornfields.

Few of us today are satisfied with such simple notions, and even if Robin Goodfellow is given the blame for crop circles, there remains the mystery of why he has suddenly become so active. Country people in the past, who have attributed the fairy rings and other such oddities to spirits, demons or witches, attached meaning to such things, and they would certainly have looked for a meaning in the modern outbreak of crop circles. This was not a mere peasant trait, for the rulers of ancient civilizations were alert to freaks and aberrations in nature. Such things were regarded as symptoms of psychic disturbance, portending some disaster or upheaval which could be averted by appropriate reforms to the administration. Priests and scholars in the past would have approached the study of crop circles

with different priorities from those we find natural today, being more concerned with the meaning of the prodigy than with its immediate cause.

It may be more useful to ponder the meaning of crop circles rather than their mechanism, but one can not avoid the modern obsession with how things work. Almost everyone who asks, "What's the answer to crop circles?", wants to know how they are made and who or what is making them. These questions are inevitable, but the nature of the crop circle agency is known only through its handiwork, and the picture thus obtained is too puzzling to justify any simple answers.

Certain clues, however, give insight into the type of forces which are involved in the formation of crop circles. An important part must surely be played by the earth, whose energies are found to have been activated at crop circles sites. On this account, it is said, the young stems of swirled-down corn continue to ripen horizontally, as if drawn to the earth, rather than raising their heads upwards. Many of the leading cereologists, Terence Meaden included, have had recourse to dowsing and have confirmed to their own satisfaction the claims of professional dowsers, that strong energy fields can be detected at crop circles. Further evidence of anomalous energies at these sites occurs in the anecdotes of malfunctioning instruments and strange animal behaviour, told by many investigators, and in the hums, chirps, crackling sounds, floating lights and other possible effects of electrical discharges from the earth.

Largely through the researches of Paul Devereux and his recent books, *Earth Lights Revelation*[8] and *Places of Power*,[9] scientists are beginning to perceive a further dimension to their studies of the energies which permeate the Earth's surface and which may constitute the essential life of this planet. These energies sometimes give rise to short-lived luminous phenomena (the so-called 'Earth Lights') which Devereux and his colleagues claim are observed on or near geological fault lines. The sites of megalithic monuments and ancient earthworks also seem to cluster in areas of geological faults, and these areas are prominent in the folklore record, as well as in modern experiences, as the favoured locations of luminous apparitions, UFOs, phantoms and other such products of the 'night side of Nature'. Archaeologists have many anecdotes, similar to those of crop circle investigators, of unexplained failures of cameras and instruments at various ancient sites.

Reviewing the evidence in this field, Devereux was struck by an observation which repeatedly occurs in reports by witnesses to mysterious light phenomena, that their experience of reality is somehow affected. Some tell of visions and psychic revelations, and a common feature is that witnesses feel aware of a mental link between themselves and the phenomena. In his category of earth lights Devereux includes manifestations which are recognised by science, though not fully explained or understood, such as will-o'-the-wisps and ball lightning. Such things certainly seem to be related to the earth's energy field, but their behaviour is unpredictable, and they often give the impression of acting in an intelligent or purposeful way towards those who see them. Devereux's conclusion, forced upon him by the overwhelming weight of evidence, is that the Earth's vital energies have a component of intelligence, similar to our own intelligence and capable of interacting with it.

To the extent that modern scientists are beginning to recognize the living, spiritual nature of the earth's vital energies, they are rediscovering the orthodoxy of previous ages. The institution of state oracles, which guided the policies of Greek, Egyptian and other ancient civilizations, were based on the premise of communication with the powers of earth. Universal traditions of geomancy also imply a spiritual link between Mother Earth and her human progeny. It is inevitable that this link will again be acknowledged, for the necessities of these times demand it. It is also apparent that the mystery of crop circles is closely bound up with the greatest of all mysteries, concerning the nature and consciousness of the organic earth-creature.

The energies which swirl down cornfields are probably located in the earth, but telluric currents are not likely to be the only factor involved. Celestial influences, particularly those of sun and moon, condition the earth's energy patterns, and its flows of current may well be susceptible to other stimuli in ways which are not yet recognized. Dowsers claim that earth currents respond to sound and music, while the old geomancers went further and recognized the affinity between the earth spirit (the ch'i of Chinese metaphysics) and the human mind. The influences which are producing crop circles could, therefore, emanate from one or more of several different sources — from the cosmos, from a star or planet, from a power within the earth, or from our own selves.

The regular geometrical patterns formed by crop circles, displaying archetypal symbols which are inherent in the structure of the universe and the human mind alike, have no obvious parallels in physical nature. They do, however, occur spontaneously in experiments on the effect of sound. Since Chladni at the beginning of the nineteenth century caused symmetrical patterns of dust to form on the surface of a suspended glass plate, vibrating in response to a musical note, many people have been fascinated by the pattern-making potential of sound waves. "In the beginning was the Word", wrote St John, and in esoteric traditions sound is held to be both the formative principle in creation and the power which binds the universe together in harmony. One possible stimulus to the energy field of the Earth, which seems capable of producing the orderly patterns of crop circles, is sound or music. The question of where such music or sound waves may originate, whether from the cosmos or from earthly source, is at present unanswerable.

Sound waves, plasma vortices originating in the atmosphere, the activity of witches, earth energies, interactions with the human mind . . . All these remain mere notions. None of them has made any significant impression on the crop circles mystery. Those who have undertaken to explain the phenomenon are no further advanced in 1990 than they were ten years ago when crop circles were first recorded. Their failure is not from want of effort or ingenuity. Many talents have been brought to bear on the problem with no apparent results, but the failure of all theories to match the phenomenon is itself significant, for it has revealed one consistent factor of crop circles, their apparently purposeful resistence to explanation. This feature has already been remarked upon, and it may be that it is not purely negative. There may be a good reason why the crop circle agency is so punctilious in confounding its explainers. Within the limits of its medium, it has done everything possible to raise the perception of its investigators, distracting attention from mechanistic theories and leading minds to contemplate the idea of other-than-human intelligence in Nature.

There is little doubt, especially as the astonishing events of 1990 continue to unfold, that the patterns in the corn have a meaning, and the meaning of such things is to be found in the way people are affected by them. Jung discerned the meaning of UFOs as agents and portents of changes in human thought patterns, and that function has clearly been inherited by crop circles, which are a continuation — a solidification, one might say — of the UFO phenomenon. We have seen earlier how exposure to the influence of crop circles has changed the attitudes and mentalities of many investigators. Such changes, if they are in accord with the spirit of the times, are both permanent and contagious. Judging by what has happened so far, there seems to be every justification for extending Jung's characterization of UFOs to crop circles, and thus for regarding them as signs of "great changes to come which are compatible with the end of an era".

Prodigies and irregularities in the natural order, such as crop circles, convey meaning in other ways. They trouble the conscience and create awareness of reasons for guilt and repentance. According to all precedent, messages from the gods of heaven or earth never convey good news nor send congratulations on how well things are going. They almost invariably come as warnings and portents of retribution. It is not, therefore, surprising that many people associate the crop circles with the ecological crisis and feel them to be a spontaneous form of protest by the mistreated earth. Colin Andrews spoke much to that effect on a BBC television programme in 1989. If the effect of crop circles is to turn minds and thoughts in that direction, it cannot be said that the phenomenon lacks meaning.

Crop circles are probably conveying much timely information, but nothing can be received or understood unless one pays attention to the message. Publications so far have largely been dominated by theories and discussions about causes, while important data, such as yearly distribution maps, are secreted in the private files of individual investigators. Cereologists, in seasons to come, would surely be best advised to forget any conclusions they have jumped at and to make a fresh appraisal of the whole phenomenon through the evidences of itself which it has chosen to present. If Nature is speaking through the crop circles, the most fruitful response is to be still and listen. The ideas which steal into the mind as one contemplates these wonderful patterns are likely to be the very ideas which they are designed to convey.

REFERENCES
1. Delgado, P. and Andrews, C. *Circular Evidence* Bloomsbury 1989.
2. Meaden, G. T. *The Circles Effect and its Mysteries* Artetech 1989.
3. Shuttlewood, A. *The Warminster Mystery* Spearman 1967.
4. Shuttlewood, A. *The Flying Saucerers* Sphere Books 1976.
5. Keel, J. A. *Operation Trojan Horse* Souvenir Press 1971. Reprinted by Abacus 1976.
6. Robins, D. *The Secret Language of Stone* Century Hutchinson 1988.
7. Jung, C. *Flying Saucers, A Modern Myth of Things seen in the Sky* 1959. Reprinted by Ark Paperbacks 1987.
8. Devereux, P. *Earth Lights Revelation* Blandford Press 1989.
9. Devereux, P. *Places of Power* Blandford Press 1990.

As old as Adam?

RALPH NOYES

How far back do the crop circles go? For the reasons given in the introduction we still know far too little about their true antecedents: there has been a tendency by researchers to keep their data unpublished, and the way has been open to anecdotal reminiscences of uncertain value.

Whatever the truth, let us remember that those first circles seen near Bratton in Wiltshire in 1980 came as a great surprise to those who found them. They were clearly no run-of-the mill event. And to this day most farmers who suffer these occurrences tell researchers that they've never seen the like before.

And yet, as the decade passed, stories began to emerge (never, let it be noted, diagrams made at the time or any photograph, except in an isolated case from the seventies on a farm near Winchester in 'haunted' Wessex) that these things had been around, albeit rather rarely and never in the complex patterns we are now seeing, for decades if not a century or so past.

A Mrs Jean Songhurst, for example, writing in *Country Life* earlier this year, tells us that she had seen circles in Donegal more than sixty years before but that the farmers kept quiet about them. They "depended on every penny the corn-merchants gave them, and rumours that something was amiss with the crops could mean ruin. So the reaction was to straighten the circles quickly and hush it up". Mrs Songhurst adds that her uncle in Scotland had also seen circles on his farm at Thurso in the 1890s.

Other similar sorts of story have been told us from other people whose memory of the countryside goes back a while. We can never be quite sure whether what is being recounted is the recollection of some roughly circular damage, perhaps caused by animals or weather, but now given the retrospective glamour of our modern occurrences. It may all be part of Hilary Evans' "anomaly-cluster" or "anomaly-spill".

Yet the feeling remains that there is something in these belated anecdotes which can't be altogether dismissed. It is as though we have always had, perhaps, a few rarish occurrences of a 'natural' kind (rare enough never to have made the standard textbooks at agricultural colleges, for example) which may have had some of the very distinctive characteristics of the post-1980 events but which remained unelaborated and few in number because (though the idea is fanciful) nobody had taken much notice of them, or took care to forget them quickly when they did. Perhaps the circles have been thriving since 1980 on the 'oxygen of publicity' which they had never had before . . .

The argument about antecedents will doubtless continue for the time being. It is another disputed area in which there has been much bad temper. Forteans could not, therefore, help enjoying the serendipity of Bob Skinner's sudden discovery, while browsing in a bookshop, of the reproduction of a pamphlet from 1678, *The Mowing Devil*. Almost simultaneously, and quite independently, it was noticed by several other people in several other places, including Jenny Randles (Intro.[4]) and the President of the Society for Psychical Research.

That pamphleteer of 1678 could hardly have expected that he would one day, more than three centuries later, provide the cover for a learned periodical, the *Journal of Meteorology* (Vol. 14/No. 143 of November 1989, in which an account is given of the find). Whether or not this is an early instance of a crop circle remains debated. It is certainly the case that good folklorists have never discovered anything else of the kind, either in illustration or in folk-tale. The last commentary on the pamphlet made by a knowledgeable folklorist, W. B. Gerish, early in this century was that the tale clearly belonged to the 'retribution' class: the kind of story told to each other by the poor when dwelling upon the unfairness of the better-off. Most of the pamphlet does, indeed, relate the occurrence to a rich farmer's refusal to pay the wages demanded by his labourer for mowing the field. "I'd sooner the Devil mowed it," was the farmer's comment — and Bob's your uncle (or anyway Old Nick). Gerish takes it for granted (by implication) that the incident itself was an invented one.

Whatever we make of the pamphlet, however, it has now done us one further service by prompting the ensuing article by Robert J. M. Rickard, the editor of *Fortean Times*.

Clutching at straws

ROBERT J. M. RICKARD

On the face of it the *Mowing Devil* (see below) seems to offer a historical account of the formation of a crop circle in 1678, couched in the imagery of contemporary folk-demonology. Whether or not it really does so is debated by the cereologists. But I was drawn to explore the cultural significance of this strange conjunction of crops, circles, whirling winds and devils.

What I found particularly intriguing was the seeming reluctance of the farmer to reap the field after this weird manifestation [Cf. that similar reluctance on the part of Hampshire farmers, even in this century — see introduction. Ed.]

It didn't take a social historian to note that in the background of the *Mowing Devil* case lay a dispute between a rich farmer and his poor neighbours. Whether the mowers were asking more for their services than in previous years, or because of inflation, the farmer obviously thought they were taking advantage of him. His angry rejection must have dismayed the mowers, who very likely depended upon this annual contract for much of their livelihood.

This kind of offhand treatment of the peasantry by secure farmers and landowners was all too common. The brooding resentment of the ill-paid workers, often in tied dwellings, was a breeding ground for the millenarianism, dissention, and social reform movements of the 18th and 19th centuries. It also formed the backdrop to the introduction of farm machinery (the vanguard of the Industrial Revolution), the Luddite reaction and the rise of the first unions and workers' cooperatives.

But in the 17th century there was no help to hand except by divine — or demonic — action. The pamphleteers of the period were at their best with the fantasy theme of retribution by supernatural powers against the profligate or greedy privileged classes. The *Mowing Devil* fits this genre well.

THE FAIRIES AND THE FARMERS

We are now beginning to understand the terrible erosion of the 'Old Ways' wrought by the spread and institutionalisation of a fascinating world-view that we will never fully comprehend.[2]

Throughout the Celtic, Gaelic, Teutonic, Scandinavian and Ugro-Finnish world the fairies or their local variants presided over every aspect of the ancient landscape, including the cultivated fields. The agricultural cults of these regions are remarkably similar — proof, if needed, of the universality of the worship of elemental forces whose genii were the 'Good' or 'Hidden' people.

The Christian missionaries deliberately hijacked the old festivals and built their churches on top of the old sacred places. The effect was to fragment the ancient lore into a disjointed ragbag of isolated images and rites which became increasingly meaningless with the passage of time. The folklorist 'Alfred' Nutt characterised these degenerate remnants of the fairy belief as "a vague but ineradicable

Licensed, August 22th, 1678.

conviction that such-and-such must be done, or the powers would be displeased."[3] It is with these fragments that we have to work and not with the vulgarised or prettified images of witches and fairies which have filled children's books since the last century and provided the stock-in-trade of the Disneys of this one.

What the ancient peoples lost was a primary form of worship. Tending the earth and its crops appeals to a fundamental religious impulse. The first agriculture must have been a practical worship of the forces of fertility and growth, decay and cyclical time (the seasons). This is still visible today in the Shinto religion, as we saw recently when the new emperor of Japan renewed his divine contract by ritually planting a sacred rice-paddy. It is only to the profane that the sexual allusions in 'ploughing a furrow' and 'planting seeds' seem crass. Agriculture in the ancient world was nothing less than intimacy with the Mother Goddess.

The cult of the fairies was also the cult of fertility and agriculture. It is difficult for us, at this distance, to imagine its grip on archaic society, which depended so directly upon the land. The fairies were credited with bringing agriculture to man, and favouring those 'horny-handed' sons of the soil above any others. Throughout the range of Indo-European cultures, the fairies were given their tithes of corn and milk at harvesting, over which they presided.

A vestige of this regulatory function can be seen in the tradition that fairies were zealous in their requirements for neatness and cleanliness, especially in household matters. They also demanded proper decorum of mortals who entered their places and dealt with them, rewarding proper observances and rituals. Unlike the devious Christian Devil, the fairies kept their word. By tradition they favoured upright men, even if they were Christians.

Consequently, as Lewis Spence observes,[4] the agricultural fairies were "a species of Providence for the worthy suffering from oppression", a pagan moral force. Tales of the fairies frequently feature rewards for virtue, and punishment of vice and greed. In this context, the *Mowing Devil* is not about the Devil at all, but can be seen as a Christianised version of fairy retribution against a greedy farmer.

It may be, of course, that the farmer's field was ruined by a natural phenomenon — one of Dr. Meaden's vortices, perhaps, or whatever else is creating our modern crop circles — and only blamed upon some remembered dispute with the mowers in retrospect. The lesson remains. The farmer had forgotten the old ways, and following this reminder from the pagan swift-kick department dared not reap the crop on which the fairies had left their mark.

GODS OF CORN AND UNDERWORLD

To widen the discussion at this point I would like to introduce the relatively little known *Kornbocks* of northern and eastern Europe. They are invisible and goat-like spirits — related to the Irish *pooka*, Welsh *pwca* and the English Puck — who live in the cornfields and ripen the grain. When harvesting destroys their homes they are invited into the mowers' houses for the winter, becoming *Hausbocks*. Once again, we hear that neatness and frugality matter to the chthonic spirits and are rewarded by good luck and a bountiful harvest to come. Among the Germans, the god Fro (known as Frey in Scandinavia), who was given Fairyland (Alfheim) as his birthright, rode through cornfields on his great boar called Gullin, whose shining golden bristles linked the sun with ripening grain. Gullin taught men agriculture, showing them how to plough with his tusks.

During the Roman occupation of Britain (44 to 410 AD) and possibly earlier (through contact with Roman Gaul), the British pagans were exposed to the pantheon of Greco-Roman gods, just as they fell under the social and economic influence of Christianity from the sixth century onwards. In the course of time the genealogies of the Greco-Roman gods became confused by the importation of foreign gods, the reassignment of attributes, and the cosmogony of various Mystery cults. This great mix 'n' match process makes specific identifications difficult, especially when our view of any ancient fertility cult is filtered through overlays of Greek, Roman and Christian cultural imagery.

One of the chief goddesses immediately significant to our present inquiry is Demeter, known to the Romans as Ceres, who personified the Earth and fertility. Demeter/Ceres was daughter of the earth goddess Rhea, and granddaughter of Gaea, and absorbed their attributes. Through Rhea, Demeter also inherited associations with the Phrygian cult of Cybele, the Great Mother, a savage goddess of caverns, wild nature, and wild beasts.

Demeter particularly represented the cultivated aspects of the Earth. Wheat and barley were sacred to her, and she is portrayed crowned with ears of corn, hence the derivation of the word 'cereals' for these types of crops. She also presided over the harvest and its attendant labours.

Where Demeter represents the Earth, her eponymous daughter, Kore, goddess of the corn (whom the Romans called Persephone), personifies the crops themselves. Kore was abducted from the face of the earth by Hades (the Roman Pluto), snatched from the middle of a field as she gathered flowers. In Sicily, Crete, Arcadia and Attica, or wherever the local cult claimed that this had happened, craters or hollows in fields were said to mark the place where the King of the Underworld plunged back beneath the earth. You can imagine the feelings of superstitious countryfolk about that strangely afflicted field in Hertfordshire in 1678 if any distant memory remained of the rape of Kore; the ground would be sacred and feared indeed.

Kore's abduction can be interpreted as an allegory of agriculture: for part of the year seeds lie in the underworld, dormant in the ground, before they, like Kore, are allowed a temporary spell in the sunlit upper regions. The myth is also an allegory of all natural cycles, especially night and day, which are so important to the growth and lives of living things.

Kore has other claims on our quest through etymology. Wherever the Great Mother cult can be found, we also find with it the deified daughter or maiden. Scholars have identified many derivations, including cardiac, kernel, carnal and carnival; the term *Kaur*, meaning 'princess', is still given to all unmarried Sikh women; and perhaps there is even a remote link with the Egyptian Karnak and Celtic Carnac in Brittany.

Also relating to our enquiry is Artemis, daughter of Demeter, and Dionysus, whom one tradition says is the son of Kore. Like so many of the Greco-Roman deities, Artemis (known to the Romans as Diana) has schizoid aspects. She was a virtuous maiden possessing the stern morality later attributed to our fairies. But as Huntress, the 'Mother of Creatures' she was goddess of forests and the chase, leading her entourage of nymphs and swift hunting dogs. By association with the sun-god Apollo (a different genealogy makes them both children of Zeus and Leto), Artemis was goddess of moonlight. She also became associated with the Great Mother worshipped at Ephesus, her myriad breasts a sign of her fertility.

During the Roman occupation of western Europe a great many shrines to local Mother goddesses were made over to Diana, much as the Christians later re-dedicated these shrines to Christ's mother. Demeter/Ceres, Diana/Artemis and the Virgin Mary all shared the title 'Queen of Heaven'.

The Fairy Queen in the British tradition was also called Queen of Heaven through sharing another of Diana's synonyms, Titania.

We must also mention Hecate, whom later the Roman Church, during the witchcraft era, demonised into a 'Queen of the Witches'. In this respect she was made synonymous with Diana. Hecate was another triple-goddess, identified with the Moon in the phases of waxing, full and waning, and with the three stages of womanhood, virgin, mother, crone. She became the female counterpart of Hades in the Underworld and presided over sorcery, charms and atonement. Her shrines were frequently at crossroads, and she too had a pack of hounds. Hecate and Helios (Moon and Sun) — often paired like Artemis and Apollo — witnessed the abduction of Kore, and revealed to Demeter her Underworld location.

THE WILD HUNT

The passage of a wild destructive force through the countryside — such as a powerful wind or even a whirlwind — is the very image of the Wild Hunt. Also called the furious Host, it was a riotous stampede of chthonic spirits which devoured, maimed, withered (or at least struck mad) all in its path. It was dreaded by all rural people, not least for fear of the frightful sight of the disintegrating dead and tormented souls forced to run along with it. At its head was a terrible horned demon or some other dangerous form of awful death, with a pack of demonic hounds adding to the clamour.

All over Europe, even to the western and northern fringes of the Roman Empire and beyond, every region had its own version of the Wild Hunt, but beneath the variations in name the same phenomenon is depicted in virtually the same imagery, an association with the decomposing vegetation of Autumn and the fertilisation of the land in Spring. It can be seen as the Old Religion's healthy awe for the great forces which surrounded them. To the Christians, however, the Wild Hunt was equated with devil-worship; they played up its bloodthirstiness and demonic details as part of their campaign to demolish local fertility cults.

The Wild Hunt embodied not merely a primitive fear of storms and cyclones, it was a symbol of Nature in all its most unpredictable, uncontrollable, implacable and most threatening aspects — the 'animist chaos', celebrated with whirling dances, which must be brought to useful fruition by cultivation, literally 'tended by a cult', with all its myths and rituals.

The antiquity and universality of the Wild Hunt and its associated cults is beyond doubt. Some of its local variations, however, have much to tell us. In northern Europe the Valkyries, Woden and his wife Frigg, and many other Teutonic gods were not only 'Wild Hunters' but shape-changers who rode out on beasts, brooms and hurdles to the *trolla-thing*, which has been claimed as a prototype of the sabbat. And the eight legs of Woden's horse, Sleipnir, were a metaphor for speed as it rushed through the air literally like the wind, the element of its master.

In the classical south Dionysus, too, had his version of the Wild Hunt. The 'Train of Dionysus' was a wild, ecstatic rampage through the woods. His entourage included Maenads and nymphs, the drunken Sileni, the Greek Satyrs and Panes and the Fauns of Italy, all of them agricultural deities, the last three goat-like and gentle if also lustful, and reminiscent of the northern *Kornbocks*.

These field-goat spirits were diabolized by Christian iconography into the form of the Devil himself — the very 'Mowing Devil' of that woodcut of 1678. The horns of fertility — celebrated throughout Indo-Europe in the great gods such as the Celtic Cernunnos as well as in the little local genii of the fields, and giving us to this very day 'horny' as an epithet of healthy desire — became one of the hallmarks of the Enemy of Mankind.

THE FAIRY WHIRLWINDS

Grimm cites a legend of the German Mark region which seems to weld together the themes of the Wild Hunt, the whirlwind, damage to the crops, and Diana the Huntress (in her local form as Hulda). It concerns "a noble damsel who loved the chase above everything," even to the point of making "havoc of the husbandman's crops", for which she was transformed into a whirlwind and "doomed to ride with the storm for all eternity."[5]

The literature of demonology and witchcraft which burgeoned from the fourth century onwards contains many references to these creatures of the Devil riding on the wind. In 1587 an Essex clergyman wrote of the belief, common in his parish, that the Devil was abroad "when there are mighty winds . . .". When the bells of a parish church were blessed, one of the powers invested in them is to put demons to flight and to nullify "the assault of whirlwinds, the stroke of lightnings, the harm of thunders, the injuries of tempests, and every spirit of the storm winds."[6]

Ecclesiastical scholars and inquisitors were quick to attribute to witches a malevolent control of the weather. In 1563, when the King of Sweden warred against the Danes, he conscripted four witches to affect his enemy's weather. The Norse believed that a wind could be raised by magic (and distinguished it from Woden's stormwind).

Many traditions, folktales and popular beliefs have made this association between witchcraft, magic and the invisible powers of the atmosphere. Fairies travel in the wind; whistling raises a wind by the sympathetic magic of imitating it; whistling may also call up fairies; "Oh, Whistle, and I'll come to you, My Lad" is M. R. James's story of the inadvertent summoning of a shape-shifting elemental; the Jinns of Arabia travel in whirlwinds; those field-goats, the *Kornbocks*, were said to "ride the breezes that ripple the stalks"; in Ireland one doffs one's hat respectfuly to an eddying wind.

Wind, weather and witches find an association, once more, with the crops (and therefore with hints of an ancient fertility cult) in a confession of the

famous Scottish witch, Isobel Gowdie, in 1662. She went flying, she said, with her witch and fairy friends, mounted not on brooms (which have their own strange links with witchcraft and agriculture) but on "cornstraws, beanstalks or rushes".

Fairies and witches flying on straws, and straws that are plucked up and flung through the air with as much choice in the matter as the dancer trapped in a fairy whirl, bring us to the circular dance and the fairy ring — and perhaps to the circles in the crops of recent years.

RINGS, DANCES AND THE FAIRY CULT

Secret assembly and ritual dancing are signs of an ancient cult, but to establish direct links between the fairy tradition and the Mystery cults of Cybele, Hecate, Dionysus, Demeter and Kore requires some speculation. Perhaps the original Mysteries, practised at specific locations in the eastern Mediterranean, were brought here by officials of the Greco-Roman Empire, posted to these barbarous frontiers, perhaps fragments of them were transmitted to the occupied people.

Only recently, Martin Henig and Graham Webster announced their opinion that many of the archaeological sites of large villas of this period have yielded paving decorated with Eleusinian and Orphic scenes, which suggests that they may not have been residences at all, but centres where bathing, sacrificing and other congregational rituals could be practised.[7]

It is interesting that many of the sites which Henig and Webster have in mind are located in the areas — Wessex, for the large part, though extending north-eastwards along the Thames-Avon axis to St. Albans — from which we have had so many of the crop circle reports. The mosaic of a stag-horned god unearthed at St. Albans and hitherto labelled 'a sea-god' could just as well be the horned Dionysus, in my view (though Michael Harrison suggests the horned Celtic god, Cernunnos).[8]

The experts mentioned above are, of course, envisaging religious centres in the form of buildings, while the pagan fertility cults would have met at outdoor locations — and certainly secluded ones after the beginning of Christian persecution. Nevertheless, it is reasonable to speculate on a benign and fruitful period before that stage, during which Roman practices might have been adapted by the indigenous peoples.

The mysteries of Dionysus and Demeter were closely related through celebrations of the departure and return of Kore. The Bacchanalia, one of the Dionysian carnivals, featured a whirling dance, influenced by the convulsive dancing of the worshippers of Demeter/Cybele, the Corybantes. Perhaps, in the indigenous culture, this became a central feature of an outdoor fertility cult of which all that has survived Christian pressure is the legend of the fairy dance and the accusations of the inquisitors about the rituals of the witches' sabbat. The reportedly tumultuous, compulsive, dangerous and

sometimes even fatal nature of the dance-in-a-ring suggests a relationship with the Wild Hunt.

But did that dance-in-a-ring account for the 'fairy ring' found in grass?

Henry More, counted as one of England's most learned men in the 1650s, and who believed implicitly in the existence of witches, agonised over whether fairy rings were made by witches or by "those little puppet sprites which they call elves or fairies". By contrast, just thirty-three years later, Dr. Robert Plot devoted eleven pages of his *Natural History of Staffordshire* to fairy rings and leaned towards a natural explanation.

We now accept that the common 'fairy ring' is caused by the outward spread of fungi. As a natural phenomenon, they were around a long time before the witch craze, when, if you were seeking out places where witches might dance in a circle, they would have been the most obvious choice. And before that, the rings became similarly attached to the imagined revels of the fairy/fertility cult. The

analagous process can be seen in the now wide-spread belief that the children's 'Ring-a-Roses' game, another circular dance, was based on symbolism of the Great Plague; it is, of course, much older.

The dangers of fairy circles were not taken lightly. Similar motifs to those of the Wild Hunt apply here also: at certain times anyone who steps into a fairy ring or joins a fairy revel is trapped, compelled to dance forever, even after death. Specifically, these were places where the fairy whirlwind could pluck a trespasser into the sky as surely as Kore was taken downwards.

In the archaic agrarian culture, the worship of the fairies was overlaid by the confusion in the mind of the uninitiated between the fairies themsleves and the mysterious doings of the cult. Even if there were no actual fairies, the behaviour of the human congregation conformed to the popular notion of fairy activity. So we must add to the list of possible identities of the fairy tribe the secret worshippers themselves. In this way the original monolithic and mystical animism devolved into organised worship and then into isolated fragments of folk-custom.

This may have important implications for the origins of early labour brotherhoods, especially among agricultural workers. J. G. Campbell hints at the possibility of such a society in the Western Isles: "In that region, if a person had what was known as the *Ceaird Chomuinn* — that is, 'the association craft' or a species of handicraft fellowship with the fairies — he could compel them to come to his assistance for planting or reaping whenever he chose."[9]

W. C. Hazlitt noted a tradition of Moray farmers in the late nineteenth century which suggests that the rites of Ceres/Demeter may have survived in part. In mid-June they would march around their cornfields with blazing torches "in memory of the Cerealia". The procession around the gathered corn or the reaped field can be ritualised as circular dancing. The fiery torches at harvest time also put me in mind of the burning of the stubble to prepare the field for winter; small whirlwinds of burning debris and ash are frequently caused by the up-draught from the fires.

In the Western Isles the farmers believed until recently that the top grain on every ear of corn belonged by right to the fairies. Where the Woden cult thrived, "when any noise was heard in the sky it was thought that Woden . . . was passing through the air . . . During the autumn when the corn was being harvested, a sheaf was often left in the field for Woden's horses."

There are many such other traditions and customs which suggest largely forgotten links with rites and practices of the greatest antiquity. As Grimm says, " . . . by our study of elves, with whom the people have kept up acquaintance longer, we are led to gods that once were."[5]

PLAITING THE STRAWS, CLOSING THE CIRCLE

From all this rich material, drawn from myth, folklore and folk-custom there emerge some curious interlinkages which — anyway to Forteans — it seems desirable to keep in mind if we feel (as some do) that scientific attempts to explain the modern crop circles, Dr. Meaden's above all, have not yet proved convincing.

The great cycles of Nature, particularly those which govern the life and death of crops, fill all of us to this very day with a sense of awe and sometimes of dread. But we have largely forgotten the myths and rituals with which men once placed themselves in harmony with these vast processes of the world. Only fragments and echoes now remain of the old beliefs and customs, and we have, in consequence, grown blind and arrogant in our treatment of the world. Perhaps the crop circles have come to remind us of the need for a little humility!

The *scientific* antecedents for present attempts to understand the circles are clear enough. Theories of

winds and whirlwinds go back as far as Pliny and Aristotle. One English scholar, William Fulke, came close to the mark when he wrote in 1571, "A whyrlewynde some time is caused by meanes of twoo contrary wyndes that meet together." And as for strange circular markings in the ground, Robert Plot, investigating fairy rings in the 1680s, behaved like the model of an investigative scientist. He went into fields and dug up the earth, tasted it, smelled it, noted the health and colouring of the vegetation, noted animal behaviour (particularly that cattle would not touch grass in the vicinity), and usually got statements from everyone concerned.

In Plot's analysis[10] — and remember that he is writing at about the time of the *Mowing Devil* incident — he discusses a variety of explanations. Dancing witches and elves inevitably came first, given the folk-lore of his times. But he boldly reserves judgement. Of greater interest to him are the natural explanations: the rutting stags, the fungi-infected soil and (his favourite) hollow tubes of lightning. All of these are familiar to us in relation to the crop circles: we have heard much about animal damage and fungi; and in Terence Meaden's latest view the plasma-vortex which he now postulates can form an illuminated tube between sky and ground and may sometimes have a hollow centre.

Yet all Plot's rings were in grassy fields; there is no mention of flattened circular areas in fields of their cultivated cousins. Given his range of interests and his network of learned correspondents (who formed the core of the recently created Royal Society), I feel sure that Robert Plot, more than anyone else, would have known of the phenomenon of the crop circles had they occurred and been discussed at that time. But he didn't. If crop circles were rare or non-existent then (and the *Mowing Devil* remains a disputed case), one of the big questions is their increasing frequency today.

It is curious how many of the theories put forward to explain the crop circles have echoes in

was a rushing sound and a rumble . . . then suddenly everything was still . . . It was uncanny . . . The dawn chorus stopped; the sky darkened . . .

The feelings of these modern observers resemble the superstitious fear and respect engendered by the forces of Nature in those who tilled the fields in earlier times. The fears of the mowers — whether or not they were members of a brotherhood or cult — were *rational* : they reflected a proper awe. It is possibly the self-proclaimed rationalist of present times who is at risk of being blinkeredly unreasonable. That unwillingness of country folk in Hampshire as recently as the post-war era to hand-reap the very simple circular disturbances which they seem to be talking about "because they though they were uncanny and had some devilish origin" could possibly make better sense in terms of the complex relationship between our species and the planet it inhabits. Perhaps this article gives us an inkling why.

Are we witnessing a modern version of the 1678 fairy retribution, enacted on a larger scale to match

antiquity. The appeal to rutting stags and hedgehogs recalls the orgiastic animism of the fairy and witch revels; and Meaden's electrically charged plasma-vortex, sometimes manifesting in luminous form, resembles not only Robert Plot's 'hollow tubes of lightning' but also the fairy whirlwinds.

From the accounts given elsewhere in this book of the manner in which — rather rarely — witnesses claim to have seen a circle in the act of forming, I have drawn the following extracts. They seem to convey the sense of many of my themes.

Suddenly the grass began to sway before our eyes and laid itself flat in a clockwise spiral . . . A perfect circle was completed in less than half a minute, all the time accompanied by a high-pitched humming sound . . . My attention was drawn to a 'wave' coming through the heads of the cereal crop in a straight line . . . The agency, though invisible, behaved like a solid object . . . When we reached the spot where the circles had been, we were suddenly caught up in a terrific whirlwind . . . [The dog] went wild . . . There

the intensity of modern farming? Are the gods of corn and field showing us their stigmata?

The commercial necessities (anyway the alleged necessities) of modern farming are perhaps the counterpart of the greed of that farmer of 1678. Many of us now feel that we are alienating ourselves from the Earth we depend upon. It is not that the older ways were necessarily the best possible, or that we should now abandon all that we have painfully learned over the centuries about the more effective cultivation of the soil (by the application of the scientific method). It may be more a matter of having temporarily lost our hearts and souls in a blindly arrogant search for maximum 'efficiency' in place of that more humble, reverent and ritual relationship with the Great Mother which the ancients certainly possessed.

Whatever 'explanation' the crop circles may ultimately prove to have, they will have served an urgent and perhaps quite literally 'vital' purpose by raising questions of this kind.

REFERENCES
1. *Fortean Times*, Issue no. 53 (Available at £2.00, post-free, from Specialist Knowledge Services, 20 Paul Street, Frome, Somerset BA11 1DX).
2 Thomas, Keith *Religion & the Decline of Magic* Penguin 1973.
3. Nutt, Alfred *The Voyage of Bran* 1895.
4. Spence, Lewis *British Fairy Origins* 1946.
5; Grimm, Jacob *Teutonic Mythology* 4 vols. 1880-88.
6. Pennick, Nigel *Lost Lands & Sunken Cities* Fortean Times 1987.
7. Newspaper, *The Independent*, of 22 September 1988.
8. Harrison, Michael *The Roots of Witchcraft* Tandem 1975.
9. Campbell, J. G. *Superstitions of the Scottish Highlands* 1900.
10. Plot, Robert *The Natural History of Staffordshire* 1686.

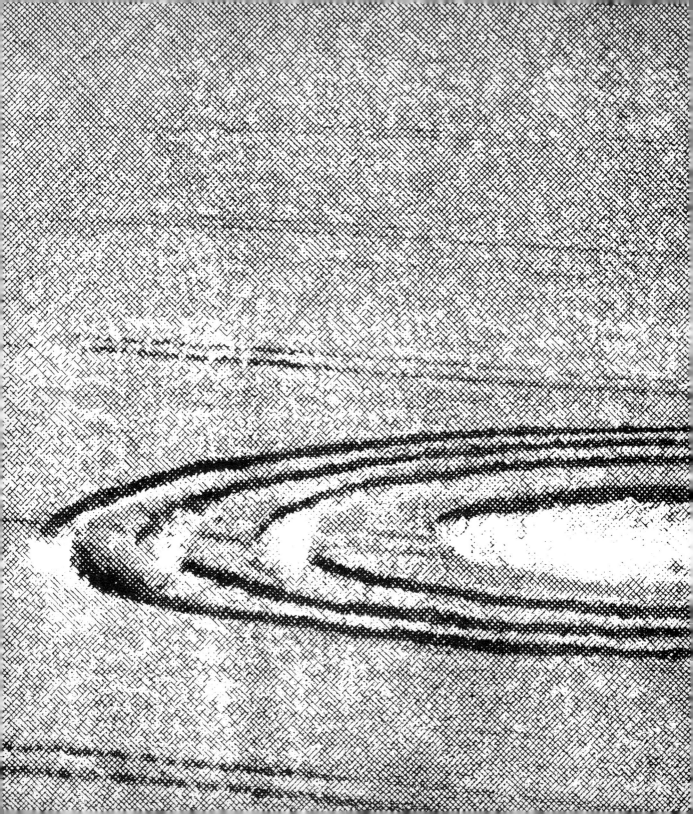

PART
2
PHYSICS AND
FORCES
PUZZLES AND
PARADIGMS

HOW ARE THEY MADE?

"What mean these Marks?" asks John Michell; and he invites us to deplore the tendency of the times "to concentrate on the mechanism rather than the message."

Part One gives much space to 'messages' and we shall return to them in Part Three. But 'mechanism' seems to many of us to be very often a necessary means of making sure that we are not carried away by a misreading of the 'messages' we receive.

Understanding the mechanism of measles may, for example, be a desirable corrective to the otherwise plausible message that our child has fallen ill from the malice of the old woman in the cottage down the road. Old women down the road would probably have welcomed Pasteur as a witness for the defence when brought to trial for witchcraft.

The myths and rituals of the corn lie deep in the history of our species. By losing touch with them and with their implied reverence for Nature, we have lost much else, including a sense of 'meaning', as Bob Rickard eloquently argues. But most of us would regret it if the entailed 'message' were read as obliging us to return to the horrendous practices, recorded at appalling length in *The Golden Bough*, which many of the archaic peoples felt necessary to ensure the fertility of the crops: some understanding of the mechanisms of growth may be a desirable part of our baggage as we resume communication with the archetypal guardians of field and grain.

There is in any case, for some of us, a wish to grasp precisely what may be happening in terms of the physical forces involved when circles form in a crop field, regardless of whether we can, or cannot, rid ourselves of the feeling that 'purpose' is also at work.

When cup-and-ring marks are found on ancient stones around the world, the means by which they are made is a desirable part of studying them. Did they appear by magic? By the whim of a passing deity? Are they the result of weathering or some other accident of blind forces? Were they made by visiting beings from other worlds? The discovery, by pedestrian examination, that they were incised by tools (and not always with great precision) reasonably suggests that the driving force sprang from the energy of an arm and a hand, probably of human size and shape. Human intention can be sensibly postulated. The all-important questions of meaning and message can then — but perhaps only then — be tackled with confidence.

How are the crop circles made? By a descending vortex? By energies at ground level or below? By other physical agencies of a more or less conventional kind (and if so, what)? By agencies of a largely novel sort?

These are hardly trivial questions if wider speculations about 'purpose' and 'intelligence' are not to degenerate into mere sectarian disputes, the choice among which is a matter of taste or faith (without so much as a *Which?* report to guide us).

In this part of the book Terence Meaden, the scientist who has grappled with the problem for longer than any other researcher, outlines, for the general reader, the present stage in the development of his atmospheric vortex model. It offers — astonishingly for most of us — some potential insights into other phenomena hitherto thought anomalous. Few of us would have expected, eleven years ago, that an attempt to account for some deceptively simple markings in a Wiltshire cornfield might come to take in (if only very speculatively at this stage) the Star of Bethlehem, the Burning Bush of Moses, sightings of the Blessed Virgin Mary and a range of UFO phenomena. If these prospects are realised, the plasma-vortex hypothesis will have proved to be among the most powerful and all-embracing of general propositions.

But no scientist expects his views to prevail

immediately without some polemical discussion. Terence Meaden will be pursuing the deeper technicalities with his scientific peers. But are there objections to be offered from the standpoint of commonsense and a close observation of the crop circles themselves? George Wingfield draws our attention to difficulties of this sort and also to a wide range of phenomena, associated with the circles, for which the evidence continues to accumulate and which, if verified, present acute problems for a wholly conventional view.

Richard Andrews completes this part of the book with an account of what dowsing (a phenomenon recognised by Terence Meaden) has suggested to him about the less accessible energies with which the crop circles appear to be associated.

Crop circles and the plasma vortex

G. T. MEADEN

For eleven years I have studied the crop-circle problem, that quixotic marvel of nature whose tantalising rings and circles have intrigued the world since their properties came to be so widely publicised a year or two ago.

The Introduction to this book, written by Ralph Noyes for the general reader, gives a brief history of the early research into this fascinating subject. In this article I want to put some scientific background behind Ralph Noyes's overview, and to explain my hypothesis of the causation of these remarkable events.

The phenomenon has much to teach us, and in more disciplines than one. The striking beauty of the circles themselves and the unusual phenomena which sometimes attend them, both before and after their formation, very readily stir the imagination of those drawn to the mystical, the paranormal and the extraterrestrial. Strange effects are, moreover, sometimes reported by psychics and visionaries. These things are most certainly not to be ignored. But I believe that they derive from a natural (though complex and hitherto unrecognised) phenomenon. In coming to understand the latter, we may well identify some of the factors which have given birth to many myths and supernatural beliefs and other socio-psychological phenomena.

A SCIENTIFIC VIEW

My hypothesis is that there exists a previously unrecognised energetic vortex, a helical or toroidal force which interacts with the crop and brings with it great power and unexpected electromagnetic properties.

Notwithstanding the difficulties of interpretation which have arisen from the amazing discoveries of recent years, including those known to us from 1990 at the time of going to press, I remain confident that the circles are to be explained wholly within the bounds of conventional science. Theoretical problems of great interest and difficulty have still to be tackled, but they will require a professional understanding of physics, meteorology, mathematics and statistics rather than idle speculation by those not versed in the scientific method.

As the Introduction mentions, there has been a steady stream of papers in *The Journal of Meteorology* since 1981. I have in addition published material in *Weather*, the journal of The Royal Meteorological Society, and in Conference Proceedings (Tokyo, Lyon, Budapest, Oxford). I have advocated a vortex solution throughout, though I have come to see it in increasingly complex terms and to attach growing importance to its crucial factor, the subsidiary electromagnetic properties due to self-electrification.

Among professional scientists Professor John Snow has worked since June 1988 on the meteorological origin of the circles, joined in 1989 by Dr. Tokio Kikuchi. Professor Heinz Wolff was introduced to the problem in June 1989 and immediately supported the meteorological approach (BBC TV, *Secret Circles*). Also in 1989 two Japanese professors of physics began applying their talents to the problem, Professor Ohtsuki via the plasma-vortex approach and Professor Hiroshi Kikuchi via magneto-hydrodynamical theory to understand the electric discharge and ionisation behaviour of the atmosphere in a circles/vortex environment. The work of these scientists led to such useful insights into the circles problem that an international scientific conference was held at Oxford in June 1990. This has led to another hardback book, *The Crop Circles Mystery*, based on the ten papers which were included in the conference booklet, *Circles Research 1*.

Scientific opinion is unanimous that no rules of science are 'broken' by the circles effect, and confidence is high following the success of the Oxford conference that all properly-monitored, unsensationalised discoveries are capable of eventual explanation, using the known laws of science and mathematics. The number of scientists supporting the principle of my atmospheric vortex theory has risen dramatically since the publication of *The Circles Effect and its Mysteries*, which is now in its second edition, and further still following the 1989 Tokyo conference and the 1990 conferences at Oxford, Budapest and Lyon.

THE NATURE OF THE PLASMA VORTEX

My work suggests that circle formation involves the descent of an energetic vortex from the atmosphere, a vortex of air which is ionised to the point at which it is better regarded as a species of low-density cool plasma producing a high-energy electromagnetic field. Not only does the assembled evidence point to a plasma source of electromagnetic radiation, with direct consequences for radio-communications interference, radar ghost-images and ionising effects on vehicle performance and animal and human behaviour, but the work explains thousands of reports of previously unidentified luminous phenomena seen spinning close to the ground or high in the air. Although a few per cent of these may have been incorrectly categorised as 'ball-lightning' in the past, a great many have been compartmentalised as 'unidentified flying objects'. My work is therefore likely to have considerable repercussions in the area of UFO research, a subject which has traditionally suffered from a temptation to ascribe unsolved sightings to extraterrestrial forces and intelligence.

The clearest evidence for the operation of this previously unknown atmospheric vortex lies in the distinctive circular-symmetric traces left in grass or in standing crops. These traces are illustrated throughout this book and in the figures in this article.

The most common finding is an area of damage, quasi-circular in shape, in which stalks of growing corn have been pushed over by an intense rotating force having axial symmetry (Photo. 1). Often the pliable stems are not broken but are bent just above ground level. In most cases a conspicuous swirl or spiral trace is discernible, extending from a tight centre up to a diameter of 60 metres or more at which there is a sharp perimeter. Both senses of rotation are found, but for some sites only clockwise circles have as yet been seen. In some cases the

Photo 1

downward blast is exceptionally severe, as at Chilcomb, Hampshire, in 1987 (see colour Plate 5). The crop is plastered to the ground like a hard carpet. At the other extreme, the descending vortex has merely brushed the crop canopy or has struck so lightly that partial crop recovery has taken place immediately.

Mature crops make the best circles. Young crops have a capability for straightening upwards which ripe crops hardly possess. Hence circles formed in green crops are not so easily seen when a few days of re-growth have occurred, whereas most circles formed in ripe cereals maintain their flattened beds until harvesting.

Some hasty statements have been made to the effect that the ripened crop of a circle continues to *grow* horizontally. I have yet to see such behaviour although I have visited many hundreds of circles. This generalisation arose from observing the stalks of *mature* corn in which, the nodes of sufficiently mature stalks were *already lignified before the descent of the vortex*: they could not possibly regain a vertical posture via the geotropic response. By contrast, when the depressed corn is green, as it is for most circle events in April and May in southern England, those nodes which have not lignified respond to the geotropic effect which permits the stalks to straighten upwards. One therefore finds in green corn the stalks bending round after a few days, the bending affecting just a couple of nodes as a rule. What the less meticulous observers have meant is that for undamaged mature stalks the corn (i.e. seed head) continues to *ripen* horizontally.

Nor should there be any mystery about the bending of the stalks at the time of the vortex event. Moving air pushes against the whole stem firmly but not harmfully. It is only natural that the bending should develop above ground level towards the root. In an extreme case in a rape-circle in May 1987, indicated to me by other investigators, the crop was severely bent, but this was because it had been planted in stony earth and the stalks had been

obliged to curve round stones as they grew. I pointed out many similar examples of upward-growing bent stalks in the untouched crop in the rest of the field.

It is often noted that in some medium-to-large circles the circle beds are layered. One can sometimes lift the flattened corn over quite big areas and find that the straws beneath are angled in some other direction. An instance is mentioned (albeit in terms with which I would not agree!) in the Editor's Introduction. Some circles have two centres, illustrative of vortex drift during the few seconds of the occurrence, and this accounts for the layering to which I refer.

The centre is not always struck down but can remain standing as a small pyramid or cone comprising bent and unbent stems (Photo. 2). Occasionally, the pyramid gets knocked to one side and is found lying flat. The pyramid effect is best explained as arising from the swirling air of a descending 'hollow-centred' vortex or ring-vortex (see below). Upon impact the rolling outwards of the expanding ring flattens the corn with a quasi-horizontal force.

Busty Taylor recorded one instance of a circle system intersecting a field edge. In 1990 one linear circle system (near Wilton House, Salisbury) lay partly in one field, partly in another.

Dispassionate examination of the evidence plainly confirms that the vortices are necessarily *descending* ones with a horizontal spreading action after impact. In this the new vortex type differs from the more commonly examined tornadoes, waterspouts, and dust-devils (which consist of inward-spiralling rising columns or tubes of air). Despite unsubstantiated claims by amateur investigators, all the evidence is compatible with the stalks of corn being pushed over by strongly moving air — *ionised* air, to be sure (as I was the first to suggest). The strength of the wind can be appreciated from some of the cases cited in *The Circles Effect and its Mysteries* of people *being thrust to the ground by an intense downblast* whose characteristics seem to resemble

Photo 2

those of an ionised or plasma vortex in descending mode. As we shall see, in order to understand the properties of the newly-recognized vortex one must determine how *breakdown* of the normal 'spin-up' situation can develop into violent vortex-descent.

Other views on the origin of the circles have been mentioned from time to time, but none has been backed by adequate theories or reasoning. In contrast to the well-supported atmospheric vortex theory, none of the other ideas has, in my view, been presented in a manner fit for scientific appraisal. On the other hand every professional scientist *who has read the latest papers on the subject and visited a few circles with the author* supports the principle of atmospheric vortices.

I do not consider that any other scientifically-based theory has been forthcoming, although wild guesses abound. The earth energy idea, mentioned in Delgado and Andrews' book as a possibility, is independently supported by G. Wingfield. Whatever its presumed origin may be 'energy' is imagined to exit from the earth as a rotating force. It is the "coming up out of the ground that causes the corn to fall" . . . "Whatever 'agency' produces the circles, it is not only invisible, but is most likely present for some time before and after the corn is found to have been laid flat".[1] How this is reconciled with the evidence of downward blasts, descending lights, eye-witness observations of circles forming, gentle vortex descent which merely brushes the crop canopy, etc., no attempt at explanation is made.

MULTIPLE CIRCLE EVENTS

The most surprising — but also most informative — of the multiple-event cases are the five-circle sets comprising a big central circle and four nearly-equidistant satellites of smaller size. Sometimes additional circles along a diagonal axis turn these into six-circle or seven-circle sets (Plate 18). Circles also form in other cluster-combinations, some with multiple rings, and some in which satellite circles combine with multiple rings. The chief types are illustrated. Patterned groups of two, three, four and five circles are relatively common. One may deduce from this that in many cases some of the vortices are interlinked and hence interdependent on one another.

To take, for example, the rectilinear triplet (three circles in a straight line, a recent paper by Van Heijst and Kloosterziel[2] has shown how a single vortex in a rapidly rotating fluid reforms as tripolar in-line vortices. That this happens in laboratory conditions suggests that triple-vortex stability may also be a natural tendency for vortex phenomena in sheared atmospheric environments as well. It is striking that such a seemingly simple experimental result as this has only just been published. It demonstrates how little we yet know about the physics and meteorology of atmospheric and fluidic vortices. No wonder that science was caught by surprise when the discovery of my proposed circles effect was announced — and no wonder that many laymen feel themselves to be in the presence of something occult and beyond conventional explanation.

EYE-WITNESS SIGHTINGS OF CIRCLE FORMATION

The number of reported eye-witness sightings increases every year. From these and other evidence, it is plain that circles can form either by day or by night.

The oldest accounts have been much cited. They are from Arthur Shuttlewood (1970s, a fan-opening spiral in grass on Starr Hill in Bishopstrow parish, Wiltshire) and Melvyn Bell (1983 in wheat, on the slopes of Great Cheverell Hill, Wiltshire). Because Delgado and Andrews[8:158] wished to generalise, using incomplete evidence, that for circle-forming "the forces's specification was total darkness operating, weather condition free, and topographically conditionless", they chose to ignore these eye-witnesses's accounts. Unfortunately for them, two more daytime sightings have since been reported, one a detailed account by Mr. Ray Barnes of West Wiltshire (3rd July 1982, a fan-opening circle in a cereal crop on the slopes of the Westbury Hills), the other a Scottish observation by Mr. Sandy Reid (late August 1989, near Duntroon Hill, north of Dundee). It is probable that these circles resulted from the phenomenon of vortex breakdown (see later section). Vortex breakdown can develop in dust-devil whirlwinds as well (Lugt 1989), as they do in tornadoes and waterspouts. This may explain the eye-witness sightings of circles made by mobile whirlwinds (as at Ross-on-Wye 1981), Marple 1988, Roundway Hill 1989, Pucklechurch 1989) (Randles and Fuller 1990; Rendall 1989, Pearson 1990).

In favour of nocturnal circle-formation is the evidence given in the next section of circles connected with luminous effects which were noted in Wiltshire and Kent in 1989 (to say nothing of August 1678 in Hertfordshire) — if we really can take that as a true instance of a corn circle at this remove in time, on the basis of a crude woodcut and without corroboration.

Finally one should mention the early morning observation of Mr. Roy Lucas of Yatesbury, Wiltshire, who witnessed three times on 16 June 1988 a spinning cloud of vapour of 'smoke' with narrow core which formed just above the canopy of a wheatfield before dissipating in the nearly still air south of Windmill Hill.[17] This was a view of up-spinning vortices of the lee-eddy type, part of which were rendered visible by condensation in the nearly saturated early-morning air. On this occasion the vortices did not 'break down' to create crop circles.

ACOUSTIC AND LUMINOUS EFFECTS

Several eye-witnesses have reported audible effects at the time of formation of circles.[11;18,19] Typical is a humming noise which sounds like the coronal discharge which accompanies high-tension electrical installations. These sounds imply the presence and motion of electric charges, just as they do for their better-studied atmospheric counterparts, the whirlwind and the tornado.

It is well known to American researchers that even the common whirlwind generates an electric field. The field is electrostatic, and arises from the electrification of dust particles which have been scoured by friction from the surface of the ground by the energy of the spinning winds. Very substantial electric-field values have been measured of opposite sign to that of the earth's normal positive electric field.

The electric field of tornadoes is known to

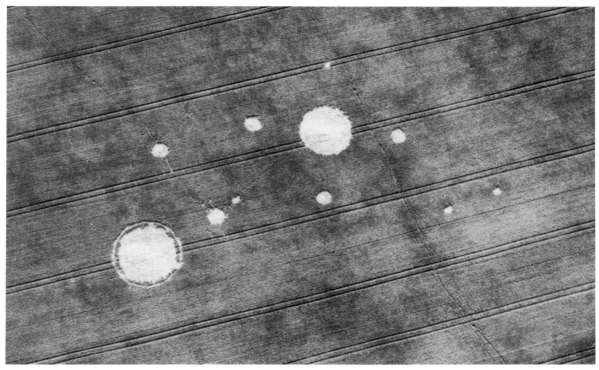

Photo 3

generate accoustic and luminous effects.[30] It is certainly the same with our circles-effect vortices. Moreover, there is a circle case from France (St. Souplet, Nord, October 1954 — date advised by Claude Maugé) in which circle formation in a plot of spinach was coincident with a red ball of light and acoustic noises (*Lumières dans la Nuit* 1976, *Nord-Matin* 6 October 1954). Two similar cases involving huge balls of light and their resultant crop circles were witnessed in England last year (29 June 1989 in Wiltshire, and 10 August in Kent). These cases have been fully recounted.[11][20] The circles were 15–18 metres in diameter. Photo. 4 shows the Wiltshire occurrence.

Light and noise imply the existence and motion of electrical discharges. This is entirely what I would expect from the circles-effect vortex which I am postulating.

RINGS ROUND CIRCLES

When rings surround circles, they are narrow rings concentric with the circumference of the main circle, and they have steep sides as well. The flattening force evidently exhibits an amazingly fine degree of control. Rings in both directions have been found. One big circle in central Wiltshire in 1989 had three concentric rings around it, and I have good reason to expect still more rings in the future. Two of the Wiltshire circles of May 1990 had triple rings, one of them with a quartet of satellites spaced on/along the middle ring. [A four-ringed circle also appeared in June near Devizes, its second ring bearing four satellites — see Epilogue. Ed.] The diameter of the biggest circle was a staggering 61 metres (200 feet) and its biggest ring a still more extraordinary 85 metres (280 feet). [The Devizes event of June exceeded even these dimen-

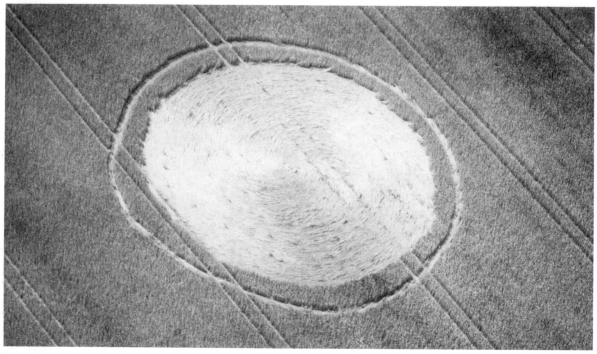

Photo 4

sions. Ed.] The width of a ring can be as much as two to three metres or as little as 10 cms (four inches) — about a hand's breadth. Photos 4 and 5 show narrow-ringed circles.

We must consider how a spinning vortex can depress the corn so neatly at the edges of the main circle and at the edges of the rings too, and how it can create multiple rings. My suggestion is that the air flowing around these rings is ionized. Whereas the rings may be formed by a boundary-interaction effect at the time of the main vortex impact, the intense flow produces electromagnetic effects. This possibly results from a flow of ions whose strength is sufficient to orient polarisable particles in the soil and so create a signature capable of instrumental detection. This would explain why residual magneto-electric effects appear to remain after the departure of the vortex, and is doubtless what the dowsers have been detecting.

DOWSING

The proposition that vortices carry electromagnetic effects with them when they strike the crop and the ground can account for the surprising dowsing effects observed in crop circles and their external ring systems. Dowsing has been studied by Richard Andrews for some twenty years, and during the last three years he has applied his abilities to the circles problem. Since 1988 I, too, have tried dowsing circles, and it seems that it works. In fact, probably everyone can do it, as Professor Heinz Wolff has recently said (BBC TV, *Secret Circles*, 1989). The reason why dowsing works for water is far from clear, but one may expect that a scientific answer will be ultimately attainable. Following a study in the US by D. G. Chadwick and L. Jensen, these two scientists from Utah State University have suggested that hand-held rods may magnify miniscule muscle movements a hundredfold or more, possibly in response to tiny magnetic field changes resulting from the presence of water masking part of the otherwise ambient magnetic field. The positive response encountered when dowsing crop circles might relate to local field changes arising from the impact of an electrified vortex with the soil if it had polarised some of the soil chemicals. My research organisation, Circles Effect Research (CERES) is intending to quantify this work by making use of electrometers and magnetometers as detectors.

VORTICES AND ELECTROMAGNETISM

Strong support is given in *The Crop Circles Mystery* for my suggestion of an electromagnetic association with natural atmospheric vortices. Plasma vortices have been created in the laboratory by Professor Y. H. Ohtsuki in collaboration with H. Ofuruton, using an electrostatic discharge in one case and microwave interference in another. Ohtsuki also reports an observation by radars of two different ships in the Pacific of an atmospheric plasma which circled both ships but remained invisible. Later, towards midnight, it returned emitting a sound and a bright light.

Theoretical work by Professor Hiroshi Kikuchi suggests the possibility of certain interactions between an axial electric field and the earth's magnetic field which could be relevant for the observations of Mary Freeman near Silbury Hill and Michael Webb at Bratton, Wiltshire, both at night in the summer of 1988.[18,21,31] Self-illuminated tubes were seen, extending from cloud to ground. [By a pleasing coincidence the Bratton event occurred near the farm of Mr. Scull, whose report in 1980 first brought the whole phenomenon to systematic attention — see Introduction. Ed.]

WHAT MAKES THE VORTICES?

I have consistently argued that the vortices are eddy processes in the lower atmosphere, set in motion by windflow past topographical obstructions. The technicalities are explored fully elsewhere[18,21] and

are being currently extended by Professor John Snow and Dr. Tokio Kikuchi.

In almost all cases the circles develop close to hills; in most others the circles appear up to 6 or 7 kilometres *downwind* of a hill — a fact which may cause untrained observers to overlook the hill effect. The distance is enough that a hasty observer may not realise that the circles are hill-induced. In July 1989 a splendid quintuplet set of circles was studied at Aylesbury in Central England. At the site the ground was flat, but the circles had been formed six kilometres *downwind* of the Chiltern Hills to the south-east.

In Scotland last August Mr. Sandy Reid was eyewitness to a circle as it formed.[22] For half-a-minute as he watched, at a distance of 15 metres, the wind was violently rustling the corn over a circular area, all the time making a strange noise, but where he stood there was *no wind at all*. Then suddenly a 'force' shot downwards and a circle appeared almost instantaneously. This was a good observation of the vortex-breakdown of a standing eddy vortex. We have proposed that similar vortices develop in the lee of hills and escarpments under the right conditions, and that circular traces inevitably result.

An essential prerequisite for vortex generation seems to be a quiet airmass with good, stable stratification which remains effectively undisturbed even in the presence of a steady *weak* airflow. Then a new airmass encroaches, marked by a microfrontal boundary with higher windspeed and usually new wind direction and different thermo-hygrometrical, aerosol and electrical properties. As the windspeed rises, vortex-tubes develop downwind of critically-shaped obstacles, like round hills and the spurs of scarps, but the final act is a system breakdown which provokes vortex descent or ring-vortex descent and leads to the circles effect. In practice, the eddy vortex may exist for a fairly long time ranging up to many minutes, whereas the breakdown state is often more short-lived.

The spiral-centred circles resulting from this

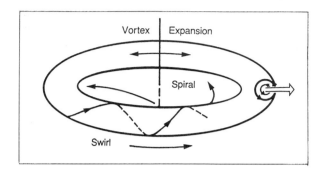

process (Photos. 1 and 2) are becoming better understood as current theory develops. Probably there are several alternative vortex mechanisms. One is the ring vortex idea, proposed by Snow and Kikuchi. Fig. above illustrates the descent and outward rolling action of one sort of ring vortex. This can explain not only the swirling pattern in the crop but also the occasionally-seen central cone or pyramid (Photo. 2).

The energy found in this violent vortex comes from the concentration of the energy of the initial encroaching airmass into the very small space of the eventual vortex-tube. The intense spin of the latter, coupled with the presence of aerosol particles or water vapour, is likely to be the key to its production of rotating electric charges and powerful electromagnetic field. Then — depending upon the relative net charge distribution within the vortex and in the crop or ground beneath — the vortex either dives hard at the crop or reaches it more gently. Occasionally, as the approach is made, repulsion seems to occur, resulting in no contact with the crop or just a soft brushing of the crop canopy. In the weakest visible rings only the ears of corn get bent over.

THE ORIGIN OF QUINTUPLET SATELLITES

The satellites of quintuplet circle systems may originate from vortex-surface interactions at the time of impact with the crop. Satellite-circle formation has been discussed by George Bathurst in *The Crop Circles Mystery*. The electromagnetic effects which are detectable in these satellites, as in the main circles, are a concomitant secondary effect. In fact a few quintuplet sets have associated rings, sometimes very narrow passing through them with all the appearance of having been formed by the circulation of ionised air.

I have been asked how I can square the idea of 'increasing order', as signified by the production of ordered quintuplets out of the disorder of air turbulence, with the Second Law of Thermodynamics which says that for a closed system entropy (or 'disorder') can only increase, if it does not remain constant. The answer is to be found at the microscopic level of inquiry. The initial stage is a relatively high degree of order over a big volume: fairly stable air above the crop and a somewhat steady wind approaching the other side of the hill. The final stage is a greatly disturbed situation with considerable turbulence over a vast volume and, only temporarily, a very limited volume with air swirling inside small satellites. There is no breaking of any law here.

SUPPOSED 'DEVELOPMENT' OF THE PHENOMENON

An oft-repeated statement (even the Introduction of this book seems prone to it!) is that recent years have seen a dramatic rise in the number of circles occurring and a sensational elaboration in their forms and patterns.

A dip into CERES's archive (which currently holds data on over 1,000 circles, as at the start of June 1990) and a rational look at the history of the circles soon exposes these fallacies.

The number of circles found annually from 1980 to 1988 (see the Introduction to this book) corresponded well with the number of *sites* discovered. Each year more *sites* were being monitored, and more circles were being found. Circle numbers leapt as aerial reconnaissance became more frequent in 1987 and 1988, and still more so in 1989 as national publicity rose.

I acknowledge, nonetheless, that 1989 can be said to have provided a notable break from that approximate proportionality between circle numbers and circle sites, the circles known to CERES numbering 305. However, this may be nothing other than a statistical effect prompted by increased 'searching hours', the sighting of smaller and smaller circles through improved observation techniques, and the character of the weather fronts responsible for the major circle outbreaks. The events of 9 May 1989 were paramount. Some 60 circles across northern and western Wiltshire were assignable to this one date, their origin attributable to the slow advance of a weak front moving south across a stagnant anticyclone which had bestowed dry, quiet weather over Britain for several days. A couple of days in the second half of June also led to the development of large numbers of vortex-circles, especially in north-central Wiltshire. These three occasions were chiefly responsible for raising the Wiltshire total to such an extraordinary magnitude (232), plus the fact that many circles would never have been found if frequent air flights had not dominated the season's monitoring activity.

Another way to analyse the statistics of 1989 is to ignore the Wiltshire total and to concentrate on the rest of England and Scotland. For these 17 counties 73 circles are known — about four circles per county. What has 'exploded' is not so much the number of circles being formed as the number of potential observers who are now looking for them, nation-wide as well as in Wessex. Once saturation point has been reached for observer-coverage of a given area (the county of Wiltshire may be the first) then statistical fluctuations about a long-term mean are to be expected. It follows that many years will elapse before real trends can be established. It is premature to suggest that circle numbers are abnormal in some way.

As to the so-called 'evolution' of circle-patterns, I believe that this is scarcely more than the result of chance discovery of whatever patterns happen to be present in a given year. There may be hundreds of different patterns, and each year we are treated to just a few of these depending on atmospheric and environmental conditions. In 1980 we knew only of single circles, in 1981 the first triple was seen, in 1983 the first quintuplets, in 1986 the first single-ringed circles, in 1987 the first double-ringed circle, and so on. But retrospective research was turning up pre-1980 evidence for some of these same formations. We learnt of a 1978 quintuplet from Hampshire (complete with photographs); of a circle triplet for 1974 (North Carolina); of a double-ringed circle for 1960 (with survey notes) and for 1977 (with photographs); and of certain pre-1980 ringed circles from other countries, we even know of a 'doughnut' circle with dot centre for 1980.

Much of the supposed 'evolution' of the phenomenon — to which some have even ascribed 'intelligence' — can therefore be explained rationally by an insufficiency of data. The more complete the archive becomes, the better this will be appreciated. [A strong argument, indeed, for the efforts being made by *The Centre for Crop Circle Studies* to secure country-wide cover of the phenomenon and the amalgamation of data! Ed.]

Admitttedly, 1990 does look to be exceptional, but just because the reasons for this wait to be clarified, it would be fatuous to decree than an alien intelligence is at hand.

CIRCLE-CENTERING ON TRAMLINES AND BARE-EARTH PATCHES

A surprising number of circles are *roughly* centred on tramlines. An explation for this curiosity is possibly associated with a second oddity: that a certain percentage of other circles not aligned with tramlines centre instead on bare-earth patches in the middle of the crop. To the uninitiated this suggests some occult force. But what would such people have made of conventional lightning discharges in the pre-scientific age? Would they not have discovered after a period of casual observation that it is tall buildings, churches, trees. . . and other exposed objects which often get hit by lightning? Would this behaviour be attributed to the selective choice, or 'intelligent mind', of some thunder-god?

Certainly, the atmospheric scientist would not. He knows that lightning follows the easiest path to earth, the path of least resistance, the path along which the local electric field is already high as a result of electron flow initiated by brush discharge or corona discharge from the highest pointed objects on the earth's surface.

It may be similar with the plasma vortex. In its final stage of descent — especially if slowly descending — the vortex may be sensing local variations in field strength. Bare-earth patches, such as the ones caused by a missed drill at seed-planting or arising from the presence of the tractor marks (tramlines), could be areas above which electric field strengths are different.

By the same reasoning certain parts of a crop could be more highly charged that average, and therefore be regions of attraction for a vortex. Dust-laden wind is known to be effective at transporting electric charges [this is a subject well researched by meteorologists]. When blowing through a crop, the wind coats the dry stalks with dust and charges the stalks simultaneously. If the stalks grow in dry, poorly-conducting soil, as is usual on the thin well-drained soils of the chalk hills of Wessex, quite high electric fields build up. There would be a tendency for this increasingly unstable electric field to break down in the damper air of the night — and if a plasma vortex was in the vicinity the path of the vortex and the nature of the resulting circle patterns would certainly be affected. One of the reasons why Wessex is favoured with so many and such complex circle systems is likely to be the presence of the underlying chalk and the thin chalky soils which

Photo 5

dry out quickly and protect the corn from rapid charge leakage into the ground.

As for the more bizarre shapes reported in 1990, including the multi-figured 'claws' or 'keys' (see back cover), these simply portray parts of the complex internal structure of the more unstable vortices which make an irregular contact with the ground.

THE APPARENT NON-RANDOMNESS OF CIRCLE-SITES ACROSS THE COUNTRY

It has been claimed that because of the distribution of circle-sites is so obviously non-uniform across the country this is the product of decision-making by some unspecified 'intelligence'. But the deductions of the methodical scientist relate vortex-formation, hence circle-formation, to topographical and airflow factors, and that is all there is to it. Certain sites are favoured because these are the places where the critical conditions are so frequently 'just right'. It is like coming to recognize that lenticular-shaped lee-wave clouds always develop downwind of hill or mountainous obstacles. We know that this is due to obstacle-related turbulence acting at a distance, but, doubtless, if the unthinking critic turned his attention to this subject, he might 'wish' the appearance of the lenticular cloud on the intervention of some divine or paranormal source.

FREQUENCY OF CIRCLES IN SOUTHERN ENGLAND

Why are circles so common in Southern England? Many dates for *circle-formation* are now known, which allows us to determine what the weather was doing at the time. On several occasions circles were associated with weak weather fronts crossing the region. These fronts have been of different kinds. The vortices develop, and the circles appear, when the right combination of atmospheric conditions blend with topographical factors which are also 'just right' and there is a suitable crop waiting beneath.

The main reasons for the high rate of circle development in Wiltshire and Hampshire must certainly relate to the topography, particularly the shapes of the chalk hills *and* their heights. The importance of chalk soils insulating electrically-changed shot from the subsoil chalk beneath was emphasized in the previous section. Another is the vast area of arable land put down to cereal production. The fourth is to do with the frequent passage of the right sort of wind system. Among the types of weather fronts which could plausibly trigger vortex formation (*and there are several*) we may mention sea-breeze fronts. In the summer months sea-breezes move northwards to penetrate deep inland, sometimes reaching a hundred kilometres from the coast by late evening or after dark when conditions have otherwise fallen calm. This means that on a quiet evening the wind can unexpectedly rise again, sometimes from a reversed direction compared with the earlier wind of the day! It even happens that it can later reverse, and become a retrograding front going south.

It takes much experience to monitor and understand such changes. Those of the 'circle researchers' in England who are non-scientists and have no training in physics, meteorology and mathematics, are unqualified to make meteorological judgments. Thus when it comes to determining wind strengths and directions on a continuous basis throughout the night and day, either a qualified person must investigate the matter or excellent instrumentation must be left in place. For example, in the period 10–18 June 1989 sea-breeze fronts moved north across Cheesefoot Head on successive evenings, 15th, 16th, and 17th June. On the last of these evenings the front went through at about 6.15 p.m. introducing cool maritime air. Later, the wind fell light to calm until, after midnight, the remains of the same front, or a different weak one, crossed the region moving southwards. This was probably the moment when a genuine ringed crop-circle came to be carved by a descending vortex on sloping high ground south of the escarpment, and may have been associated with a peculiar acoustic noise (if the sound was not a hoax) reported by C. Andrews, P. Delgado, G. Wingfield and others who were on the hill that night, but whose thoughts lay more in the preternatural.

LUMINOUS PROPERTIES AND BALLS OF LIGHT

The luminous properties, mentioned earlier, are sometimes coloured and sometimes pulsate. Reds and orange-tinted lights are most frequently seen, colours which correspond to the emission spectrum of atmospheric nitrogen and its oxides. Radio-frequency effects are sometimes noted. I exemplify with reference to the Japanese circle event which happened in the mountainous part of Yamagata Province in August 1986. Overnight on 8th–9th an almost circular area 6m diameter was blasted into a pond 6 km from the town of Mishikawa, and identified by a strongly-marked radial pattern in a floating bed of reeds; at the same time 20 tonnes of water vanished from this rice paddy. At 8 p.m. on the 8th at a nearby house a period of severe television interference was possibly associated with this event, as also a report of the descent of a bright orange light of 'ball lightning'. Various examples from other countries of the world can be given[18] including the St Souplet circle cited earlier.

Radio-frequency effects have been inferred for various reasons. There are numerous incidents of radio-communication interference in the vicinity of spinning balls of light.[18] Hundreds of examples of previously-unexplained cases are known. Sometimes pulsed lights are reported; and of course it is well known that tornado vortices can be tracked by their severe sferics or RF emissions. Tornadoes, too, generate luminous RF pulsed emissions and the Blackwell, Oklahoma, tornado is a meteorologically-monitored case.[12] In our plasma vortices too, the origin of the emissions is certainly the vortex's exterior region — the plasma-pause, the shell where the ion density is greatest. So, coloured lights, occasionally pulsating, and with an audible hum if one is near enough to hear are all authenticated. What would religiously-motivated people have thought of such a vision, especially someone near enough to hallucinate or be 'entranced'?

VISIONS

In our theory of the luminous vortex we find an answer to the miraculous visions of the past which 'faith' has supported on the part of the religious but which have gone unbelieved by the non-religious. An obvious case is the mountainside apparition of 13 May 1917 near Fatima in Portugal. The vision that the three young witnesses claimed to see could well have been a plasma vortex. Unexplained until now, we can understand the sighting in terms of an electrified vortex of the type under discussion.

The burning bush of Moses is another event awaiting reinterpretation as a luminous incandescent light of plasma vortex origin. Even the Star of Bethlehem had a reported motion which was incompatible with that of any astronomical light, so it can be better explained by the movement and hovering of a self-sustaining luminous vortex. Many other examples can be cited, from Will-of-the-Wisps and spooklights to 'angelic' appearances and Virgin Mary visions. So many of these happenings took place in hilly country, as do the luminous vortices of Britain. We can appreciate that spiritually-minded people had an innate susceptibility, then as now, to assign such revelations to the supernormal, and that, in any event, most such witnesses had neither the desire nor the philosophical training to allow them to seek explanations of natural origin.

SOME CONSEQUENCES FOR THE UFO PROBLEM

Serious workers in the UFO field will recognize how the plasma vortices which I have been studying for so long may be relevant to the UFO Problem. By this I mean, first and foremost, those observations of luminous phenomena which hover in the sky or descend towards or away from the ground but which, for lack of scientific recognition, have been given the sobriquet 'UFO'. I also include those further reports which involve electrical failures to cars, unexplained effects on animals and humans, etc, in connection with proximal light forms of unknown origin.

But now a whole new class of observation has acquired scientific understanding, validity, respectability. We can say that the UFO movement has been monitoring a genuine physical effect all the time — one of which the scientific community was unaware, and which will be of the greatest importance to the physical sciences in the future. The result is a substantial increase in the number of IFOs and a reduction in the number of true UFOs.

In their book *Controversy of the Circles*, Paul Fuller and Jenny Randles provide examples of three species of observations thought to be UFOs but which they now regard as better re-interpreted as plasma vortices. These concern close-encounter events well-known to ufologists: Tibet in 1947, Nelson (Lancashire) in March 1977, and Todmorden (Yorkshire) in November 1980 (a close encounter of the fourth kind). Fuller and Randles emphasize that many hundreds, if not thousands, of other cases need re-examining in the light of my

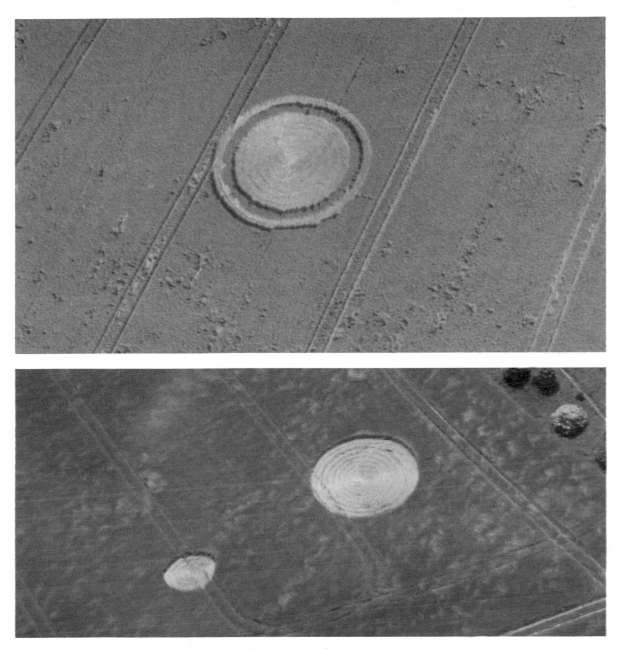

Plate 20. This single-ringer was formed on the last night of the White Crow experiment at Cheesefoot Head under bizarre circumstances which are described on pp. 104–5 by George Wingfield.

Plate 21. The larger of the two circles is the one we sat in on the evening of June 18 1989, when we heard a strange trilling noise. This has been documented and spoken of on a number of occasions. From a height of eight hundred feet you can still count the seven concentric rings in the main circle.

Plate 22. This photograph, which was taken at Hungerford in August 1988, gives the impression of a very large comma. One of the other satellites in this quintuplet set was only half-formed.

Plate 23. This photograph, taken at Bishops Cannings, shows how fine the rings have now become. The rings are so thin that you will have difficulty in trying to walk them without damaging the surrounding corn. This appeared on June 1 1990.

Plate 24. One of the more original designs of 1989 was the appearance of the 'Tadpole'. This was a clockwise circle with a 22 metre tail leading into it. In this photograph, taken from the pole, the concentric rings are very visible and their dimensions can be judged by the person standing in the photograph.

Plate 25. The last two circles of the 1989 season were the most spectacular of the year; the first one, seen here, consisted of an outer ring followed by an outward splay of corn with three contra-rotating rings in the middle. You can see that the circle is trying to form segments in the outward splay. This appeared on August 5 1989.

Plate 26. The last circle of 1989 (August 12) was the most spectacular that I had ever seen and was a real surprise. It was to leave us to ponder over the winter what to expect next year. This masterpiece of nature we called 'the Swastika'. My 1985 photographs from Salisbury Museum included a similar circle design to this.

Plate 27. This close-up of quartered segments shows the unbelievably perfect combing of the quadrant boundaries. This circle, when viewed from the air, was one of the most magificent sights that anyone would wish to see.

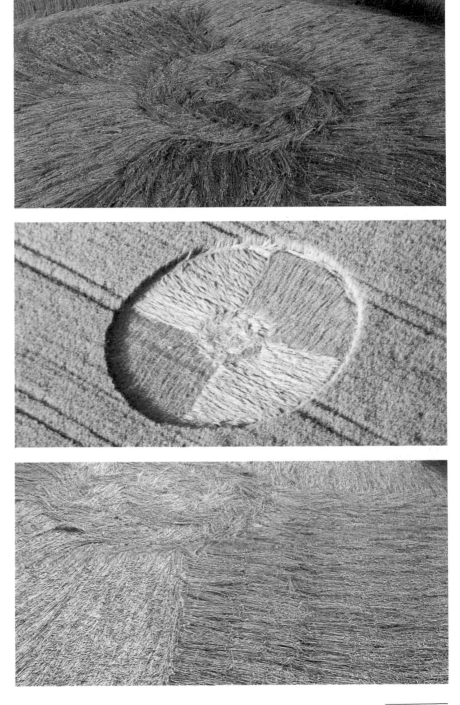

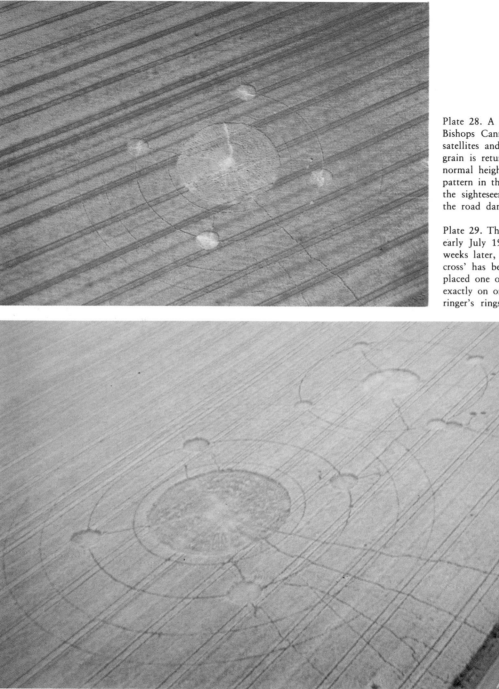

Plate 28. A four-ringer at Bishops Cannings, with four satellites and outliers. The grain is returning back to normal height, making a radial pattern in the circle. Note how the sighteseers' tracks in from the road damage the crop.

Plate 29. This photo, taken in early July 1990, some three weeks later, shows a 'Celtic cross' has been added, and has placed one of its satellites exactly on one of the four-ringer's rings. *Michael Green*

Plate 30. A giant circle near Bishops Cannings taken on May 19 1990. The main circle is some 180 feet across with three outside rings, in immature barley. There were some 24 small 'grapeshot' satellites, and again you will notice the pattern effect that develops in the corn after the event.

Plate 31. On May 27 I noticed that this same circle had developed a fourth outer ring and ten additional satellites running across the middle of it; more grapeshot had also appeared elsewhere in the same field.

Plate 32. One of the most puzzling formations in the extraordinarily rich repertoire of 1990 was this triple-ringer with the interrupted inner ring which was found on June 6 on the Longwood Estate. What was truly remarkable was how the segments of the inner ring neither overlapped nor ended short, but precisely on the same radius. This circle measured over 29 metres.

Plate 33. The scale of the interrupted triple-ringer can be seen from the figure and also the precision of the curved edges. The outer ring was clockwise, the next ring was anticlockwise, the next ring was clockwise and the inner circle was clockwise.

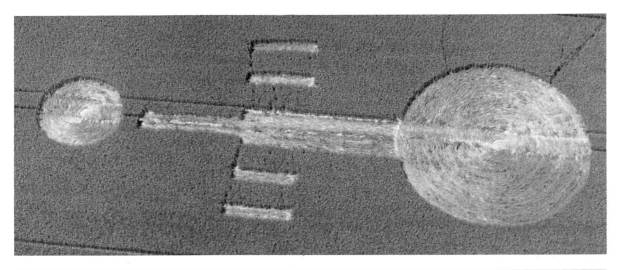

Plate 34. The first 'Pictogram' of 1990 was formed at Cheesefoot Head in wheat on May 23. This picture was taken when it was three days old, and you can see a path connecting the boxes; originally there wasn't a mark in the crop, but this has been made by people walking through it.

Plate 35. A close-up of the first Pictogram, showing how it is balanced on the tramlines. This pole shot shows Don Tuersley, a fellow researcher, taking notes, and gives a perspective as to the size of the circle.

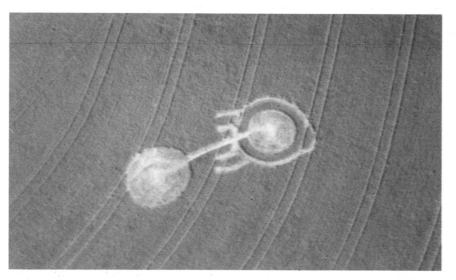

Plate 36. The second pictogram was formed on June 2 at Cheesefoot Head in winter wheat. It is quite asymmetrical and the outer ring has been 'pulled' into the second tramline.

Plate 37. The second pictogram close-up. This was in immature wheat and was soon damaged by sightseers.

plasma-vortex theories. They re-analyse many of these in their latest work *Crop Circles: A mystery solved.*

I will cite another case well-known to French enthusiasts. This happened at Chapelle-Taillefer around 2.30am on Sunday March 19 1967.[3]

Three witnesses saw a big red-orange light, diameter estimated as 10 metres, descending from the sky at about 45 degrees near them. It crossed the first barn of the village and terminated its downward path in a field only a few metres away from them. It was egg-shaped with the more pointed end at the top, and was surrounded by a halo of white sparks 5 metres long which were brighter than the orange-red ball. The sparks were likened to those of a Catherine Wheel, as was the sound it emitted which was further described as "a loud purring noise, the sound of a car's starter, the sound of the old windmill wheels". The ball seemed to be engulfed by the ground as it sank into it in a burst of sparks. It had been visible for 15 seconds. A fourth witness, a motor-cyclist, also saw the ball pass overhead. Next day a circular patch seven metres in diameter was found in the grass, some of which was said to be slightly yellow. The night was cold, several degrees below zero, and slightly overcast but not in any way stormy, and there was no wind. The investigator, R. Dupire, wondered whether it might be ball lightning, Mr. Steuart Campbell[3] agreed, but in a later article[4] attributed the event to a misidentification of the magnitude 0.92 star Antares rising in the south-east (the object was seen to the south-west)!

In fact the great size of the object makes it an unlikely candidate for conventional ball lightning (still less an astronomical event), but we can see how well the details of the story fit the requirements I have spelled out for the new plasma-vortex. This description is just one of many thousands in the literature of UFOs and ball lightning held in the specialised collection of GEPAN, TORRO, BUFORA, CUFOS, and other research bodies in Europe, America and the rest of the world. Even two of the cases studied in the Condon Report (cases 10 and 38) are explicable in terms of the ionized vortex.[18] For instance, case 10 refers to an observation made by a nuclear physicist at Haynesville, Louisiana, on 30 December 1966, which was a dark rainy night. "A pulsating reddish light seen below treetop level from a highway at night became brilliant white briefly, then resumed its earlier character".[5] It pulsated regularly, ranging from dull red to bright orange with a period of about two seconds.

CONCLUDING REMARKS

A crop circle is a thing of beauty, laden with mystery and deserving of the interest that it is attracting worldwide, both popular and scientific. A solution to the circles, while continuing to be arduous, is nonetheless within the bounds of scientific understanding. For years to come scientists have a splendid problem with which to grapple, firstly on the observational plane, then on the experimental and theoretical. Fortunately, this is an exercise in which co-operative, enthusiastic amateurs can helpfully add to the general fund of knowledge, and those who live in England must count themselves lucky to have it on their doorstep. But the circles occur in other countries too, although with lesser frequency, so keep looking wherever you may be.

The scientists see a powerful research tool before them whereby the cropfield impressions offer new possibilities for studying the behaviour of the lower atmosphere and the electrical effects that develop there. This will be the circles' greatest achievement. The extraordinary circle complexes reported from southern counties this year are helping in this task. The much-publicised Alton Barnes circles demonstrate aberrations from circularity which positively help the generalised vortex theory. For instance, it has been suspected for some time that some vortices have complicated but symmetrical internal structures which lead to the well-known quintuplet formations or broad multi-ring systems, but at Alton Barnes crop and ground impact of unstable vortices gave rise to less regular patterns and exposed for analysis something of the satellite- and ring-forming elements in a 'miscarriage' situation. By studying imperfect cases like these we are learning more quickly about the working details of the complex vortices, and are also demonstrating how effective a research tool the study of imperfect circles can be. At the same time, much that is of interest to the UFO community is being uncovered on account of the aerial manifestations involving light, sound and electromagnetic effects — all of them related to the intense spin regime of the swirling vortex.[32]

It is thought that these additional phenomena — less tangible and at first sight even more extraordinary than the incontestable circular traces — may cause actual physiological effects to sensitive people. This realization could go some way toward explaining a few of history's 'mystical' experiences, including some which may have had far-reaching religious and sociological consequences. Indeed, psychology and mythology are further areas of useful research — including trying to understand, by direct observation of an unfolding phenomenon, how and why myths grow and prosper. Although this is said to be an enlightened scientific age, the cultural consequences even now can be important for some, perhaps many, people: especially those who seek solace in beliefs that are beyond science, beyond our norms, beyond reality.

REFERENCES

1. Anon. S'Agissait-il de foudre globulaire? Phenomenes Spatiaux 12, pp. 17–23, 1967. (Groupement d'Etude de Phenomenes Aeriens et d'Objets Spatiaux Insolites (GEPA, Paris).

2. Anon. Quasi-atterrissage a Saint-Souplet (Nord). p. 22, mars 1976. *Lumieres dans la nuit*. Also *Nord-Matin (Lille)* 6 October 1954.
3. Campbell, S. Ball lightning at Chapelle-Taillefer in Central France, *J. Meteorology*, vol. 8, 103–105, 1983.
4. Campbell, S. A ball lightning report objectively reconsidered. *J. Meteorology*, vol. 11, 204, 1986.
5. Condon, E. U. *Scientific study of Unidentified Flying Objects*. Bantam Books, New York. 1969.
6. W. D. Crozier. The electric field of a New Mexico dust devil. *J. Geophys. Research* 69, 5427–5429, 1964.
7. . . . . 1970. Dust devil properties. *ibid*. 75, 4583–5.
8. Delgado, P. and Andrews C. 1989. *Circular Evidence*. Bloomsbury.
9. Freier, G. D. The electric field of a large dust devil. *J. Geophys. Res.* vol. 65, 3504, 1960.
10. Fuller, P. and Randalls, J. *Crop Circles: A Mystery Solved*. Hale 1990.
11. Harris, P. 1990. Nocturnal eyewitness observation of circles in the making. Part 1: East Kent, 10th August 1989. *J. Meteorology*, vol. 15, 3–5.
12. Jones, H. L. The tornado pulse generator. *Weatherwise*, vol. 18, 78–79, 1955.
13. Meaden, G. T. Mystery spirals in a Wiltshire cereal-field. *J. Meteorology*. vol. 6, 76–80, 1981.
14. . . . . . . Mystery spirals in cornfields. *ibid.*, vol. 8, 11–19. 1983.
15. . . . . . The quintuplet formations of 1983. *ibid.*, vol. 9, 137–146. 1984.
16. . . . . Advances in the understanding of spiral patterns in cereal fields. *ibid.*, vol. 10, 73–80. 1985.
17. . . . . The vortices of vapour seen near Avebury, Wiltshire, above a wheatfield on 16 June 1988. *ibid.*, vol. 13, 305–311. 1988.
18. . . . *The circles effect and its mysteries*. Artetech 1989, 2nd ed. 1990.
19. . . . . Nocturnal eyewitness observation of circles in the making. Part 2: North Wiltshire, 29th June 1989. *J. Meteorology*, vol. 15, 5–7. 1990a.
20. . . . . Quelques consequences pour la recherche ufologique de la decouverte d'un nouveau phenomene electromagnetique dans l'atmosphere: le vortex plasmatique et ses traces circulaires visibles au sol. Fourth AESV
21. . . . (Editor) *Circles from the Sky – The Crop Circles Mystery*, Artetech. 1990.
22. . . . . Eye-witness sighting of a cropfield circle in the process of formation, Scotland, August 1989. *Weather*, vol. 45, 273–274
23. . . . . (Editor) *Ball lightning studies*. Artetech. 1990.
24. Pearson, J. F. 1990. Whirlwind circles. *J. Meteorology*, vol. 15, 219.
25. Randalls, J. and Skinner, R. The mowing devil or strange news out of Hertfordshire 1678. *J. Meteorology*, vol. 14, 381–389, 1989.
26. Rendall, P. D. 1989. Circles made by a whirlwind, Avon County, 5 August 1989. *J. Meteorology*, vol. 14, 414–415.
27. Simpson, J. E. Inland penetration of sea-breeze fronts. *Quart. J. Roy. Met. Soc.*, vol. 103, 47–76, 1977.
28. Snow, J. T. and Kikuchi, T.. 1990. Possible mechanisms for the production of crop circles. *The Crop Circles Mystery*. Artetech.
29. Van Heijst, G. J. F. and Kloosterziel, R. C. Tripolar vortices in a rotating fluid. *Nature*, 338, 569–571, 1989.
30. Vonnegut, B. Electrical theory of tornadoes. *J. Geophys.* vol. 65, 203–212, 1960.
31. Wingfield, G. 1990. The English Circles in 1988, in *The UFO Report 1990* (Ed. T. Good).
32. Compare *J. Meteorology*, the five issues dated Oct. 1990 to Feb. 1991, which give the latest theoretical and observational advances in the crop circles problem.

Beyond the current paradigms

GEORGE WINGFIELD

The extraordinary circle formation (Plate 34) which Robert Trevelyan spotted beside the A272 near Chilcomb, Hants, on May 23 1990 probably drove the final nail into the coffin of the atmospheric vortex theory of circle creation. This circle formation, of a design never seen hitherto, included four rectangular 'boxes' which quite clearly could not have been formed by circulating air or plasma. Yet they were also quite clearly an integral part of the formation and had not been added later by jokers. Many researchers had dismissed the vortex theory long before, but this surely dispelled any lingering doubts. And, as if to emphasise the point, the mysterious agency which is responsible repeated its trick with a further similar Pictogram design (as some cereologists are calling it) nine days later, casting doubt on whether we should even refer to 'the circles' any more since circularity seems no longer a necessary characteristic.

A further demonstration that the atmospheric vortex (or plasma vortex) hypothesis is not tenable was given on June 12 1990 when the author discovered that a giant triple-ringed circle near Devizes had grown a further concentric ring outside the original three. This thin ring, approximately 1000 ft in circumference and about six inches wide, had appeared in a perfectly concentric position around the giant 300 ft diameter triple-ringer formation since my previous aerial reconnaissance on May 22, when photographs showed no trace of it. The only conceivable explanation for such an addition seemed to be that the unknown energy field, which causes the corn to fall, and which is detectable through dowsing long after the event, had been reactivated again in some way to produce the new outer ring. (See Plate 31)

I make these points in refutation of the possibility of some random natural process for the benefit of those who have no first-hand experience of the circles, for even a brief acquaintance soon tells the observer that there is very little that is random about them. The geometric patterns are non-random; the positioning of formations is non-random (for they seldom, if ever, overlap field boundaries or paths); and even their surreptitious appearance seems non-random. For this reason we simply cannot consider the circles to be a phenomenon within current scientific paradigms, such as a meteorological effect would be. To the honest observer, the undeniable impression of intelligent manipulation is overwhelming; and this intelligence must inevitably be either human or non-human.

Having reached such an initial conclusion, many researchers have, like myself, thought at first that the circles really have to be man-made hoaxes. Very clever ones, perhaps mechanically produced ones, but nevertheless man-made. I hope that most people will agree with the reasoning so far. It is what comes next which may cause the armchair pundit to part company from the field researcher, for it does not take much observation to realise that the fine structure of the circles completely precludes the possibility that they are all man-made hoaxes. There are indeed hoaxed circles — jokers manage to produce several each year (sometimes to very mischievous effect as, for example, during the *Blackbird* operation in July this year) — but if they are examined when fresh, the faked events can usually be seen to be hoaxes by anyone familiar with the genuine article. There is no need to dwell on the reasons why the circles are definitely not all hoaxes, since that ground has been covered often enough [not least by Dr. Meaden (Ed.)]. All those who have done any fieldwork are in total agreement that this is the case.

So, by this reasoning, I maintain that what we are dealing with is the product of some kind of non-human intelligence, the nature of which we will try to examine in so far as we are able. But first, many will ask: "How is it that other researchers have come to the conclusion that the circles are the result of a perfectly natural phenomenon such as fungus growth or a meteorological vortex?" This is a fair question, and quite easily answered. Those who maintain that circles are caused by fungi (or helicopters, or subterranean archaeological features, or even by animals chasing round and round, for that matter) have quite evidently never visited any genuine crop circles, done any fieldwork, or bothered to look at the data which CCCS and other researchers hold. These views can be dismissed out of hand.

Nevertheless there are some who insist, however impossible it appears, that the circles must be caused by a natural phenomenon for the sole reason that they cannot envisage that it could be otherwise. Often they cite Dr Terence Meaden who has done considerable fieldwork on the circles and still maintains that they are the result of a natural atmospheric vortex of a rare and previously unrecognised type.

But Dr Meaden has changed his theory several times in a dogged though unsuccessful attempt to accommodate the changing behaviour of the circles.

While his current theory, the 'plasma vortex', might seem plausible to those unfamiliar with the circles, the developing complexity of the formations in 1990 has underlined its complete failure. One look at the Alton Barnes Pictogram (see back cover), which is more complex and articulate than anything seen previously, should be enough to dispel the notion that this is the result of a blind meteorological vortex.

The 'plasma vortex', if it exists, would have to be endowed with almost magical properties, including some sort of evolutionary process, if it is to explain all the characteristics of the circles. I am not aware that Dr Meaden has yet published any figures for rotational velocities, etc., or equations to explain the formation and supposed modus operandi of the 'plasma vortex'. Merely calling this agency, which allegedly produces the circles, a 'plasma vortex', and the dogmatic assertion that this explains everything, is neither scientific nor does it advance understanding of the phenomenon one jot.

CHARACTERISTICS OF THE CIRCLES

So let us return to precise observation, rather than to any attempt to cram the data into preconceived ideas. To attempt an understanding of the nature of the circles, we must first list some of the physical and other characteristics of the phenomenon which need to be taken into account. My list is not comprehensive, but will do for a start:

* Geometric, but imperfect, precision of most circles
* Circular, annular, elliptical, rectangular, triangular etc., shapes
* Sharp cut-off between flattened and standing crop
* Vanishingly few reports of circles overlapping boundaries
* Stalks of corn, etc., bent, but generally undamaged, when first found
* Continued growth and ripening of flattened corn, often horizontally [see Terence Meaden's article for

the contrary view that continued 'growth' does not occur, only continued 'ripening'. Further research seems needed. Ed.]

* Multiplicity of 'lays': clockwise, anticlockwise, radial, straight, swastika, complex, etc.
* Layering, 'veining' and twisted bundling, etc., of corn
* Frequent signs of formation alignment with linear ground features such as tractor lines
* Generally nocturnal and usually elusive formation
* 'Revisitation' or additions to some circles at later date
* Extraordinary variety of multiple and ringed formations
* Increasing complexity of circle formations during 1980s and 1990
* Increasing numbers of circles appearing during 1980s and 1990
* Appearance of non-circular features and elaborate designs in 1990
* Possible historic reports of simple circles. Then gradual reappearance from 1970s
* Tendency to 'infest' certain locations, espcially in Wessex
* Tendency of proximity to ancient sites, tumuli, etc.
* Some UFO reports preceding new circle appearances
* Witnesses see no visible agency, or else 'UFO' which descends and vanishes
* Anomalous visual effects: blue flashes, black darts, small luminous points, etc.
* Anomalous audible effects: 5 kHz trilling noise, tapping noise on tape
* Very consistent and lasting dowsing patterns in circles
* Apparent symbolism of many formation types, especially in 1990
* Numerous channelled messages by psychics relating to the circles

Not included in the above is perhaps the most important characteristic of all, which I have already mentioned: the impression of intelligent design of purpose. This, and perhaps several of the items towards the bottom of the list, will be rejected by the sceptic, but solely because his mind-set cannot encompass such things. Whichever way we look at it, we undoubtedly have the most bizarre and unprecedented kind of phenomenon for which to seek a viable explanation.

THE CIRCLE PHENOMENON FROM DIFFERENT PERSPECTIVES

The list of circle characteristics offered above encompasses effects which fall into several disparate areas of knowledge, between which there appears to be no clear connection. Rather than discard certain areas because one's preconceived ideas and prejudices exclude them, I propose that the whole subject of the crop circle phenomenon is only explicable if we attempt a solution which involves a synthesis of those different aspects, which clearly do apply.

There are four relevant areas of knowledge which apply, and it is instructive to study the way in which they are related. First is the realm of the physical sciences, which is best understood and largely explains the workings of the physical world. Next is the area of ufology, which might well be called 'Sky Mysteries'. Then we have 'Earth Mysteries', which includes the subject of ley energy and dowsing. Finally there is the realm of the psychic, or spiritual, otherwise called metaphysics. I maintain that no study of the crop circle phenomenon can afford to ignore any of these four aspects.

My diagram represents the relationship of these areas of knowledge as a quincunx, with the crop circle phenomenon itself as the central element. Although the fact that this is also a favourite crop circle configuration is hardly a coincidence, I would not want to invoke any mystical significance for it! It can be seen from the diagram that opposite

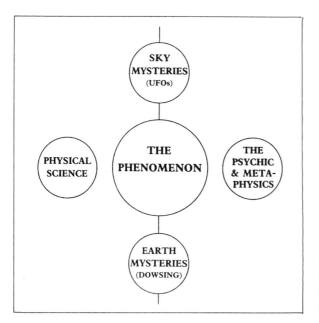

Another way of looking at this diagram is to recognise that there are just two unlike realms, the physical and the psychic, which are divided by the vertical line down the centre. The areas of ufology and dowsing each straddle the line, since in each case we are looking at phenomena which occur at the interface of these two realms. Denying the existence of the psychic solves nothing; it is a different domain from the physical, and, in it, different rules apply. Physicists can think of the analogy of the surface of a liquid. Different laws are applicable to the behaviour of the vapour above and the liquid below; yet it is quite possible for molecules from above to penetrate the surface, and those from below to move into the gaseous domain above. If we can conceive that many of the phenomena we are dealing with result from the analogous penetration of the boundary between the physical and the metaphysical, many of these things are seen more clearly.

RELATIONSHIP WITH THE UFO PHENOMENON

One characteristic of the circles, which is listed above, is their undoubted link with the UFO phenomenon. Those who are unfamiliar with UFOs may react to this statement in either of two ways: they may say that UFOs are nonsense, or they may envisage UFOs as alien spacecraft piloted by little green (or grey) humanoids, which is the unfortunate image that Hollywood and the sensational tabloids have combined to create, since they appear incapable of understanding the nature of the phenomenon. But UFOs are not nonsense, and their nature is very much more complex than the simplistic idea of their being spacecraft from other planets.

A study of modern ufology soon reveals that there is a very strong element of the psychic involved in UFO close encounter experiences. Such events tend to happen to certain people (and possibly others who are with them at the time) and frequently these people also undergo other psychic

elements are not easily visible to each other, which is why advocates of one particular discipline tend to deny even the existence of the opposite. Physicists frequently dismiss the realm of the psychic as rubbish and imagination, whereas psychics often maintain that the importance of the physical world is illusory. Equally some dowsers will scoff at the relevance of the UFO phenomenon to the circles, and ufologists will often deride the significance of the 'earth mysteries' aspect.

It is easy to see that certain cereologists remain firmly entrenched in their particular camp, which might be any of the diagram's outer circles. They may venture out a little, going either to the left or right, but probably prefer to explain the claims of the adjacent camps in terms of their own subject. This, I believe, is the wrong approach, and what we require is a synthesis in order to obtain a complete picture. I will leave the reader to decide in which camps the different circle researchers belong. For myself, I will remain firmly in the central circle and try to observe the phenomenon as a whole.

experiences. An essential book, which well illustrates the nature of the UFOs, is *The Gulf Breeze Sightings*, published in 1990.[2] In this Ed Walters, who lives in Gulf Breeze, Florida, describes his experiences of continuing visitation by UFOs (and indeed the entities which appear to be associated with them). The UFOs are illustrated in dozens of his photographs, which have been authenticated and exhaustively tested by experts. There are many other witnesses to similar sightings in Gulf Breeze, which has undergone a UFO 'flap', rather like the Warminster one, in the last few years.

This particular case is relevant to the crop circles because a mysterious circle in long grass was reported during 1989 from Gulf Breeze, close to the venue of Ed Walters' UFO encounters. This single clockwise swirl was 7ft 8in across, and looked very much like crop circles that have appeared in England. Other crop circle occurrences are reported from Australia and Canada, together with just a few other countries, but on nothing like the scale which we have experienced here in England.

I have written at length of a dramatic UFO sighting[3,4] by a Marlborough woman, which immediately preceded the appearance of the Silbury Hill circles in July 1988. On this occasion a large intensely luminous object was seen in the sky near Avebury. From it a long narrow beam of light shone towards a field near Silbury Hill at an oblique angle. This was where two giant quincunx sets of circles subsequently appeared. (Plate 12)

A further UFO sighting was directly associated with the appearance of a ringed circle at Silbury Hill in June 1989. In this case a local man watched a luminous orange sphere descend into a field on the south of the hill, seemingly bounce, hover, and then blink out. This man appears to have been deeply affected by this event and is said to have undergone a radical personality change as a result.

More usually, UFO sightings associated with the appearance of crop circles occur these days in places where circles have not previously been seen; it is as if the 'sky mysteries' (or UFO) event has seeded a new site with circles! In 1990 there were further instances of UFO sightings preceding the appearance of circles at Bickington in Devon and at Hopton in Norfolk. At Bickington a mysterious object with bright flashing coloured lights was seen over the site where a circle surrounded by seven satellites was found the next day (see Plate 43).

The more recent case in Norfolk which still has to be assessed is apparently connected with the formation of another circle with multiple satellites. Yet again this was at a site where circles had never been seen before. The connection between these 'UFOs' (whatever a UFO might be) and the circles seemed unmistakable. Our meteorological friends might say that this was a 'plasma vortex', but that does not explain things any better. (I suppose one could call the highly structured objects which appear in the photographs taken at Gulf Breeze 'plasma vortices', but this terminology does not explain the phenomenon any better and smacks strongly of self-deception.)

A reappraisal of Arthur Shuttlewood's many books on the extraordinary UFO events around Warminster in the late 1960s and the 1970s, shows that some crop circles (and other shapes) were being reported then in conjunction with the mass of UFO sightings which were occurring. In just the same way, these UFOs appeared, almost invariably at night, as luminous, and sometimes structured craft, which frequently blinked out in thin air. Sometimes formations of UFOs were reported resembling the patterns of the quintuple, the linear triplet, and the equilateral triplet crop circles, which we have been observing through the 1980s. Moreover these sightings were in exactly those places such as Warminster, Upton Scudamore, and Westbury, where we are getting circles today. The inescapable conclusion is that the circles phenomenon sprang from these beginnings at Warminster in the 1970s, and has evolved over the past twenty years. The fact that it is an evolving phenomenon is incontestable, since right now in 1990, we are seeing the circles appear in new formations, and in multiplying numbers never previously observed.

THE TRILLING NOISE

Certainly the circles give a strong impression of purpose, and their precision and elaboration is such that all but the most hardened sceptic will concede that they seem to be the work of some intelligent agency. But what indications do we have of the actual nature of this agency? The following description of an event which took place at Cheesefoot Head in the early hours of June 18 1989, immediately after the White Crow surveillance project, will possibly throw light on this, although explanations in terms with which most people are familiar are not forthcoming.

Six participants of White Crow, myself included, decided on the final night of the project to sit within the larger of the two crop circles (Plate 21) at Cheesefoot Head, which had formed three weeks earlier, and see whether, by relaxing our minds and waiting, we would be able to establish any kind of contact with whatever this intelligence might be. With me were Busty Taylor, Pat Delgado, Colin Andrews and also Rita and Steve Goold. Rita is a well known medium, whom we were lucky to have with us that night, and it was felt that she might be key to such contact.

Shortly after midnight the six of us went to sit in the circle. A moon, which was nearly full, afforded excellent visibility all around, and the night was decidedly cold after a hot summer day. There was a possibility of the aurora borealis being visible, following an intense solar flare which had been reported earlier. We settled down, leaving it to Rita to attempt communication, if it were possible, with whatever might be contactable.

After about twenty minutes I became aware of a strange trilling noise which had started up very close to us. Indeed this seemed to me to have actually come out of the circle itself, or even from out of the heads of the six of us who sat there. We looked at each other in amazement, realising at once that all of us could hear this thing. But nothing visible was to be seen.

The trilling noise appeared to move about and had now established itself perhaps fifty yards from the circle. Intense, yet not loud, its whirring, chattering quality seemed to penetrate one's head like no noise I have ever heard before. It sounded vaguely like a large cricket, or cicada, but this noise was certainly not produced by any insect. Colin Andrews said at once that this was the same noise which he had heard briefly near circles at Kimpton, Hants, on June 30 1987. He then described it as being like the chattering noise produced by the electrodes of an electric arc, prior to the arc being established. Although it can only be speculation, it is possible that this was the noise of the actual forcefield, which appears responsible for laying the corn in the circles.

For a time the noise kept its distance from us like some wary animal that circled round but would not approach. Rita tried to talk with whatever this was, but the only positive response which I remember occurred when she said: "If you understand us, stop!". The trilling did indeed stop for a second or two, but was otherwise continuous. Gradually, it approached us, and after a time it came right up to the edge of the circle through the standing corn. We could not tell whether there were one or more sources producing the noise, but I think none of us had the slightest doubt that it was behaving as though it emanated from some animate and, indeed, intelligent entity. But at no time did I see anything physical which could have produced this noise.

When it was at its nearest, the trilling was intense and the effect hypnotic. Some of us got up and walked slowly towards the edge of the circle, where this unseen presence moved about. Surprisingly, none of us appeared to experience any fear of whatever was out there. Standing within a few feet of the noise's source, and speaking aloud, I said: "Please will you make us a circle?"

In retrospect this request, addressed to a seemingly empty cornfield, may seem absurd. But it appeared — one can say no more than that — that my request was granted, for early the next morning a new ringed circle (Plate 20), which was absent on the previous evening, was found about 500 yards away in the direction in which the trilling noise eventually moved away. No new circles had been found at Cheesefood Head, or indeed anywhere else in England, so far as we knew, during the previous 8 days, which is to say, the whole period of the White Crow surveillance project.

Soon afterwards three other participants in the White Crow project entered the circle, having heard the mysterious trilling noise from the road at the top of the hill. I waved at them, indicating they should get down, but it appears that this arrival caused our unseen visitor(s) to withdraw to a position near the hedge, about fifty yards down the field. Despite our attempts to entice the trilling back to us, we all knew the moment had passed and, soon afterwards, all nine of us went back down to the caravan which served as headquarters for the surveillance project.

By then it was just after 2am, which meant that an hour and a half had elapsed since we had first heard the trilling. This realisation amazed me and the others. It seemed to the six of us who had originally gone to the circle that the events just described could barely have occupied half that time, but we were reluctant to accept that we had experienced 'missing time'.

Ron Jones, one of the three late-comers, told us subsequently that when he, then alone, had first heard the trilling noise from the road, he had walked towards the circle, where he came on a most unexpected sight. In the circle six figures sat huddled on the ground but directly above them in the sky, he saw a luminous object, as bright as the moon, which was also visible. This was shaped like a pair of horns. Rather alarmed he stopped for some moments, not certain what was happening; the trilling noise was now at its loudest. None of us in the circle saw this light above us, as far as I know. Apparently it faded away soon afterwards and then Ron Jones and the other two who had arrived, proceeded into the circle. In view of the forecast of the aurora, we might suppose that this explains what Ron had seen, but other explanations are certainly possible. A 'don't know' is the most honest assessment.

One might be forgiven for supposing that what we had heard and experienced was some kind of psychic entity conjured up by the redoutable Rita Goold. It is indeed possible that Rita provided the link which enabled whatever it was to manifest. But, once it had done so, it assumed an independence which was undeniable. Long after Rita and Steve had driven home to Leicester, and about an hour after we had come down from the circle, I went back up there with Colin Andrews and Ron Jones. We listened, and could still hear the trilling, fainter now, and further away down the field.

Grabbing a tape recorder, Colin and I led the way back into the field and along the hedge, towards where the noise came from. We closed on it, but as we walked further and further into the corn along one of the tramlines, the trilling always kept a short distance in front of us. At one point Ron Jones raced up to join us. He had heard a loud crackle of this strange sound from close beside him in the hedge and said that he had got the impression that he was being 'herded'. Eventually we halted, as the sky grew lighter in the east. We decided to turn back, since it seemed likely that the trilling, which had then lasted for over three hours, might persist even during daylight, which would be with us soon. It was a decision that I bitterly regret, since, if we had followed, as it seemed we were meant to do, we might have witnessed a crop circle forming.

THE SIGNATURE OF THE 'CIRCLEMAKERS'

This trilling noise was the same as that heard two

years earlier by Colin Andrews at Kimpton. Sometimes, it is described as being like an electrostatic chattering or crackling, sometimes as a high-pitched wavering or whirring noise. The tape which was recorded that night has since been professionally analysed at Sussex University. It was not possible to identify the sound, which is unlike any known insect noise, but its peak frequency is about 5.2 kHz.

A similar sound was recorded by members of French UFO group (Groupe 52–55) at Cheesefoot Head in June 1989. They had no idea what this was until they heard Andrews' tape. It has also been heard several times since then by Pat Delgado, Colin Andrews and by Ron Jones and others, on separate occasions. The most public appearance of the trilling noise came when it was heard in broad daylight during the filming by BBC TV of a sequence featuring Andrews and Delgado in the giant Beckhampton ringed circle, which formed in July 1989. The invisible source of the trilling moved about in the centre of this circle near Pat Delgado and was clearly heard by those present. But very often the sound is only heard by certain individuals who seem to have enhanced psychic faculties, and other people are unable to hear it.

Although we cannot say for certain that this is the sound of the 'agency' which lays down the crop in the circles, there seems strong circumstantial evidence to suppose that this is the case. The new ringed circle at Cheesefoot Head, which formed on the night of 17/18 June, when we heard and recorded the trilling noise, was in exactly the direction in which the noise receded from us. Now consider something rather similar which occurred at Warminster back in the 1970s:

"Londoners Steve Evans and Roy Fisher have made frequent trips to the Warminster area since 1971 to try to spot UFOs. They claim to have seen at least 30 and to have had two even closer encounters . . . The first happened as they gazed at the sky from the top of Cradle Hill, one of several vantage points around the town. 'A forcefield seemed to move through the grass like a snake, crackling furiously like static electricity', Evans said. 'It came straight for Roy's feet, then veered suddenly to the right. Sheep in the field were going frantic. When daylight came, we found flattened grass, as though something had landed'."[5]

Looking carefully at some circles, we can see sometimes just how they have been laid down. With complex formations, such as the one at Winterbourne Stoke in August 1989 (Colour Plate 26), or some of the Pictogram formations at Cheesefoot Head found during 1990, one can see that certain features of the design have been laid before others, since the flow of the corn flattened earlier lies under the later flow. It seems as though something like an invisible stylus has swept about tracing out the design.

There is ample reason to believe that this 'stylus' is, in fact, a forcefield of unknown variety, which has moved around in the crop, bending it as it goes. It appears capable of contracting to very narrow width or expanding to a few feet wide as it sweeps out the pattern. Often one sees its tendency to follow the empty tramlines momentarily, before it corrects its course to execute the pattern. Where complex features of a design are being 'scribed', such as the rectangles of the Pictogram formations, this 'stylus' needs sometimes to move through the standing crop to a position from which to start to draw a new feature. In those cases in which it does not have an empty tramline to move along without trace, one can often see where it has left a thin line of fallen corn, just an inch or two wide, in order to reach the required position.

Back in about 1983–1985, quincunx circle-sets often had a thin, but just visible, arc of 270° connecting the four equally spaced satellites. This corresponded to the path of the moving 'stylus'. Later this track was no longer seen and it looked as if the 'Circlemakers' had perfected the design without leaving this give-away. But, when the giant quincunx sets of circles arrived at Silbury Hill in July 1988, further unexplained tracks were often seen leading directly between opposite satellites. Although these were then suspected of being footmarks, it now seems possible that they were caused by this forcefield, scribing what was then a new formation type.

Taking the analogy of the stylus directed by the unseen hand still further, cereologists will be quite familiar with the fact that the geometry of the circles is often short of perfect. The satellites of a quincunx are not always placed in an exact square, and are often of slightly differing sizes. In fact the design is more like the handiwork of an artist, rather than a draughtsman. This concept of the 'cosmic artist' is reinforced by the way that new circle designs are often repeated with improved results. The swastika design at Winterbourne Stoke (Plate 26) was preceded by an almost identical circle a few days earlier in which the pattern of laid wheat was similar, but less well executed (Plate 25).

The three 'crucifix' (or long-shaft cross) formations of circles, which appeared in Wiltshire in June 1989, were similarly not all perfect. The first, found at Scratchbury Hill, was pretty well executed, it must be said. Another at North Down, which most probably occurred earlier, left much to be desired, since three of the satellite circles were incomplete. One had the impression that the 'artist' had made a duff first sketch! The third 'crucifix' at Cherhill was good again, though some have complained that the base circle was slightly out of alignment (Plate 18).

Whether or not this concept of perfecting a design can be justified, it is certainly persuasive. With some Pictogram formations, which have appeared in 1990, the components of the design are often the same, but the proportions have been altered. Also various features have been repositioned in other parts of the design. There seems little doubt that this is intended, and we await new developments of these formations with anticipation.

While considering this aspect of circle formation, it needs to be said that this method of executing a 'design' cannot apply to all circles. Very often, plain circles show none of these indications, and satellite circles usually have no trace linking them to other parts of the formation. Similarly 'grapeshot' or small circles which sometimes accompany a large formation, appears to have come down at random rather than being connected to the larger components. One has to be extremely careful about generalising when it comes to the circles, which seem to delight in proving wrong any rules one sets for their behaviour!

THE EARTH MYSTERIES ASPECT

Having explored the apparent aerial aspect of the production of circles (the UFO phenomenon) to some degree, we must also consider the ley energy aspect. These energies, which are detectable by dowsers, appear to reside on the earth's surface, but are not, as far as we know, detectable by conventional scientific instruments. Some would maintain that this is because the dowsable energies are of an 'etheric' (or higher) nature, and therefore only able to interact with the human psyche or consciousness. Nevertheless the dowsing effect is perfectly real, although there may well be rather variable results and interpretations, when we compare the performance of different dowsers.

I must confess that when I first heard of the dowsing aspect of the circles in 1988, I groaned inwardly, since dowsing was something which I could neither understand, nor trust. However, since then, its relevance to the circles phenomenon has been demonstrated again and again and I have no doubt that the dowsing factor is an important element of the Circles Mystery, though by no means the whole story. Being no expert, I will not dwell on a subject which is covered in far greater detail by acknowledge dowsing experts in this book. For those who doubt this, it would be well to consider the undoubted association between circle locations and ancient sites, such as Avebury. Long before the circles arrived to perplex us, students of earth mysteries were well aware that such places were the source of dowsable energies which can be detected in stone circles and some tumuli. Study of the locations of major crop circle formations near Avebury and Silbury Hill during the last two years strongly suggests that these fall along lines radiating outwards from this important area. Moreover, some stone circles show remarkably similar dowsing patterns to the crop circles, which may well indicate that they were built to mark the site of equivalent crop circles of long ago.

In particular, one is impressed by the consistency shown in the pattern of dowsable concentric rings in main circle formations. This persists for long after the corn is harvested, and may remain for years. The pattern remains active, in so far as it will usually reflect changes of polarity which occur in other circles in the locality, and perhaps further afield. This illustrates the inter-connectedness of the circles, which may give support to some psychics' interpretation of them as merely the outwardly visible sign of energy fields, which are capable of interaction with human consciousness.

THE NATURE OF THE INTELLIGENCE

Having concluded quite unequivocally that we are dealing with some kind of non-human intelligence, which I have called, tentatively, 'the Circlemakers', I must address the question which arises: "Can we know anything of their nature?" Certainly there is no indication that these are physical objects and I am unaware of anything physical being left behind in any of the circles. The name 'Circlemakers' is not intended too anthropomorphise this intelligence or consciousness. The forcefield, which may well be associated with the trilling noise, gives every indication of intelligence, but it would be a mistake to assume that the intelligence is, in fact, that forcefield, or resides in it. The latter may be no more than an instrument manipulated by the intelligence, but it is obviously impossible to say. If the Circlemakers are non-physical, the most that one can say is that they do not reside (if that is the applicable word) within the dimensions of our physical world.

If we are speaking of an intelligence, the next question must then be: "Is communication with this intelligence possible?" The answer here must be "Yes", in so far as the Circlemakers have already shown themselves with their circles, and in the events of June 18 1989 at Cheesefoot Head. In fact their communication appears to take two forms, the indirect and direct.

The indirect communication is embodied in the symbolism of the circles, which is something quite apparent to cereologists, if not the public at large. A number of formation types display a symbolism which is discussed by other contributors to this book. Some of these symbols, such as the Christian, or long-shaft, cross, which appeared three times in Wiltshire in June 1989, are strikingly plain, but in other cases the symbolism is most likely perceived at a subconscious level rather than a conscious one. Certainly, for me, the most definite and articulate symbol which has appeared was the quincunx with three equal and one unequal outer elements (satellites), which was found in three formations near Silbury Hill in July 1988. This is the symbol of the 'quinta essentia' or the unity of consciousness, which was described in, among other places, a book by Carl Jung written thirty years earlier.[6]

Possible direct communications, if they do come from the Circlemakers, may take the form of channelled messages which are received by mediums. Over the last few years a number of psychics and mediums have sought out the cereologists with information of this kind. This, in itself, has been another unexpected aspect of the phenomenon and all the time more psychics have come forward as the public has becomes increasingly aware of the circles.

The channelled messages which are received are generally of a similar nature, and purport to come from non-physical beings, who are variously called

Alphas, Watchers, or Elohim (see pp.. 168–169). The messages speak of the raising of human consciousness, which is to be gradually achieved through a downpouring of 'energies', the outwardly visible sign of which is the circles. Additionally, there appear to be some lower level communications (perhaps 'astral') by other entities associated with the circles.

Quite clearly many people will regard such communications as unacceptable, unreliable, and as something without a shred of proof to substantiate them. This is nothing but psycho-babble, they will say, and quite unworthy of inclusion in a serious article. And I would agree, except that several of the messages have contained information on the circles which has subsequently been confirmed by events.

These communications should indeed be treated with reserve, but the following instances of verifiable predictions are remarkable. Isabelle Kingston, a psychic, received messages that there would be a 'sign' at Silbury Hill shortly before the giant quincunx circles appeared there in July 1988, when no circles had been recorded there previously. This was told to a number of people before the circles appeared. She and another medium independently forecast that there would be a dramatic increase in the number of circles around Silbury Hill in 1989, which was indeed the case.

Most extraordinary is that Janet Trevisan, who channels in Malta, and Isabelle independently received messages indicating that the circles would be very different in 1990, with different formation types, different swirl patterns and different physical manifestations. These predictions have been dramatically confirmed in ways that we would not have thought possible. Almost every major circles formation (i.e. excluding 'grapeshot') found so far in 1990 has been of a type never previously seen, and the complex designs which we are now being shown by the Circlemakers are unlike anything that has gone before.

Richard Andrews checking George Wingfield's dowsing reactions.

In previous years, we did indeed get elaborations and, more rarely, new formation types such as the double-ringer (Aug 1987) (Plate 6), the Celtic Cross (Sept 1988) (Plate 15), and the Crucifix (June 1989) (Plate 18). But 1990 was unbelievable. Multiple-ringed circles of enormous size were found near Devizes. One giant triple-ringer measured over 300 ft across the formation; it was this one which subsequently grew an extra outer ring to become a quadruple-ringer, shortly after the discovery of the first quadruple-ringer (with quincunx satellites) less than a mile away. Extraordinary, dumbbell shaped designs, the Pictograms, appeared near Cheesefoot Head. Segmented ring circles (Plate 32), never previously seen, soon followed, all during the first few weeks of the circles season. Then came the giant double Pictograms near Alton Barnes in the Vale of Pewsey. (Plates 47, 48, 50, 55–57)

After this we shall listen with great interest to anything these channellers tell us, though I doubt whether the sceptics who made up their impenetrable minds a long time ago will be in the least bit swayed. A further channelled message of uncertain origin should also be mentioned although I am sure it will cause great controversy. Several people have suggested that this part of the circles story should be suppressed, since it is not to their liking, and seems too bizarre for words. But without offering an opinion on this particular comunication, I will include the episode simply because it happened.

During the course of the White Crow project an anonymous letter was received by Colin Andrews. It was marked "Utmost urgency to read" and "Read before Saturday". Two pages of handwritten verse were enclosed and a note said that this was "a communication by our group". In part it read:

"Where I be is all around. Listen hard
You'll hear my sound.
It seems you work from back to front
Looking for the cause of such.

Find us first, the next you'll know
All will be clear for rings to sew.
In your hands you have the key
To talk to us, we are so free.
One soul is there, they have signed in
Who has the mind to link within . . .

And — I will tell you what to do.
Get this mind and sit around
In quiet of dark upon the ground,
Listen hard for every sound.
Not white of bird? But us around . . ."

This letter was produced at the White Crow project site and read and discussed by several of the principal participants. Most of us considered that it must be a hoax. There seemed no doubt that Rita Goold was the 'one soul' referred to in it, but there is no reason to think that Rita wrote it. Whether authentic or not, we decided that it was worth trying out what was suggested, and shortly after Saturday midnight, the six of us walked up to the circle.

What happened has already been described, and regardless of the anonymous letter, was something quite astonishing and incredible. The fact that this letter apparently foretold what was to happen is strange enough, but if this was a channelled communication, what are we to make of its interpretation of what occurred? That is something which I think must be left to each individual reader, and I certainly hesitate to take it literally.

The circles phenomenon has crept up on a materialistic and unsuspecting world that is little prepared for such strange events. Yet they have happened, and they continue to happen. What the future will bring is anyone's guess, but already the circles have radically altered the perception of the world held by those of us engaged in this research.

REFERENCES
1. Meaden, George Terence: *The Circles Effect and its Mysteries*, Artetech, Bradford-on-Avon, 1989.
2. Walters, Ed and Walters, Frances: *UFOs: The Gulf Breeze Sightings*, Bantam, London 1990.
3. Wingfield, George: "Did Avebury UFO cause the Silbury Hill Corn Circles?", *Flying Saucer Review*, December 1988. (FSR Publications Ltd.;, P.O. Box 12, Snodland, Kent, ME6 5JZ.)
4. Wingfield, George: "The English Corn Circles in 1988", *The UFO Report 1990*, edited by Timothy Good, Sidgwick and Jackson, London 1989.
5. Blundell, Nigel and Boar, Roger: *The World's Greatest UFO Mysteries*, Octopus Books, London, 1983, pp. 131–2.
6. Jung, Carl: *Flying Saucers: A Modern Myth of Things Seen in the Skies*, Routledge and Kegan Paul, London, 1959, p. 114.

The living countryside

RICHARD G. ANDREWS

Knowledge is a treasure,
practice is the key.

I farmed with my father until the 1960s and then managed an estate in Sussex. When working in the country you become attuned to the seasons and the weather patterns which control your farming life. I learned from an early age that being in tune with Nature gave me more benefits. Observation and attention to small details and changes in the woodland, open spaces, cattle, birds, plants, etc. are all part of country living in the best sense.

We used to dowse on the farm to find land drains. Knowing that water could be picked up by this method, I found that dowsing made me aware of subtle energy effects as well. These appeared to be organised in lines over the ground which were later identified as part of the known 'ley line' system. I began to realise that circles formed where some lines crossed. I called these invisible patterns 'line prints', and, 'circle prints' some of which seem to have subtle effects on living things.

In 1985 I found for the first time that the work I had been doing on the energy lines for the previous fifteen years in relation to animal and human behaviour, now seemed to apply to the circles phenomenon. It was then that I started to devise a dowsing technique which could give me a reliable reading of the energy flows in the corn circles. The first observations surprised me when I realised that the circles had a crossing line in the centre, and rings within the floor pattern. These were quite distinct from any visual effects. Looking at the surrounding area I found that some major lines were equidistant from the edges of the circle pattern.

The following year I was not only able to check the original work, but to expand considerably the links with topography. It soon became clear that some lines associated with ancient sites I had looked at in conjunction with my original work on lines were linked in some way with these systems. The biggest problem I had was to try and find other, more scientific ways of recording magnetic, electrical, radiation or earth energy present. This has proved more difficult as the instruments I have used with professional help were not reliable enough to record on a regular basis. What I needed was a quick, reliable way for identification of the different types of line encountered by dowsing. Up to now, nothing else has been able to read the potential with a high degree of accuracy, except where sophisticated equipment was in a fixed position, as they all seemed to need time to settle down before they were used. Digital readouts didn't seem to stay in a reliable state after continuous movement to different locations. That is why dowsing, practised in much the same way as we find water and many other things, has been used as the most reliable method of collecting new information that will help build a computer model of the phenomenon.

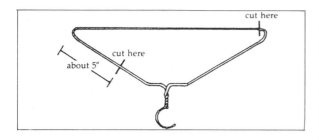

DOWSING WITH ANGLED RODS

Angled rods can be made from two wire coat hangers, which can be cut with a pair of pliers.

Cut each hanger as shown in the drawing, which will give you two angled rods. Then bend the short piece until it is at right angles to the longer piece. You will now have a pair of angled rods ready for work. Hold them in your hands, so that the ninety degree angle is about 2.5cms above your index finger knuckle, and with your little finger lightly round the bottom of the short piece. Now bring them up until the long pieces are parallel with the ground and walk forward. A little practice will soon produce results.

DOWSING RESPONSES

Walk forwards, holding the angle rods in front of you. Your first response will either be crossing or a widening of the rods. Crossing will be 'yes' or positive, depending on which is appropriate. Straight out in front of you, the rods are at neutral — no response. Splayed out will be 'no' or negative. These are the only responses you will need to consider at the beginning.

When you have your first results, make sure that you have approached a line at right angles, otherwise you will get a protracted reading, or a pulsing which will mislead you. Most of the lines you will pick up are either East/West or North/South approximately. Walk down a line and the rods will pulse almost like a heart beat; in one direction the rods will turn inwards and the other direction they

will turn out with a pulsing action. There are other responses the untrained mind will pick up, so you must be very specific about what you are asking, i.e. I want lines, or I want circles. Most times you will only be picking up the basic responses, but occasionally your concentration will wander from the job in hand, and this will clutter your results.

Note: Do not continue to dowse for long periods of time or be in too much of a hurry, as this will confuse the result. Regular practice is the best way to learn dowsing. After each identification of lines put your arms down to your sides and shake them, for this will discharge the energy absorbed and leave you ready for the next line. Don't dowse for more than an hour at a time, you will only become confused. Once you have this discipline, you should be able to have reasonable success. Reading about dowsing will *not* make you a dowser, only practical application will do this. If you become impatient, or think you cannot dowse, you won't!

You will need to practise for about a year before you begin to recognise basic lines, and this is better done away from corn circles. The best training ground is your garden. Once you have made a chart of the lines in your garden, you will be able to check your readings at the start of each session, and compare your note with someone else who can dowse.

The dowsable patterns of the corn circles are complex and at different levels which will confuse dowsers used to ordinary dowsing. Until you have been instructed in the special technique for corn circles, you will not be able to check sufficiently to make an accurate chart for future reference.

DOWSING CORN CIRCLES

Circle configurations have evolved over the last decade from single circles, small and large ones in varying sizes, quintuplets, or dice five, which were first seen at Cheesefoot Head near Winchester in 1983, to circles with one, two or three rings around

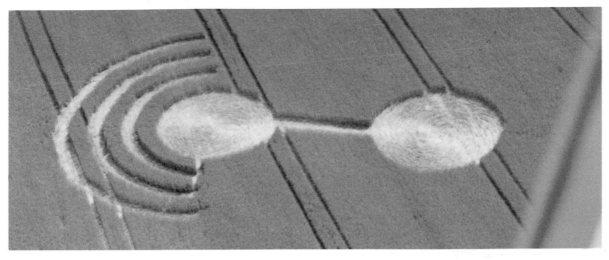

Plate 38. This Pictogram, the third, named the 'Phoenix', was formed in wheat on June 16 in the same area. The four boxes have disappeared, but arcs have manifested. *R. G. Andrews*

Plate 39. A new complexity in this Pictogram, formed in wheat on June 28 on the Longwood Estate, has a ring-and-hat effect.

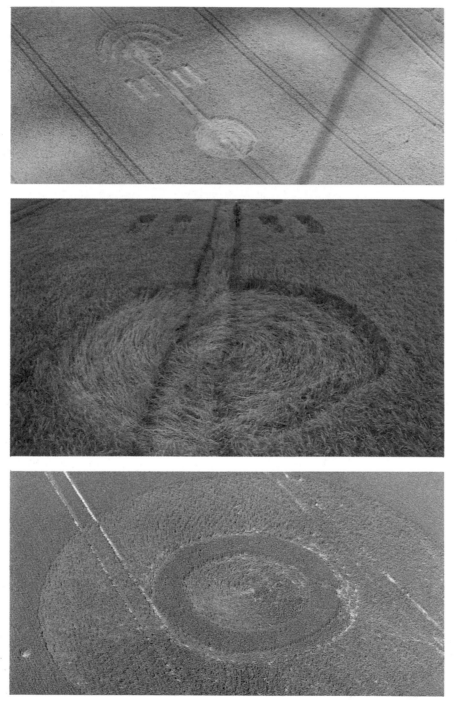

Plate 40. The fourth pictogram found at Litchfield on June 23 is a variation on the last. It has four boxes as before and two semi-circular arcs. As with the others, both circles are swirled clockwise. *Mac Smith*

Plate 41. Another view of the fourth pictogram, which was the first to appear outside the Winchester area. This was in barley at an old circles site, unvisited by the 'Circlemakers' since 1985. Nearby is a group of tumuli.

Plate 42. This inverse ring – a concentric band of standing grain in a large circle – known as 'the doughnut' appeared in May 1990 in the Punchbowl at Cheesefoot Head. *Mac Smith*

Plate 43. The first reported circle configuration in Devon appeared at Bickington, near Newton Abbot. It is the only formation reported to have had seven satellites around a central circle.
West of England Newspapers

Plate 44. This lovely quintuplet at Exton, near Bishop's Waltham, has the very essence of a lush early summer English landscape. *R. G. Andrews*

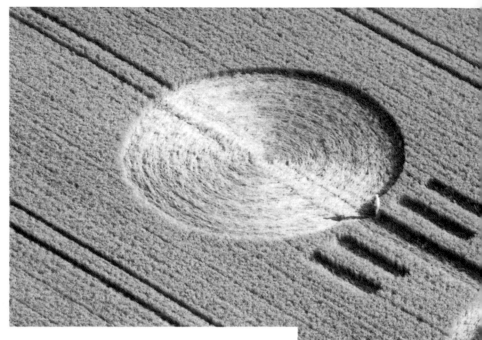

Plate 45. This extraordinarily beautiful and pristine Pictogram appeared at Crawley Down, north of Winchester, on July 13 1990. The third circle at the top anticipates the double Pictogram. *Mac Smith*

Plate 46. A shot from Busty's 30ft pole shows the vast scale of the Crawley Pictogram.

Plate 47 (left). The 1990 season reached its climax a month early on July 11 with this wonderful configuration, over 120 metres long at Alton Barnes in the Vale of Pewsey. It was the first of a series of 'double Pictograms'. The little ringed circle with its satellite has been noted on some ten other configurations, and is known as the circlemaker's 'trade mark'.
Alick Bartholomew

Plate 48 (above). The Alton Barnes complex created a national sensation, with thousands of people making pilgrimages to experience its lovely atmosphere, from all over the country. The farmer showed foresight by charging a modest fee, making sure that the visitors walked down the 'tramlines'.

Plate 49. This curiously decorative device, called by some the 'hand of God' appeared in the Vale of Pewsey, close to the Alton Barnes double Pictogram.

Plate 50. A short distance down the Vale of Pewsey, probably on the same night as the Alton Barnes double Pictogram, this twin appeared near Stanton St Bernard, pointing directly towards the Allington White Horse.

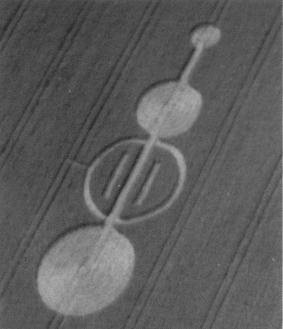

Plate 51. The seventh Pictogram which appeared on Chilcomb Down on July 6, was one of more than a score of such formations which appeared in Hampshire and Wiltshire in 1990.

Plate 52. A very different type of large Pictogram; this appeared on Pepperbox Hill, near Salisbury, in July 1990. *R. G. Andrews*

Plate 53. This design is called a 'winged circle'. It appeared at Amport, near Andover.

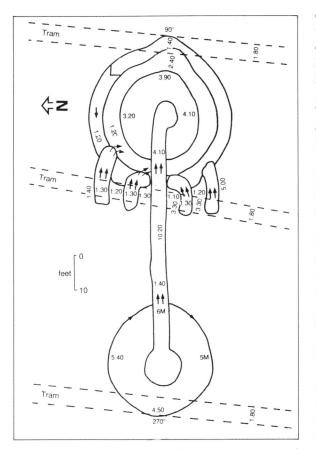

Figure 1. The second Pictogram at the top of Cheesefoot Head June 2 1990 (see also Plate 36).

circle appears with a single ring outside it having the same flow of the crop as the floor pattern of the circle. This was the single ringed circle of the Longwood Estate in 1989. Since this time we have had every combination of directions of flow on lines and rings associated with the circles phenomenon. The first major happening after this was the highly complex pattern of the floor of the single circle that had quartered at Winterbourne Stoke in August 1989 (see front cover and Fig.00). I found, looking at my daily dowsing of the print formation of floor patterns that these had been changing every day during the crop circle season, but when a circle 'fires' only the pattern that is then present will become visible. It was the daily dowsing of certain areas that has given the enormous amount of data that is helping with the understanding of this very complex phenomenon.

But even more dramatic, in 1990, when for the first time, the dumb-bell formation, with two and four boxes. All conform to the dowsable pattern, which is the most complex yet, and will need considerable work to find out more about about the reason for their appearance. Several circle floor patterns have changed after they have formed, which shows that energy is still present, or is being topped up. The boxes only form when a three-line ley crosses the positive line of the shaft between the two circles (see Fig. 2).

DOWSABLE LINES

The main lines that concern us are:

1. *Single Positive Line.* Up to 1988 I found this was indicated by a single crossing of the rods; then the line started to grow wider. Most times we see it at about one metre wide, crossing in the centre, but as it grew wider it gained a negative on either side, and when pulling away from the negative, the rods will both turn in one direction. This will be the direction of energy flow in the line. All lines have a flow direction on their edges, as described. Positives

them. Then in 1988 a quintuplet with a ring connecting the four satellites, which had been just discernable as part of a ring before this time, but hardly noticeable. The same year there were the three circles grouped in a triangle pattern, the floor pattern of which changed after formation to seven consecutive rings and forty-eight spokes. One thing that was apparent before 1989 was that the dowsed print rings or lines showed a change of flow direction on each alternate line; the rods predictably moved first left then right. Then for the first time a

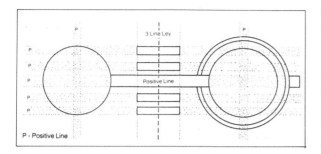

Figure 2. The energy lines at the Longwood Pictogram June 28 1990.

Figure 3. Measurements of the Longwood Pictogram.

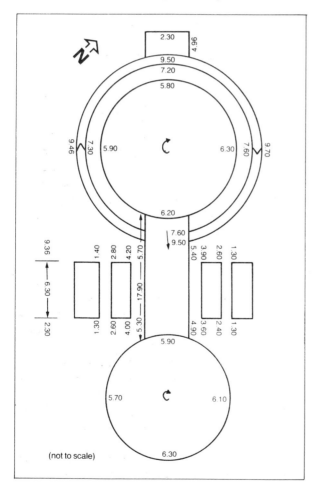

(not to scale)

seem to have surges of energy that may be instrumental in triggering the circles.

2. *The Negative Line.* This is when the two rods open and oppose each other. This line has changed, in that it has grown wider. Negative lines seem to be connected directly to earth energy, and to be instrumental in the discharge of other line energy. We have also found in recent years, as line prints and rings have become wider, that they have developed a negative response on either side of the line complex. It appears that this negative line is responsible for the cut-off between the standing crop and the floor pattern.

3. The three lines that run together, which are known as a *Three-Line Ley.* These lines are present in churches and tumuli, etc., but are the ones the circle configuration forms between. Having looked at several hundred circles now, I have never found a three-line ley passing through the centre of a circle. Three-lines leys are fairly common — about 100 metres apart — and have quite different applications to the other lines. For example they are found going longways through churches and long barrows. They have properties of telepathy when thoughts are focussed (as in prayer), and of unconcious healing for both animals and humans. Three-line leys have to be present for the boxes to form in the new dumb-bell formations.

4. *Rods Both Pointing Right or Left.* This shows the flow of energy in line (but it can also indicate flowing water underground).

5. *Whirly.* The rods will start to spin round as you walk through this line. This is a powerful line and is always present in a tumulus or long barrow and seems to be dominant when it is present. Many people new to dowsing the circles may find that both rods spin as if out of control, but this will be due to inexperience. Whirlies are less common than other lines but seem to be instrumental in transporting energy in greater quantities than positive lines do.

6. *Where Lines Cross.* The rods will spin round at one spot because of the vortex made by the lines crossing, so you will need always to check where you are when you get this reaction.

7. Where there are *multiples* of four lines (i.e. 4, 8, 12, 16 etc.), the rods will point alternately left and right, until you meet a negative line which marks the edge of the complex.

This is only a guide to some of the lines you will find in a circle, as the lines are joining together now and showing different characteristics. However, that involves a more advanced form of dowsing that would only confuse you at this stage. Keep everything simple and you won't have any problems. If you think you can work without strict discipline you may find yourself with more problems than you had when you started. Undisciplined energy work can be disturbing.

Each circle configuration, or group of them, will have the same dowsable pattern as any other one of the same grouping, and if one pattern changes, they all change. This may show after the formation of the floor patterns in the physical formation.

Figure 4. The Winterbourne Stoke 'swastika' showing how the crossing of the energy lines has triggered the quartered laying of the grain floor pattern (see Plates 26 & 27).

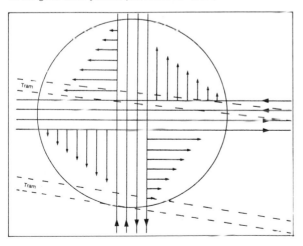

I remember, in 1988, finding that the pattern had changed in one formed quintuplet. I travelled round all those I could find to check them to see if they had all changed, and found that once one of a type changed, they all changed at the same time.

The quintuplet pattern is probably one of the best to check, and this will be done in the autumn after the crop has been cut, which means that you can peg it out and check its relation to all the lines. The rule of thumb is to find the two three-line leys and walk between them, and you will find the pattern neatly placed on crossing positive lines. On dowsing the circle pattern, you will find there are several dowsable rings where your angle rods will move either left or right, giving you the directional flow. Each circle floor pattern will finish with a negative response on the outer edge.

ENERGY SOURCES

Over the past few years we have had a great increase of energy entering the Earth's atmosphere from the Cosmos. The Sun has also reached a maximum of sunspot activity which has affected our planet quite considerably. The circles in the corn are partly a response to this, so also is the increase in earthquake and volcanic activity.

SOLAR FLARES

There were two events that seemed to be connected with this phenomenon. The first was on the night of 24/25 June 1988. I was waiting for a new corn circle to appear in the Punchbowl at Cheesefoot Head, near Winchester. At about 10.30 pm that evening, only one circle configuration — three circles grouped together in the centre having appeared on 4 June — was visible. When I returned at 6.40 am the following morning there was a large, two-ringed circle in the corner of the field nearest the road.

A second event on the same night was when 5,000 racing pigeons were released in France. The weather was fine for the flight to their homes. However, the solar flare storm hit our atmosphere during the night and upset the earth's magnetic field, thereby disrupting the pigeons' navigational senses, and over 3,500 perished in the Atlantic Ocean. The instance was reported by the media on 1 July. This shows that birds navigate by the lines of our standing energy field.

AURORA

The Aurora on 13 March 1989 bent the Earth's magnetic field to such an extent that drilling for oil in the North Sea had to be stopped, and the compass was put out by 8° from Magnetic North. This upset all navigation, which left airliners having to switch to visual navigation during this very violent solar storm.

LIGHTNING

Strikes of lightning have quite some effect on our line grid system, and are one of the causes of the energy increase, or at least of helping to sustain it.

On 6 July 1989, I saw a strike of lightning in my garden at 3 pm, and another strike on the other side of the house, during a thunderstorm. I had dowsed my garden on a regular basis for the previous two years, observing the change in the lines. I had looked at them that morning, but I checked again after the lightning and found that a seven ring circle print had been formed. Then Andrew Budd, who lives immediately behind my house, came over to say he had seen the lightning strike in two places to the east, once in a field of barley and once in the grass field in front of his house. It was then that I realised the strikes had all been consecutively in a straight line, and on dowsing all the strikes I found that a seven ring dowsable print had formed on each lightning strike point.

However, the most interesting point was that all the strikes were on a positive line and only where

Figure 5. Markall Close, Arlesford, Hampshire. Diagram shows how the lightning strikes occurred on energy line crossing points, or nodes.

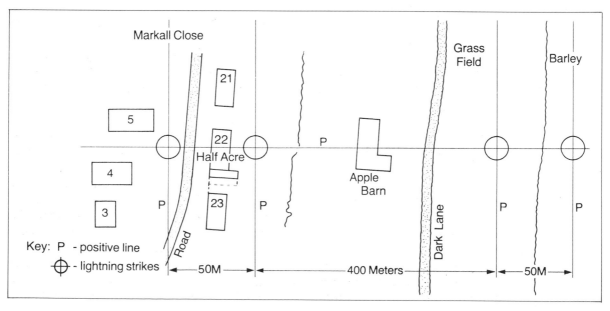

there was another line of the same value crossing it at 90°. These crossing points, or node points, are the same in the centre of corn circles. This led to the discovery that lightning strikes only on these node points, and it seems that it is when some are more active than other nodes that the strike will use that line of nodes. Observation over the year has shown this to be the case, and that the strikes on node points can happen more than once, as there was a second strike in the garden in the centre of the circle print, which made it larger, on 9 May 1990. The other interesting point is that the seven rings have changed polarity several times over the year at the same time as have the circle traces of corn circles, which has shown they are directly linked with the energy grid system.

LINKS WITH THE TOPOGRAPHY

The lines are part of a grid system over the face of our planet, which seem to have energised over the past fifteen years, getting stronger as the input from solar flares and radiation from the Cosmos has increased, also from lightning in our own Earth space. These inputs of energy are affecting televisions, fridges, computers, wirelesses, etc., when they are situated on positive lines. It is as though the energy grid was becoming overloaded, so that a lightning strike will cause an excess of energy in certain electrical appliances. I have many instances of televisions that are not connected to the mains electrical supply, showing little squares of blue and red on the screen, which show there is enough electrical power on the lines to filter through the electronic system to light primary colours as dots on the screen. Over a space of time the dots will change position until they group at the centre of the screen and disappear. Also I have seen many instances of small transformers used for radios and answerphones that have melted into a solid, useless state, and there have not been any surges in the electrical grid system, as this was the first thing I checked.

As you have seen from previous chapters, the corn circle configurations have evolved in a dramatic way. Do they have links with ancient civilisations? It would seem that they do, because some of the energy lines associated with the ancient megaliths and tumuli are also to be found in and around the circles, and many circle configurations are near to these formations. Busty Taylor's aerial photographs often show the proximity of some ancient workings to circles that have formed.

On 21 October 1988, Busty and I went to Stonehenge, in Wiltshire, to check the lines that were present, as I had found these on previous occasions. There were fifteen whirly lines, and twelve three-line leys radiating from the centre. Only one of these lines went straight through the centre of Stonehenge, and this was the three-line ley on the axis, which went down the Avenue to the water source, and beyond . . . The other features about Stonehenge are the way the standing rings of stone spiral in or out in the same way as the floor patterns spiral in or out from the centre of the crop circles. In addition, the centre is not central to the outside rings.

The other point that is common with the corn circles are the dowsable rings (which, incidentally, at sunrise can be seen as slightly higher grass rings going out beyond the standing stones). The erecting of stones in a particular formation could well have been in order to denote the importance of these circle and node points, or to enhance them in some way. This had shown the importance of some of these node points, which I believe to have been used by past civilisations for healing and fertility rites, others for astrological and mental communication.

There are hundreds, if not thousands, of tumuli in Hampshire and Wiltshire, where we have the highest concentration of corn circle activity anywhere in the world. In 1988 I was standing on the tumulus at the top of Telegraph Hill, just after dowsing the pattern associated with it, when I felt a jolt through my body, like an electrical shock, and

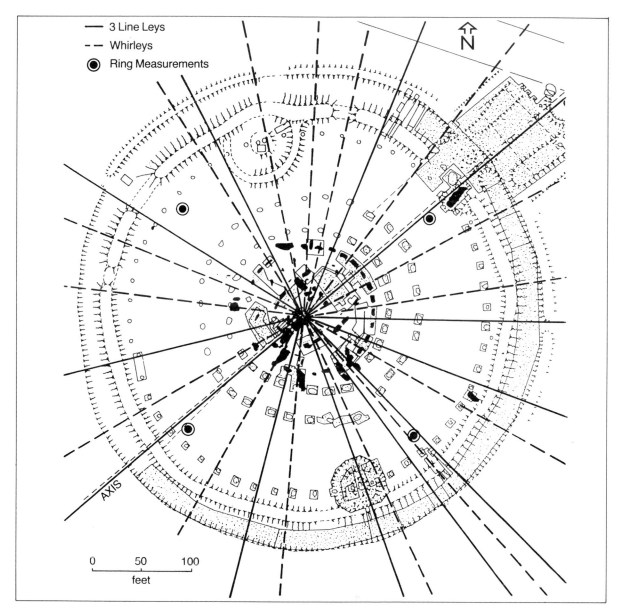

Figure 6. The enigmatic Stonehenge has always commanded attention by the prominent position on Salisbury Plain. The dowsed pattern shows the energy lines of two distinct types, 15 whirlies and 12 three-line leys. In the southern half note that the lines run alternately, three-line ley — whirly. The groupings of the lines in the northern half consist of two pairs of whirlies at 70/90° and 280/290°, with two single whirlies at 45° and 333°. Finally, there are whirlies grouped between the two three-line leys, 30° and 340°. This grouping of lines may be very significant in astrological calculations, or the focusing of energy onto a specific point, as they do in the circles in the corn.

this was strong enough to clench my fist as a response. On checking again, a wide positive line had added to the dowsable pattern, and was flowing down into the Punchbowl at Cheesefoot Head. This was very strong, as the rods in the flow position on the edge of the line would not stay still, rather like weeds flowing in the strong current of a river. It was not long after this that the two-ringed circle formed in the Punchbowl. This could be one possibility for circles triggering.

Tumulus print. A tumulus will have a dowsable, wide positive line round the base, which interrupts all but whirly lines. When a positive/negative or three-line ley comes against the positive, they are funnelled round to the opposite side of the tumulus, and continue in a straight line, as before. Only the whirly cuts through this line into the centre of the mound. Sometimes it will be deflected when it hits the dolmen at the entrance and changes course by up to 90°.

It was noticeable that a circle print I had dowsed in 1988 on the Longwood Estate, showed a three-ringed circle in 1990. The difference to all three-ringed circles was that the crossing lines in the centre were whirlies, being the first time I have found a whirly crossing in the centre of a circle, and the effect was a complete surprise, as the whirlies had gone through the outer, positive ring, and cut the next two rings into opposing quarters (see Fig. 8). Although the rings shown by the circle print of 1988 were full rings, the effect has shown that the whirly was probably the reason for the quartering and firing from one line to the other in the physical circle.

The dowsable rings within the outer, positive, ring of a tumulus show as full rings, although, if they 'fire', they may be quartered in the same way as the circle. The dowsing of the prints of tumuli are different to dowsing the stones and archaeological remains. The energy flow under the ground is opposite in direction to the flow above ground, as the first foot above the ground is negative. (Try this

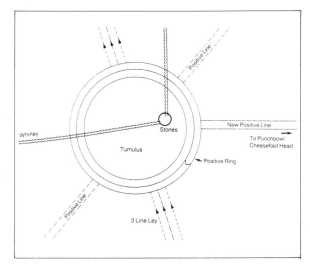

Figure 7. A tumulus at Telegraph Hill, near Salisbury. Some tumuli seem to have very powerful nodal energy effects in the landscape.

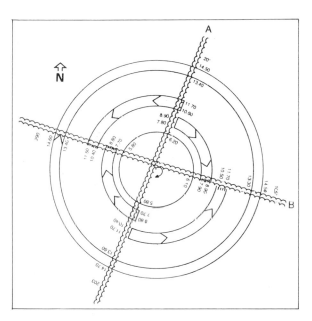

Figure 8. Interrupted three-ringer circle at Cheesefoot Head, 1990, where whirly 'A' triggered the broken pattern, and whirly 'B' cut it off. June 6 1990 (see Plate 32).

when you dowse anywhere.) All tumuli are connected by lines. Similarly, lines also connect some of them with corn circles, but the caution is, it won't always be the nearest one, or the nearest to which you think it is in line. This must be thoroughly checked before you commit yourself to what you think is right. I have found that it is better to check this with another person, because it is too easy to assume that you have the right one. This is the commonest fault of the undisciplined dowser.

TREES

Walking through woodlands over the past thirty years, I have noticed that there were quite a number of dead trees scattered throughout planted areas, and that this was increasing through the years. The hedgerow timber also had the same problem. The question I asked myself was, "Why are there dead trees here, when there were others of the same variety standing next to one another?" So, this was not some infection of the kind we had with Dutch Elm disease, which spread like wildfire through the elms as soon as it had a hold. Why? was always the nagging question, because I was not satisfied with the rather glib answers, such as bad summer, good summer, disease — it was obvious that the tree just died! They were becoming too numerous to fit into the quick answer meant to stop further discussion. Since the corn circles have appeared with regularity, albeit only a few at first in the 1970s, the number of trees dying has increased, as the numbers of circles have increased. Are they linked in some inexplicable way?

On dowsing, I found that the majority of dead trees were all on a positive line, which is the same as the ones we now find in the corn circles. But there is more to it than that. As these lines have become wider over the past three years, different varieties have died at different times. In 1987 and 1988 more cherry trees died than other varieties. In 1988 and 1989 it was beech and Scandinavian spruce. In 1989 and 1990 more oak were apparently affected. So it seems that the line itself was weakening the tree, and making it susceptible to secondary strike, either by disease, infestation or other natural causes. The ability to mobilise its defensive system seemed to fail. When you see some of the oldest and best of the trees, along with the young ones, dying as they stand, you realise that quite a change is taking place.

You only have to look at the gardens now to realise that something more than gales, and what we consider as normal weather, must be at work. Have you noticed the number of Leyland cypresses that form hedges that are failing in odd places? And that more trees and shrubs have failed more than usual? If you dowse them, you will more than likely find that there is a line going through the bush or tree. Do not replant on the same spot, as its successor will also fail. Now dowse the width of the line, plant the new shrub on either side of this, and it will grow normally. I have been able to advise many gardeners who have sought my advice on my discoveries in the garden. This work has also been shown to the Alice Holt Research Station, near Farnham in Surrey. As the scientific establishment recognises the value of dowsing and other alternative methods, so we are going forward together.

BIRDS

When out in the country you often take the birds for granted, and don't really observe them, but when you do, many wonderful things are revealed. The flight home for the night is usually on an energy line. It is only when they sight the landing area that they break formation and begin to select their own landing point. In the spring, if you look over ground that has been prepared for a crop, or sown, you will notice that some birds appear to be grouping and resting in the morning.

Last year, I saw seagulls resting in a field at about 9.30 in the morning, and thought it odd that they were in two groups, very tightly packed together. Carefully, I walked in their direction, and found, as I approached, they were gathered in a circular formation, with only two birds outside this configuration. I slowly walked between the two groups with my dowsing rods, and found that a line went through the centre of the two groups, and the two birds outside were on the line. I walked slowly towards the smaller group of gulls, and I could see that they were all sitting down tight to the ground, and they did not start to fly off until I was about twenty-five metres from them. (Usually, wild birds in an open space would have flown before this.) They all lifted off the ground fairly quickly, and when they were high in the sky they all took a straight line to another point about three hundred metres away, and started to descend in a clockwise direction, and on landing, resumed their resting, as before. When I arrived in the area where the birds had been, I found a seven-ringed circle by dowsing, and I found that the droppings from the birds were deposited within the outside ring of the dowsed circle pattern.

Since this first observation, I have seen this many times, and as the droppings seemed to be within the dowsed configuration, I deduced that they seemed to be charging up from the circle energy, as they do not seem to do this elsewhere. When landing in a circle configuration they spiral down the way the vortex is spinning. Sometimes they land clockwise and sometimes they land anticlockwise, and they also seem to do this when they land in a formed corn circle, and there you can see that they match the spiral of the floor pattern. *Note:* As I have not seen birds land in a bomb burst floor pattern, I don't know how they would approach this. By the afternoon, the birds will have broken away from the ring, and are foraging all over the fields before going home in the evening.

In the winter, when it is frosty, I have often seen pheasants and partridges sitting or walking up and down in a line. These birds sit very tightly when I

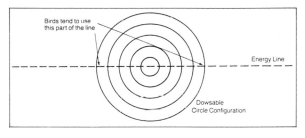

approach, to the extent that I have been able to get within about five metres of them before they fly. But this time they are on a line , and I wondered why they tend to use only a small stretch of it, a well-used little path. I have found by dowsing that the part of the line they use tends to lie within the outside ring of a dowsable circle configuration; it seems that the birds are able to keep warm along this strength: Once again, here is evidence of circle energy having the ability to hold birds within the outside ring. This might be why some people feel safe on one area, but not in another, because the energy within a circle has certain beneficial qualities. When you are out in the country in the winter, or spring, see how often you can observe this.

Crow Damage

Quite often I see what looks like a circle in the corn. On further inspection, I find that instead of a precise, well formed floor pattern, the stems have been randomly bent over at about 15cms above the ground. This is certainly not consistent with the floor pattern of corn circles. Watching crows attack a patch of corn that has been laid by the weather one can see them stripping the soft grain from the stem, and when they want more they open their wings and fly up against the standing corn, peck the stalk to make it bend, and then continue eating. Where there are many crows, they attack all round the edge of the laid area, hence the formation of the circular pattern.

ANIMALS

Animals use some of the lines when they travel from one point to another, and you can often see this where cattle walk across grass fields. As you walk beside a hedgerow, look for paths that go through the hedge and undergrowth, and you will find, on dowsing, that there is a line, and the track will follow it across the next field. This seems to be one of the ways that animals track across open land, rather as we use roads.

In the early morning, when the day starts up and the sun comes over the eastern horizon, the animals rouse from their sleep. Deer in the wild often walk for some time in a straight line across open ground, e.g. the New Forest in the south of England. Sheep will do the same after waking from their sleep. On further inspection, I have realised that they have been walking on the three-line configuration in our line system. Interestingly enough, the same three-line system is present in our churches. These lines seem to have a very beneficial effect, especially to those animals which are in poor health, as they spend much more time on the line, unless they meet a fence or hedge. The very fit ones soon come off the lines and start to graze. I have seen sheep in a circle formation all facing in the same direction round the perimeter of a dowsable circle pattern. As with birds, there seems to be something they can find or use to their advantage. Quite a number of people have reported this phenomenon to me.

MOLES

I have done test diggings and found that the worm count is higher where the line shows by dowsing, and the moles have pointed this out by digging for their dinner. This suggests that the lines are also under the ground, as well as above. Worms do not appreciate cold ground, and will go deeper when the temperature drops below a certain figure. But in a fine winter, you will still see molehills on the surface, as they haven't had to go lower for the winter, and the worms are available without them having to dig deeper.

DEER

Stags will call their mates in spring from powerful positive crossing lines, which I call node points; these seem to be giving the extra power that is needed for the stag's supremacy, as they will stand proudly on these points and call. These are just a few examples of the line and circle properties which I have found in the living countryside. What a wonderful world we live in as we begin to realise what is available to us.

We are part of the Earth's delicate ecology, and we will prosper or fail with it. Let us understand it now, as we bring scientists to the new frontier.

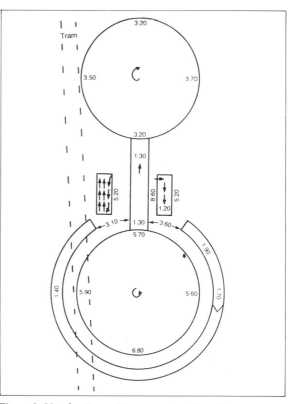

Figure 9, Hazeley Down Pictogram (see Plate 51)

Sheep, rods and pendulums

RALPH NOYES

We cannot leave that absorbing account of dowsing and the 'earth energies' to which it seems to relate without giving you three remarkable anecdotes.

The first comes from the unlikely source of the *Journal of Meteorology* (Vol. 14/No. 13). Dr. Meaden reports that a correspondent, Mr. J. C. Belcher, had witnessed in August 1988 some strange behaviour by sheep on Baildon Moor, near Leeds, Yorkshire. They had been seen forming very precise circles, as shown in Mr. Belcher's sketch.

The incident, said Dr. Meaden, had been reported to him "because of my well-known interest in circle phenomena." Mr. Belcher's own suggestion was that "perhaps some mysterious radiation was emanating from below or above." In his comments Meaden remarks that "instead of hypothesising extraordinary and peculiar forces of unknown origin, why not, as always in science, first check to see what sort of known forces might have been operating?" He offered for discussion by readers the possibility that "inoffensive whirlwinds may have played some role. For suppose that the sheep were initially fairly close to one another but distributed at random within the group, then following the start-up of some minor whirlwind in their midst the disturbed sheep drifted apart just by easing themselves placidly beyond the reach of the mischievous wind till the wind-speed, being low enough, they felt able to settle again and graze in peace." Readers of this book may care to ponder the problem and perhaps to watch for similar oddities of animal behaviour.

The other two anecdotes have reached us from Barbara Davies and Lucy Pringle, members of the Council of the Centre for Crop Circle Studies.

At its inaugural meeting during Easter 1990 the CCCS Council had been shown by Busty Taylor some specimens of mature stems of oilseed rape, collected from a circle which had formed in a field of that crop the year before. The bending — without breaking — of this somewhat brittle crop at near to ground level and through nearly ninety degrees was strikingly evident. (CCCS awaits further evidence for this kind of occurrence and an explanation of what causes it.) Barbara Davies, who is an experienced dowser (and a transparently sincere and credible witness) was reminded of a remarkable experience she had had in 1985.

"I was using a Y-shaped hazel rod and getting a variety of reactions to underground water, etc., though I was hoping to identify the points where ancient trackways crossed the modern road north of Fowey. About a quarter of a mile south of Castledore (a prehistoric ditch-and-bank enclosure), as I was passing a field gateway on my right, I felt the right-hand arm of the rod give way. My first reaction was disappointment — I must have broken it, and it had been responding well. Then the arm stiffened again, but in a new shape — it had acquired a ninety degree bend half way along. It was as though it had temporarily turned to plasti-

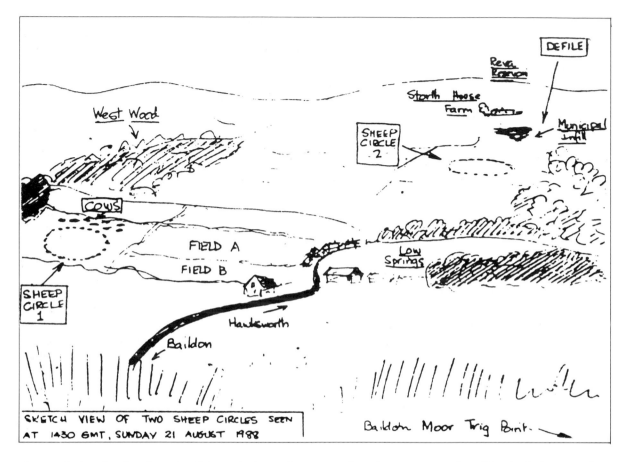

SKETCH VIEW OF TWO SHEEP CIRCLES SEEN AT 1430 GMT, SUNDAY 21 AUGUST 1988

cine, and then hardened again. I kept it for a few months, but eventually threw it away as by then there was no proof that it had not grown in that shape (though it would not have been one suitable for a dowsing rod!)"

Incidents of this kind have many parallels in psychical research, including that maddeningly elusive nature of the evidence! They come unbidden; they seem to have no 'meaning'; they leave behind them only the flavour of some Puckish joke. They have been called by Mary Rose Barrington (a well known researcher into things psychical) JOTS — "Just One of Those Things". They happen to most of us during the course of a lifetime, but we don't usually mention them, even to close friends. It is convenient to ignore them — but we probably make a great mistake if we do. Whether or not they have anything whatever to do with the crop circle phenomenon time may, perhaps, tell us. But at this stage in the weird behaviour of the phenomenon we had better neglect nothing!

Our other anecdote is from Lucy Pringle (whose profound commonsense and brisk handling of business is excellently serving CCCS in her combined roles of Hon. Treasurer and Hon. Membership Secretary). In her own words:

"I have used a pendulum since I was in my teens but never with any great consistency until I became fascinated by the Crop Circles. Suddenly my pendulum has become a most treasured friend once more. When I go into a Crop Circle configuration I always start in the usual way by asking my pendulum if it will be happy to answer questions — luckily the answer has always been in the affirmative! I then proceed to stand in various locations and ask if this area or spot is negative or positive or, as the Chinese call these energies, the yin or yang, representing negative or positive, female or male. One instance I would like to tell you about, was the time I went into the configuration shown on Plate 38. I had a violently positive reaction in the circle without rings and when I went into the top circle (surrounded by the three half-circles) the pendulum also gyrated rapidly, this time registering negative. The energy in both circles was so powerful that whilst I was swinging the pendulum straight backwards and forwards, asking the questions, it started to jump before answering. This I understand happens when there is a strong energy force. Having dowsed the centre and perimeter of the first ring (positive) I did likewise in the top one and on standing at the perimeter it swung around so powerfully that it flew off, having snapped the chain. Goodbye pendulum I said to myself. The velocity must have carried it yards into the standing wheat, so . . . imagine my amazement when I glanced down and there within three to four inches of the edge of the circle was my pendulum lying in the standing crop! What force had stopped it dead in its tracks so that it plummeted to earth instantly without any rebound? There it lay and I scooped it up with joy.

"I believe that what happened to me is in fact a well known and accepted dowsing phenomenon and one which has turned many a sceptic into a believer when it has happened to them. It would seem that as soon as the pendulum moves out of the orbit of the attraction area, the energy no longer being present all movement abruptly ceases: rather similar to turning off an electric switch. This would indeed appear to be the case as demonstrated by a dowsing friend in another crop circle. His pendulum instantly ceased to move the moment he stepped outside the circle."

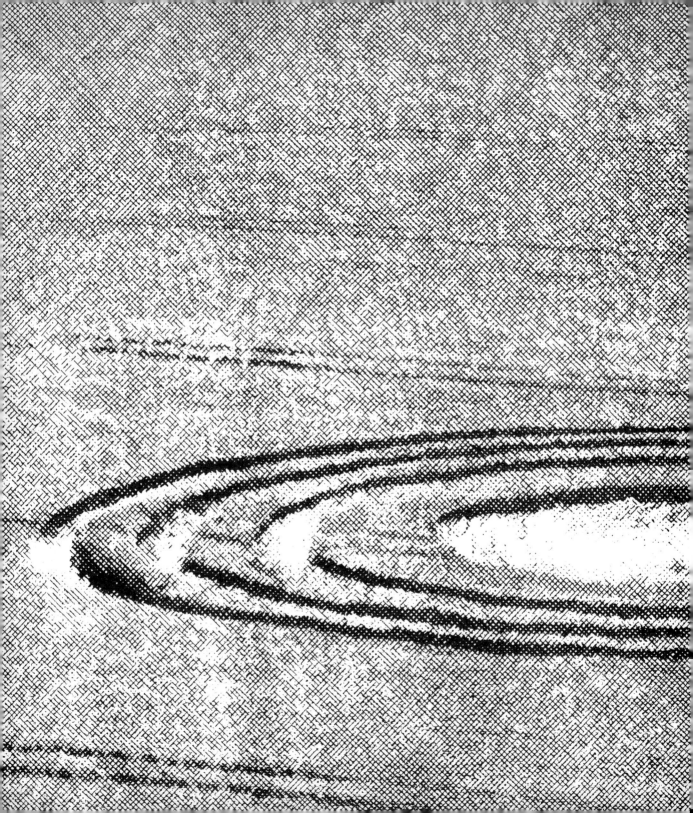

PART

3

MEANINGS AND METAPHYSICS

MEANINGS

As Michael Green says in his Preface, the impression is irresistable that we are witnessing the manifestation of something which shows the strongest signs of design, purpose, intention — in short, something which in any other field we would call intelligent. Many of us who thought this idea whimsical in 1987 were put firmly with or backs to the wall by the events of 1988 and 1989. Figure 3 in the Introduction, which looks no further than the latter year, is enough to demonstrate the problem confronting those who were still hoping, up to the end of last year, to find an explanation in wholly conventional terms. The diagrams on the frontispiece put beyond doubt that we cannot — perhaps *dare* not! — evade John Michell's question. The problem of a possible 'meaning' has become urgent.

What do we mean by 'meaning'? The question has often been debated by philosophers. What 'meaning' is seen by some tiny ant in the abrupt intrusion into its world of the crumb of bread which falls from your sandwich, like manna, on a summer's afternoon (from you, that Great Invisible, which the ant will never see or comprehend)? What 'meaning' should we poor humans read into the shrugging of Gaia's skin which destroys, in a moment, 50,000 of our fragile kind in Iran or Armenia?

It is possible that the 'meaning' of the cropfield patterns will escape us forever. Perhaps they mean nothing; perhaps they mean far more than we can hope to understand. But we'd better try . . .

In the following two articles Michael Green and John Haddington show some remarkable parallels between the cropfield events and a number of ancient and venerable symbols which have haunted the imagination of our species from the earliest times. The coincidences are striking; and we are, perhaps, beginning to learn or re-learn that coincidences are not to be ignored. Neither of the two articles offers us an *explanation* for the extraordinary events which are now in train; it is not their aim to do so; they simply give us some astonishing parallels.

But parallels, as Euclid once remarked, meet at infinity.

The rings of time:
The symbolism of the crop circles

MICHAEL GREEN

I am a child of earth and
starry heaven, but my race
is of Heaven alone.

Orphic tablet from Petelia, Italy, 3rd or 4th century BC

A celebrant of the Ancient Mysteries standing on the summit of Silbury Hill in Wiltshire, England at the dawn of the summer solstice in 1989 would have noticed something strange and new in the landscape. Emerging out of the golden mists that surrounded the mound were to be seen the intricate patterns of the crop circles in the fields below (Plate 14). They had not been there a few days before, but now the two sets of quintuplets shone in the corn on the north side of the hill, together with a single circle on the very summit. The circle formations reflected the sun and the full moon in the sky together on that beautiful morning, with the star Aldebaran, the 'eye' of the constellation Taurus, glowing between them. Aldebaran, the Hebrew Aleph, God's Eye[9,385] was regarded in the ancient world as the leading star of the heavens, harbinger of Light, Illumination and Sound; and in Christian parlance, the Light of the World.

Within the elaborate patterns of the major circle formations around Silbury and elsewhere were grouped smaller circles, or 'grapeshot', which look like constellation patterns. In this connection it may be significant that shortly before the first quintuplet appeared in July 1988, a motorist in the vicinity saw a "constant beam of white light which stretched from the clouds to the ground" near Silbury Hill.[24,55]

If the crop circle phenomenon is, literally, extraordinary, Silbury Hill is unique amongst prehistoric monuments. The largest man-made hill in Europe,

it has been dated by radio-carbon analysis to around 2800–2600 BC. Excavations between 1968 and 1970 failed to locate a central burial, or indeed any ostensible reason for its creation. However, it was established that, beneath the earth cover, it is a masonry faced structure of pyramidical form (with rounded corners) built on six levels.[22,99] Interestingly its nearest parallel is the ancient Egyptian stepped pyramid of the pharaoh Djoser (Netjerykmet) who ruled c. 2630–2611 BC during the Third Dynasty, almost exactly contemporary with the creation of Silbury. Djoser's pyramid at Saqqarah is also built with six steps.[20]

Strange phenomena round a mysterious prehistoric monument: these are not the subjective fancies of an impressionable occultist or ufologist, but hard physical facts, a structural expression of metaphysical realities if you like in the landscape of Britain in the 1980s, and now increasingly in other parts of the world.

THE ANCIENT WISDOM

The sight of the crop circles at Silbury brought back memories of another morning half a lifetime ago when as a poor student the writer had been browsing through a second hand bookshop at King's Cross, London, now long defunct. In a battered copy of Waring's classic study of prehistoric ornament[31,55] was an engraving of solar and stellar sym-

137

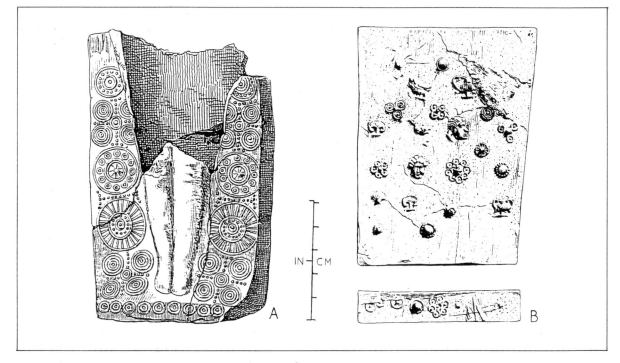

Fig. 1. Romano-Celtic Circle Symbols (1B drawn by M. Stroud)

bolism (Fig. 1A). These had formed patterns which decorated the sides of a small Venus shrine of Gallo-Roman date from Brittany, now lost, but of a type characteristic of second century AD *ex-votoes* made in Gaul.[14,38] The elaborate concentric circles arranged singly and in quintuplet patterns bear a close resemblance to the configuration of the crop circles, but in the case of the Venus shrine are to be identified with the symbolism of the Celtic Tree of Life.

The circles of the Tree, the Welsh *cantrefi*, are analogous to the Kabbalistic *sefirot*. A *cantref* in old Welsh means a canton or subdivision (literally a hundredth) of land, and was used in a metaphysical context to denote the seven states of consciousness,[7,173] which together with the primordial Trinity constitute the Ten, the Causal Consciousness of the Cosmos. Likewise the *sefirot* are also ten, each *sefirah* being a container of light or an Attribute of God.[16,327] The crop circle phenomena may therefore relate to the symbolism of the Ancient Wisdom of north-west Europe.

The Ancient Wisdom, that great body of esoteric knowledge, deals with the nature of Deity, the origins of the manifested creation, God's expression in the natural world and His relationship with mankind on the Wheel of Life, where humanity finds its spiritual apotheosis. The teaching is profound, complex and scattered throughout the ancient and modern writings of the world. It shines like threads of gold in the tapestry of each great religious system. It vibrates with the timbre of their cultures, whether the *Sufis* of Islam, the *Kabbalists* of Jewry or the *Mystics* of Christendom, but the density of the weave is dependent on the quality of their spiritual systems.

In the Hellenic world, Diogenes Laertius (third century AD) quoting Pythagorian traditions of the fourth century BC lists four esoteric schools which had analogies with the Greek philosophic systems of the Ancient Wisdom. These were: the *Magi* of the Persians, the *Chaldeans* of the Babylonians, the *Gymnosophists* of the Indians and the *Druids* of the Celts and Galatae (Diogenes Laertius, *Lives of the Philosophers*, book 1, preface). Each of these systems of the ancient Indo-Aryan world are cultural branches of the Ancient Wisdom, of whom Ammianus Marcellinus (AD 330–391) singles out the Druids as having "a loftier intellect, and bound by the rules of brotherhood as decreed by Pythagoras' authority, were exalted by investigations of deep and serious study . . ."[6,26]

Unlike the other traditions, however, the Druidic and earlier religious beliefs were never committed to writing. Apart from brief references by the classical writers, only the symbols, iconography and monuments of the prehistoric belief systems of north-west Europe have survived to give any hint of the character of their beliefs. Nevertheless it is necessary to relate this evidence of these lost systems to the patterns and structure of the crop circles, for they are closely related.

AN APPROACH TO THE CLASSIFICATION OF THE CROP CIRCLES

It is significant that none of the published studies of crop circles has made an adequate attempt to classify and group the evidence by type.

This may in part be due to the fugitive nature of the phenomena and the poverty of the resources so far made available for their proper study. It is also, it must be said, a reflection of the inordinate professional jealousy and commercial rivalry which has unfortunately marked the study of the subject to date, and has led to a hoarding of essential information. One of the first casualties of such negative attitudes is a cripplingly inadequate data base for their proper scientific study. Above all, perhaps, it

shows a failure to understand at this time the crucial importance of what an earlier age would have clearly interpreted as metaphysical symbolism.

Consequently neither the surveyed plans of the phenomena are available for study, nor their accurate topographical relationship to the surrounding terrain plotted by site, let alone any adequate distribution maps published of their national and international coverage.

Because the crop circles tend to nucleate round particular focii, there is also a need to unpick the palimpsest of markings. This is comparatively easy where the circles form part of a tightly structured group, but much more difficult where there appears to be a random addition of single circles and satellites. Meaden has demonstrated[24,10] just how complicated this process can be in the case of the circles at Bratton, Wiltshire in 1987, where additional circles and satellites were added to already existing features.

Even more interesting is the now clear evidence for what might be termed experimental prototypes of certain types of phenomena, sometimes taking a period of years to reach fruition. For example, a quintuplet found at Bratton in July 1983[24,65] has traces of what Meaden describes as an "ion race" linking the satellites. This feature appears in a fully developed form in a quintuplet (the Celtic Cross type, see below) on Charity Down, Goodwood Clatford in July 1985 (Plate 15) and near Devizes in 1990 (Plate 29). The amazing swastika cross circle from Winterbourne Stoke in 1989 (cover illustration) was the outcome of earlier attempts in the vicinity where the quarterings were not quite so defined. The circle at the top of Cheesefoot Head, Hants, in 1989 (Plate 24) which had a tail giving it the appearance of a comma, also had a prototype. This appeared with only a vestigial tail at Hungerford in 1988.

Another problem arises over the elliptical shape of some circles, indeed it is rare for any of them to be perfectly circular. Two notable examples are the

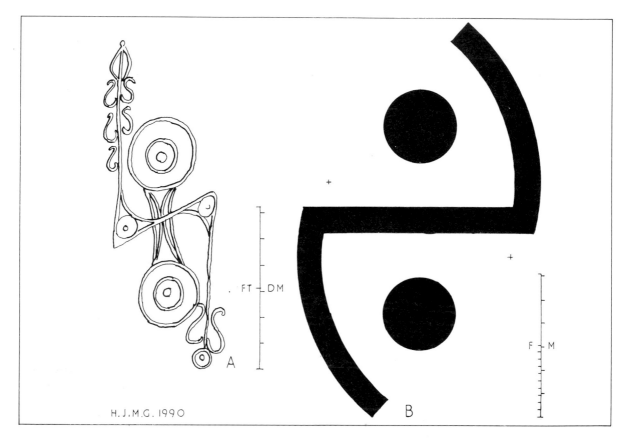

Fig. 1A. The lightning-strike symbol.

formation with two satellites found at Whitehome, Westbury in 1987. Whether these are a separate type or a distortion of the ordinary circle is uncertain. Meaden suggests that ellipses are due to an oblique vortex tube action [24] [68] and the Whitehorm case suggests that the energy forms may have struck the ground obliquely.

Taking all these factors into consideration and bearing in mind the progressive elaboration of the phenomena since 1980, a tentative classification can be put forward under six headings.

First there are the basic circle types, of which there appear to be at least seven (Fig. 2). Second, these can be subdivided in certain cases into five or more subclasses by the addition of satellites, a process which became marked in about 1988. Of the basic circles only nos. 4, 5 and 6 are subdelineated by satellite patterns, which usually consist of single swirled circles. Nos. 4 and 6 have one to four satellites laid out rather like dice patterns around the central circle. In each case there is a variant of the two satellite type. Type 5, however, appears to be missing the two satellite patterns. Third, there are the very small circles (grapeshot), not more than about 2m in diameter, which are forming increasingly complex patterns, both around the main circles and on their own. The configurations sug-

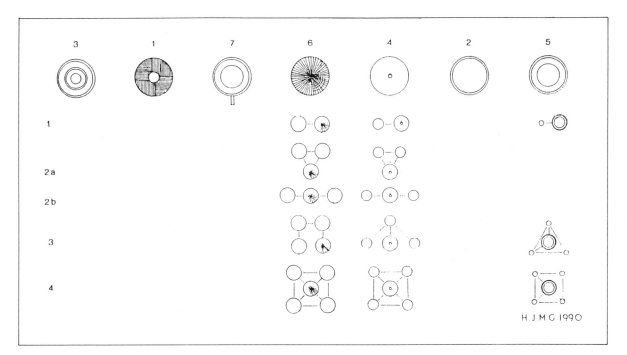

Fig. 2. Planetary Type Crop Circles

gest possible constellation and other patterns (Plate 3). The fourth group which started in 1987 appears to be thematic formations representing certain cosmic principles. The fifth group which appeared in 1990 are symbolic figures of the Sun God (Solar Logos) and Earth Goddess (Planetary Logos) and have a range of attributes illustrating their different functions. The sixth group, and the most spectacular, are great composite, non-symmetrical formations which bring together aspects of the previous group. At least one of these formations at Alton Barnes, Wiltshire, appears to represent the outer planets of the Solar system (back cover of book). None of the figures in groups five and six has subsidiary satellites.

It is proposed that if the main circles represent symbols of different types of cosmic energy and their subdivision in certain cases, the thematic formations represent certain cosmic principles. The grapeshot patterns further define the source and nature of the energies involved possibly at both a macrocosmic and microcosmic level.

THE PLANETARY SYMBOLS

It seems inconceivable, at least to this writer, that such complex, symmetrical formations, which often have features added over several weeks, can fail to be explained except as a consequence of intelligent activity. If indeed these are symbols, what do they refer to and how does this give a clue to their origins?

It has occurred to certain research workers in this field, notably Busty Taylor and John Michell[25] that the circles bear some sort of generic resemblance to pre- and proto-historic symbolism that occurs in the British Isles.

However, a remarkable discovery made over

twenty years ago at a Roman villa in Sussex for the first time really breaks the metaphysical code of the circles. Villa II at Chilgrove, near Chichester, was excavated by Alec Down in the sixties.[11] It was probably a tenant farm of a large estate, of which the main complex has only recently been discovered. In an outhouse dating to the early fourth century AD a mosaic had been constructed with a pattern of seven circles across the centre of the room and two additional circles near the doorway (Plate 68). Behind the main group of circles large patches of burning had partly damaged the mosaic in the late Roman period. At the time of the excavation neither Alec Down nor the expert he consulted, the late Dr. Jocelyn Toynbee, had any idea what the circles meant, except that there was some indication of a ritual significance since the room was provided with a niche for a domestic shrine (*lararium*).

The Chilgrove circles are symbols of the planetary deities presiding over the days of the week. The sequence starts with *Saturn* at the south end (a circle with four lobes encircled by three rings), followed by *Sol* (sun rays and a swastika pattern), *Luna* (handled mirror), *Mars* (convex shield), *Mercury* (ring with central dot), *Jupiter* (a plain ring) and *Venus* (a four-lobed circle with a single ring). The days

represented are of course Saturday to Friday, consecutively. The additional two circles at the east end of the room probably represent *Ceres* or Earth (circle with broad outer band) near the niche and a circle representing the etheric or mystic centre which has two rings round a three lobed centre. In esoteric terms the latter symbolises the Unmanifest Deity, the Central Spiritual Sun (the Light behind the Light of the physical Sun). The three lobed centre in this context represents the Primal Causal Triad of manifestation functioning within the Ring-Pass-Not which separates the inner Ring-Cosmos from the outer Ring-Chaos.[12 15]

It would appear that the room at Chilgrove villa was used for storing cult floats (*fercula*) dedicated to the various deities of the week, which were carried in religious processions (*pompa*). A painting of a *ferculum* from Pompeii shows it to have been of a light timber construction carried on the shoulders of the celebrants, rather like the images of Catholic saints on a Roman feast day.[15,209] The evidence of burning on the mosaic suggests that the stored floats were burnt in situ.

If the symbols of the planetary deities from Chilgrove are compared with the different types of crop circle, the resemblance in many cases is remarkable (Fig. 2 and table 1 below).

TABLE 1			
DEITY	PATTERN	SITE EXAMPLE	RAY
Saturn	Triple ringed circle	Cheesefoot Head, 1988, (Plate 19)	3
Sol	Swastika pattern	Winterbourne Stoke, 1989 (Plate 26)	1
Luna	Ringed circle with spur	Whiteparish 1987 (Delgado & Andrews 1989, Plate 27)	7
Mars	Cartwheel pattern	Bishops Canings 1990 (Plate 30)	6
Mercury	Circle with central dot	Goodworth Clatford 1985 (Delgado and Andrews) 1989, Plate 9)	4
Jupiter	Single ring	Kimpton 1987 (Delgado & Andrews 1989, 62)	2
Venus	Ringed circle	Winterbourne Stoke 1987 (Plate 7)	5
Ceres	Circle with broad ring	Cheesefoot Head Bowl 1990 (Plate 42)	
Spiritual Sun	Double ringed circle		

A modern astrologer might object that these symbols are completely different (with one exception) from the planetary signs that are in use today. This is true, but as S. F. Tester comments, the current system is of recent origin and is not found at all before Byzantine times.[30,31] The Chilgrove symbols appear to be a much older system and probably represents it in its most developed state, although Romanised in character, immediately before the introduction of Christianity. Odd examples occur elsewhere along the south coast of Britain in non-Belgic areas during the Roman period and also in northern Gaul. A similar pair of circles, possibly representing the Sacred Marriage, appear on the entrance threshold of Temple 1 at Springhead, Kent (Arch. Cant. 72 (1959) pl. 11c). The glyphs on the Venus figurine from Brittany have already been mentioned: another rather simpler version with eight 'Venus' circles occurs on a similar ex-voto from Allier, France.[14,38] An interesting shale plaque (now lost) from Halton, Chesters (Fig. 1B) shows a number of similar circle formations,[17,92] and the tradition survived in the north of Britain with examples of Pictish art showing the Sacred Mar-

Fig. 3. Symbols of the Sacred Marriage

H.J M G 1990

riage (see illustration, the Dunnichen Pictish stone, p. 175).

Each planetary symbol has a long history stretching back into the prehistoric past in which the basic type survives, but differs in interpretation according to its cultural context. To take two examples: the mirror of *Luna* symbolises at a superficial level the Moon reflecting the light of the Sun. At a deeper level it illustrates the principle of form or matter reflecting the illumination of the spiritual Sun; or again at the human level the dichotomy between the soul and personality. At an earlier period a similar glyph is shown, but is given an explicitly sexual character where the relationship between the principle of spirit and matter is viewed as a union between the fertilising male principle and the female principle of form. Many prehistoric petroglyphs from both the Old and the New Worlds show these symbols of the Sacred Marriage (Fig. 3E). The ethnologist Rivett-Carnac ,when working at Ayodhya in India in the nineteenth century, found one of these cup and ring petroglyphs and consulted a fakir as to its meaning. First he drew the concentric circle and asked what it meant, "*Mahadiva*" (god of generation) said the fakir. Rivett-Carnac then drew the spur into the circle. "*Mahadiva*" he said again and relapsed into his normal comatose state. The fakir was of course quite correct, the symbol represents sexual intercourse as

Photo 2. Mosaic at Rockbourne Roman Villa, Hampshire.

a cosmological principle at both macrocosmic and microcosmic levels.[21,97] This principle is explicitly stated in the crop formation from Cambridge (Fig. 3D) and Hampshire (Figs. 3A & B; Photo. 39 & 45): *cf* with the Cochmo stone, Glasgow (Fig. 3C) — circa 2000 BC.

The swastika symbol of Sol is another glyph which hides a palimpsest of sacred interpretations. Before it was irredeemably tainted by the Third Reich, it was a symbol of great beauty and power. Only at the most superficial level does it represent the passage of the physical sun around the Earth. Esoterically it speaks of the Wheel of Life, the Great Turning as it was known in the ancient world, and symbolises the states of consciousness through which mankind must pass in the light of his own inner, spiritual Sun. A mosaic at Rockbourne Roman villa, Hampshire, of second century date, illustrates this higher interpretation (Photo. 2). The swastika image has at its centre the eightfold wheel representing the four states of Being and the four states of Becoming; the first represented by the spokes of the wheel, the second by the bolts that hold the axle in place. This is further reflected in the surrounding pattern which has four spokes on the quarters, the one on the south passing to the outside of the pattern. Within each of the four segments there is a swastika pattern representing movement or development. The 'becoming' in this context relates to the five great spiritual initiations which lead to the apotheosis of man, the last taking the initiate through the etheric centre and off the Wheel of Life. This is an immensely ancient mandala of the Timeless Wisdom, and the Rockbourne pavement probably represents one of its last statements as a living tradition in Britain. A much older example, but setting out precisely the same truths, is to be found represented as a petroglyph on the swastika stone of Woodhouse Crag, Ilkley Moor, with its four stationary points and four moving positions encapsulated within the arms of the swastika (Fig. 5B). The date of the petroglyph is not known.

The expression 'states of Being and states of Becoming' is my own, but the principle is succinctly set out in another Indo-Aryan branch of the Ancient Wisdom.

> The visible forms of my Nature are eight: earth, water, air and fire: ether, the mind, reason and the sense of 'I'.
>
> But beyond my visible nature is my invisible spirit. This is the fountain of life whereby this universe has its being.
>
> *Bhagavad Gita 7*

The relevance of this mandala and its teaching to the crop circle enigma is this: each of the seven manifested States of God symbolised by the deities of the week, together with the eighth, the Earth itself, determine the quality of one of the eight positions on the Wheel of Life. It is the symbols of the Cosmic Energies of Deity which are appearing in physical form in the corn fields of England today.

THE COSMIC SYMBOLS

Since 1989 the relatively simple crop circle formations of the early years are being replaced by elaborate patterns of an entirely new type. The new class of phenomena represent, in my view, certain cosmic principles of the Ancient Wisdom which were implanted in the matrix of human consciousness millennia ago and were recorded by glyph and symbol.

The Circle with a tail type. The earliest cosmic symbol to appear is this type, which is appropriate since it represents the principles of cosmogenesis. As mentioned above the type first appeared in 1986 and in a fully developed form at the top of Cheesefoot Head in 1989 (Plate 24).

The symbol appears in great swirls of energy on the stone ball from Towie, Aberdeenshire, which would appear to date from the third millennium BC (Fig. 12). It represents the spiral manifestation of Spirit within the circle of infinity (*Ceugant* in the came forth from it . . . Thereupon a Holy Word (*Logos*) descended on that nature and upward leapt pure fire . . . the Light-Word is the Son of God".[23,4]

The Crucifix type. Perhaps the most profound of the cosmic symbols to appear has been a formation which consists of a quintuplet with an extra circle in alignment to give it the form of a crucifix. Two cases appeared on the south side of Silbury Hill in 1989 where the adjoining quintuplet shared the same satellite. This might have been an accident, but this was certainly not the case of the formation at Cherhill, Warminster, which appeared in June 1989 (Plate 15).

The crucifix is of course pre-eminently the symbol of the Son of Man, the Christ energy, the Second Ray of Love and Wisdom in the Theosophic system, which is also the determining characteristic of the Earth Logos.

All things were made by Him: and without Him was not anything made that was made. In Him was Life, and the Life was the Light of men.

St John 1: 3 and 4

If the Christ energy is the supreme motivating force of creation, then the parlous ecological condition of the planet is a reflection of the fact that in spiritual terms "the earth is regarded as a turning point or battle ground between spirit and matter, and is therefore, from that very consideration of great importance . . . The animating principles of allied constellations and systems, watch the progress of the Son with the keenest interest".[3242] The cross is also a reminder that suffering and purgation are a necessary condition before healing and restitution can take place. It is interesting that the crop circle formations and the spiritual centres with which they are associated are places of healing, both psychic and physical. "Many of the places on the earth's surface . . . which are famed for their healing properties are thus noted because they are magnetised spots, and their magnetic properties

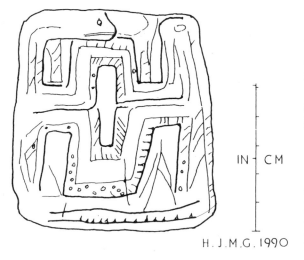

IN ⊦ C M

H . J . M . G . 1990

Photo 3. Bronze Age chalk plaque from Stonehenge.

Celtic systems) in opposition to the inert nature of lifeless matter (referred to as *Annwn*, the abyss). To put it another way "we have the prime spin of the Ring-Cosmos; the reaction giving rise to the Ring-Chaos; the attraction of the Ring-Chaos introducing a secondary spin in the Ring-Cosmos which forms the Ring-Pass-Not".[12,14] It is significant that the physical properties of the crop circles appear to demonstrate those features.

This quality of generation is symbolised in the Ancient Mysteries as a great serpent or dragon, and appears on a Bronze Age chalk plaque from Stonehenge (Photo. 4). The coils of Being are also seen on the great west kerbstone from Newgrange (c.3200 BC) where they emerge from the abyss (Photo. 5). In the *Corpus Hermeticum*, Poemandres speaks of this cosmic conflict and transmutation: "I saw a Darkness . . . coiling in sinuous folds, so that methought unto a snake . . . after that an outcry inarticulate

Fig. 4. Cosmic Egg Symbols

demonstrate as healing influences."[2,130] The crucifix formation is therefore of critical importance in setting the tone and character of the other cosmic symbols of the crop circle phenomena.

The Cosmic Egg Type. In June 1990 a strange variation of the circle with three rings appeared at Middle Warren on the Longwood Estate, Hampshire. The two inner rings are broken alternately to form quadrants (Fig. 4A, Plate 32).

The type is well known on petroglyphs from the Irish megalithic monuments. It represents the breaking apart of the Cosmic Egg, or the disintegration of the primal centre to form the elements of the manifested cosmos. The process is shown on the side of the great stone initiation basin in the eastern chamber of the Knowth passage grave (Fig. 4B). The theme is elaborated on another stone from Knowth (kerbstone 5). This shows in symbolic form the Sacred Marriage with the *lingam* of the male principle of spirit in the broken egg on the left-hand side and its penetration into the female *vulva* of matter on the right-hand side in the other half of the egg (Fig. 4C). The resulting fertilisation produces the third element of the primal trinity, the sacred child, the Son of Man, evidenced as a great spiral of cosmic energy between the male and female principles. The formation at Cheesefoot Head illustrates this principle (Plate 63). The eighteenth century Welsh mystic Iolo Morganwg expressed it thus: "When God pronounced His name, with the word (*Logos*) sprang the light and life . . . And in the declaration was His Love, that is constantaneously with it sprang like Lightening all the universe into life and existence, co-vocally and co-jubilantly with the uttered Name of God, in one united song of exultation and joy — to the extremities of *Annwyn*.[32,17] The cosmic orgasm, the 'big bang' in every sense of the word, was essentially threefold in structure: "form and sound; and one unitedly with (these two) was life . . . and in Life was God".[32,19]

It is significant that within the ring-pass-not of the outer circle, the crop formation has split into five parts, a segment on each quarter with a centre. When the Hellenic philosopher Apollonius of Tyana asked the Brahmin sage Iarchas "of what the cosmos was composed", he was told "elements". "Are there then not four?" asked Apollonius. "Not four," said Iarchas, "but five . . . water, air, earth, fire and ether . . . the stuff of which the Gods are made."[8]

The Celtic Cross type. First evidence of a variation of the quintuplet first fully emerged at Charity Down, Goodwood Clatford in July 1988 (Plate 15). Unlike the other quinquux formation where the satellites stand isolated, these satellites are bound together by a single ring emphasising their totality with the centre.

The wheel symbol is universal in the Indo-Aryan world, and indeed appears in British contexts during the Wessex-Middle-Rhine phase of the Beaker culture early in the second millennium BC, a period for which there is no evidence of spoke-wheeled vehicles. The lack of internal division or spokes forces attention back to the four points on the rim, which have analogues with Bronze Age wheel amulets in France and Germany.

To regard this quaternio of points as merely a definition of the primal elements would perhaps be simplistic. In my perception this symbol represents the principle of rotative activity about the hub of cosmic consciousness, a process in which all life forms are impelled to circulate through all states of consciousness so that they may be imbued by their energies. In Celtic tradition this process of the Little Turning was termed *abred* (*ab*, from; *rhed*, a course), the principle of development and progression for all sentient matter. Iolo Morganwg stated "As there is a special knowledge in each form of existence, which cannot be had in another, it is necessary that we go through every form of existence before we can acquire . . . every species of understanding and consequently renounce all evil and attach ourselves to good"[32,331] In this sense the process is part of the karmic law of development, in which an obligatory factor is a pattern of reincarnation for every spark of God, as the individual soul is known. A necessary part of this process is to pass successively through the mineral, vegetable, animal and human states, even though part of this process may have been achieved aeons ago in systems far removed from our solar system.

The Seven Rays type. A variation of the circle and satellite formations is the crop circle arrangement near Bickington, Devon, reported in June 1990. A central circle was surrounded by seven satellites, symmetrically disposed (Plate 43). In my view this is one of the easiest symbols to interpret in this series, and relates to the Seven Rays, the seven principles of Manifested Deity.

The seven are the Progenitors (*Prajapatis*); the givers of life to all on this planet. They are three and seven making the ten of the Kabbalistic *Sephiroth*. At a cosmic level these Existences are symbolised by the seven *Rishis* of the Great Bear. In their totality they make up the Body of the Grand Man of the

Heavens, the *Logos*. At the level of our solar system, of which the Sun in its turn embodies one of the principles (centres or chakras) of the *Logos*, they constitute the seven planetary spirits, whose classical symbolism and identity has been identified above. From the standpoint of the Earth they are the seven *Kumaras* of the East and the *Angelic* Beings of the West.

In planetary terms they constitute the Living Principles which infuse the matter and form of the third aspect of the primal Trinity of the *Earth Logos*. Since the fourth millennium BC these principles have evidently been understood in the teaching of the Ancient Wisdom of the Indo-Aryan systems. At Newgrange the capstone of the north chamber has a marvellous carving, a mandala symbolising these beliefs (dating to c.3200BC), depicted in the anthropomorphic form of the Earth Logos (Fig. 5A). Three circles represent the head as the primal Trinity. The body is a circle with eight divisions, of which the eighth is distinguished from the others; for whereas the Earth, Gai, is a transient vehicle of the Earth Logos, the Seven Spirits are eternal. The principles of this system are set out in a Vedic hymn 'The Birth of the Gods':

The birth of the Gods . . . in the primeval age, . . . as Being emerged from non-Being . . . Thence did divisions follow into existence . . . From the Infinite (i.e Spirit) Intelligence (i.e Matter) was born . . . Eight were the sons of the Infinite born from herself. With seven she approached the Gods, Martanda she . . . brought forth for the sake of generation and dissolution (*RGV. X 72*).

As mentioned above, the eightfold wheel (with the ninth principle forming the centre) became the prime symbol and mandala of the Celtic peoples (Fig. 5C). As the Great Turning it embodied the ancient Indo-Aryan system of spiritual initiation, and incorporated the principles of the elements.

The Seven Spirits constitute the stations or 'houses' of the Wheel together with Gai, the physical body of the Earth Logos. The Logos Himself, as the motivating spiritual principle of our system, forms the centre.

THE SYMBOLS OF THE LOGOII

In 1989 and 1990 the crop formations have exhibited an entirely new symbolic series in the form of stylised figures. They fall neatly into two classes identifiable from the associated symbolic attributes, namely the Solar Logos and the Earth Logos. Each type has started as a simple form exhibiting the type, and has been followed by others drawing attention to particular characteristics of the two Beings.

The Solar Logos. The formation found at Telegraph Hill, Chilcomb in June 1990 represents the undifferentiated Solar Logos (Fig. 6A, Plate 38). The stylistic convention adopted for all these figures is the double circle linked by a column. In this case, however, the 'head' has a halo of three half-rings representing the primal Trinity (Fig. 6A). The quality of the figure is essentially the male principle of Spirit.

The identification as the Solar Logos is clear from the halo type, which is one of the earliest symbols to appear in Europe. The half-circle glyph occurs in many of fourth and third millennium passage tombs in western Europe, and in particular in the initiation basin from Knowth dating to c.2000 BC which has the characteristic three ringed head (Fig. 6D) and the solar rays. The symbol has also appeared on stones from Knowth (Figs. 6C & 8B) where it shows as an eye. A variation with attributes of the sacred marriage appeared at Cheesefoot Head (Fig. 6B).

The Solar Logos is the controlling Entity of this solar system, whose centres comprise certain planetary Beings as already indicated. He in turn forms part of a greater cosmic Entity, and indeed it is on this principle of morphic resonance as Rupert

Fig. 5. Symbols of the Great Turning

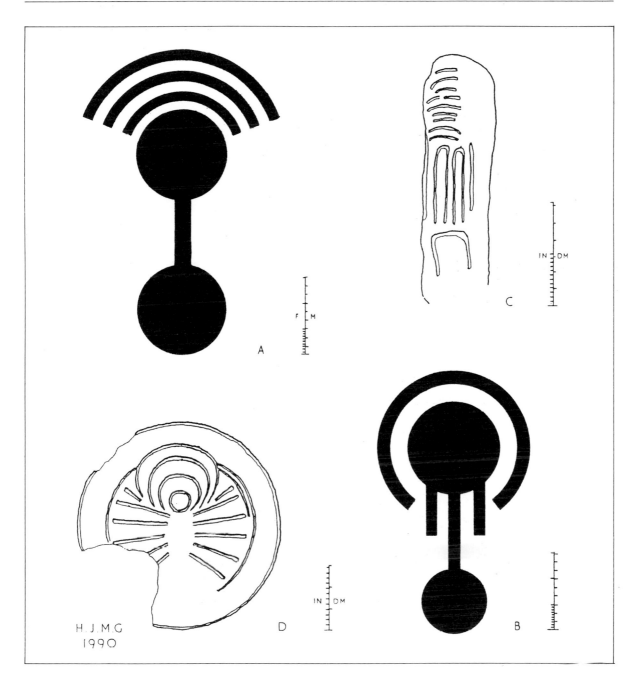

Fig. 6. Symbols of the Sun God

Sheldrake terms it, that the cosmos is constructed. As the oft quoted saying of the Ancient Wisdom has it, "As above, so below that the one thing may be achieved" (The Emerald Tablet of Hermes Trismegistos). Two other things may be said briefly about the Solar Logos. He is, like all Beings throughout the Cosmos on a path of spiritual development, and is thus in this sense an Imperfect God. Secondly His primary characteristic is that of 'unconditional love' reflecting the nature of the centre which he occupies in the 'Grand Man of the Heavens'.

The Earth Logos. In June 1990 an extraordinary new formation appeared near Chilcomb, Winchester. The innovatory features included the dumbbell shape of the body and the rectilinear boxes on either side of the figure (Plate 34 and Fig. 7A). Although sharing features with the Solar Logos type, its symbolism suggests analogues with the Great Mother, the physical form of the Earth Logos.

The earliest symbols of this type appear in northwest Europe in Epi-Palaeolithic painted pebbles (Fig. 7B) from Mas d'Azil, Spain (c.9000 BC) and on cave paintings (Fig. 7C) from Ciaque, Spain (c.6000BC). A stone Helladic figurine (Fig. 7D) of uncertain provenance dated to c.5000–3500 BC illustrates the basic type in iconographic form. All consistently show the Great Mother in a timeless pose, holding her breasts as succourer of all terrestrial life forms, or as a worshipper. She is indeed the One "in whom we live and have our being" as Djwhal Khul expresses it.

Fig. 7. Symbols of the Earth Goddess

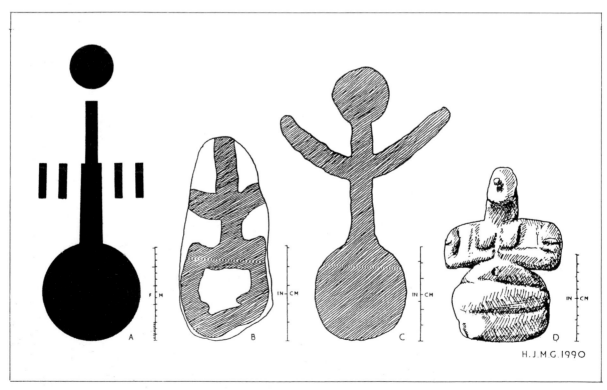

H.J.M.G. 1990

Plate 54. The third double Pictogram to appear was at East Kennett. This lovely shot shows how the configuration is aligned to Silbury Hill. *George Wingfield*

Plate 55. The East Kennett double Pictogram was formed late in the season, July 26, and the wheat is now quite brown. *Kate Bartholomew*

Plates 56 & 57. (opposite) Pole shots of Busty's give some idea of the complexity of the East Kennett double Pictogram.

Plate 58. Just over the hill west of the Kennetts, these strange new designs appeared in a field near Beckhampton. There were two large 'scrolls', some smaller ones, and a triangle with four 'boxes'. *Kate Bartholomew*

Plates 59, 60 & 61. The 'scrolls' and the triangle were found by some to be particularly powerful. A Japanese t.v. crew found their equipment failed, and the magnetic bearings in the field were sent awry.

Plates 62, 63 & 64. The last double Pictogram formed on August 11 1990 in Barn Field near Cheesefoot Head, Winchester. The circlemakers, ever inventive, created 'horns' at each end.

Plates 65 & 66. (opposite) Pole shots of the Gallops double Pictogram, which formed on August 4.

Plate 67. This lovely early evening shot of the top of Cheesefoot Head shows The Gallops double Pictogram in relation to the second Pictogram of the season.
George Wingfield

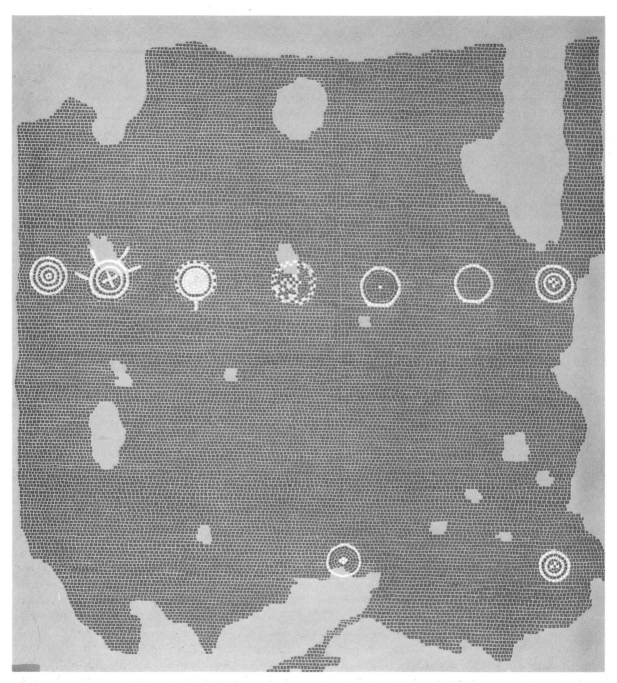

Plate 68. The Pavement at Chilgrove Roman villa (to go with
"Rings of Time").

The same sentiments are conveyed in the great hymn to Isis by Apuleius (second century AD) in the *Golden Ass*:

I am Nature, the Universal Mother,
Primordial child of time
Sovereign of all things spiritual . . .
The single manifestation of all gods
and goddesses that are . . .
Though I am worshipped in many aspects,
Known by countless names and
Propitiated with all manner of different rites,
Yet the whole round world venerates me.[18·228]

Although the general symbolism is clear enough, the detailed attributes are also worth careful examination. The rectilinear boxes for example mark the position of the outstretched/folded arms of the Earth Goddess, but why should they be depicted in this form, and why four?

The rectilinear shape has always in the Ancient Wisdom represented the manifested form, a balanced amalgam of earth, fire, air and water. The symbolism appears on the Newgrange petroglyphs, for example on kerbstone 67 (Fig. 8A). In the case of the Chilcomb crop formation it appears to be a brilliant means of symbolising the *quaternio* of the elements as the creative aspect of the Great Mother, the role of Her arms and hands if you wish.

The Earth Goddess as lover. A completely different symbol of the Great Mother appeared in June 1989 near King's Bromley, Staffordshire (Fig. 9A). A circular formation of what was described as swathes, or short radial boxes, had a 'bib' of the same formation on one side. What may be regarded as 'prototype' formations occurred elsewhere in the same field.[26·73]

Petroglyphs on rocks at Alta, Finnmark on the northern tip of Norway, and within the Arctic Circle, show similar symbols (Fig. 9B). A stick figure from the same area shows this object to have been a cloak, tied beneath the chin, which has been thrown over the figure's head,[18,43] and probably dates to the earlier fourth millennium BC (Fig. 9C). Similar symbols occur at Loughcrew and New Grange (Figs. 9D & E). This may also be the basic symbolism of the Maze representations from northwest Europe. Examples may be cited from Tintagel, Cornwall (Fig. 9E) and the Hollywood Stone, Ireland. The maze is a powerful mandala representing the Little and Great Turning of personality and spiritual development, all encompassed within the aegis of the Great Mother in her procreative aspect.

In short the type symbolises love and desire as a necessary function of the Great Goddess by depicting a form of erogenous display, a timeless 'come on' gesture. The Sheila-na-Gig series of fertility figures of early medieval date in northwest Europe express precisely the same beliefs.

It may be significant that the symbol in its earliest representations is restricted to northwest Europe, and may perhaps be associated with the appearance of the Aurora Borealis in those latitudes, to which the panoply of the cloak may have been likened.

The Divine Hermaphrodites. In June 1990 new types of symbolism occurred in connection with the Solar and Earth Logii. The first to appear in the Cheesefoot Head area had the same dumbbell shape as the Great Mother type, but carried different attributes (Plate 36, Fig. 10A). The *Quaternio* boxes which had represented the arms of the Great Mother type at Chilcomb, here form a fringe below the ringed circle of the 'head'. A protuberance also occurs on the top of the ringed circle 'head'.

Similar representations occur on the stele of the megalithic passage graves of the Morbihan region of Brittany dating to the fifth millennium BC. On a slab from the Gavrinis tomb is carved a figure with a ringed oval 'head' with a 'bib' or necklace below (Fig. 10B). Comparison with other 'guardian' figures from Breton passage graves, especially those from Les Pierres-Plats monument indicate the type. They are sacred hermaphrodites which on the one

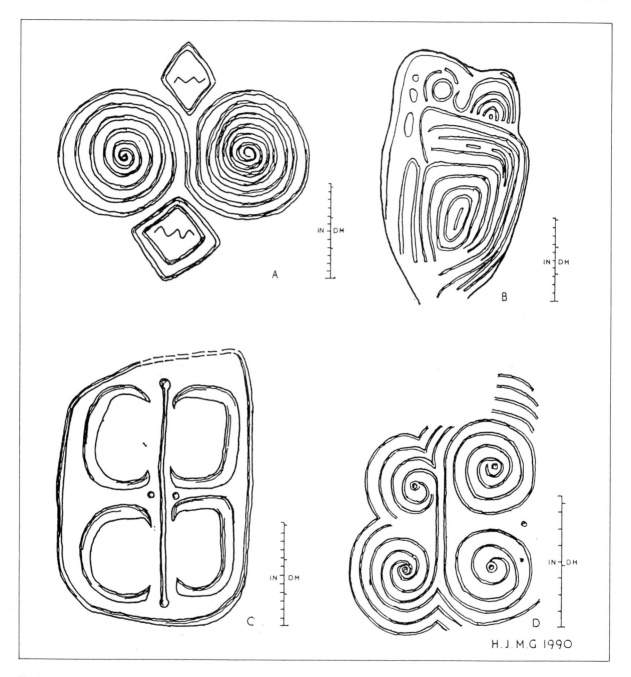

Fig. 8. Symbols of the Quaternio

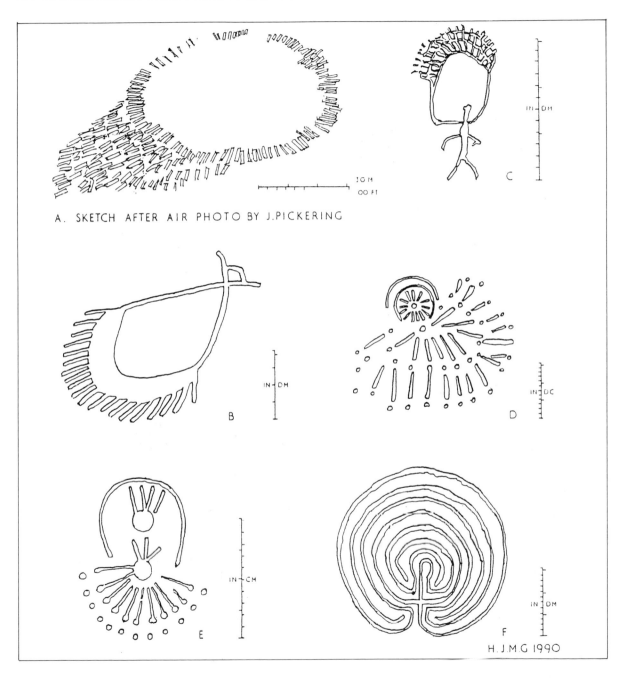

A. SKETCH AFTER AIR PHOTO BY J.PICKERING

H.J.M.G 1990

Fig. 9. Sacred Cloak Symbolism

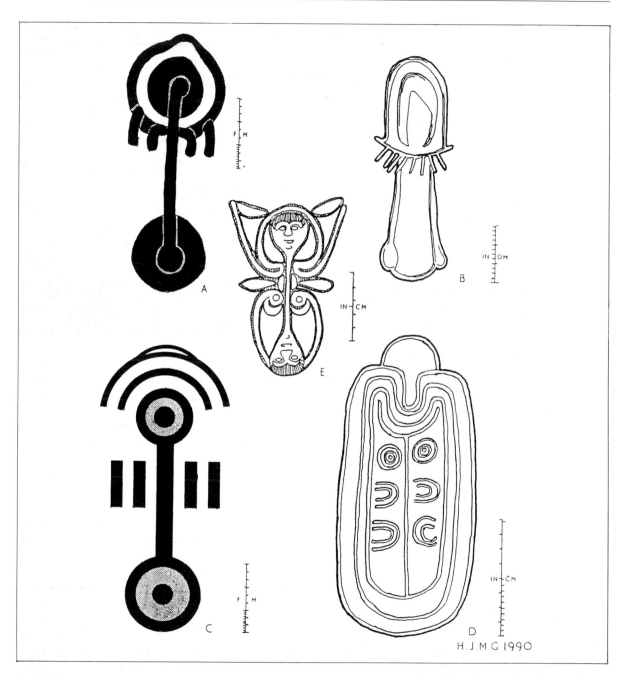

Fig. 10. The Divine Hermaphrodite

Photo 4. The great west kerbstone at Newgrange (c.3200 BC)

hand have the symbols of the Great Mother consisting of a necklace, and in some cases breasts; but also have the male characteristics of lingam, with the penis head having a lip on the top. This latter feature in certain cases also cleverly combines the features of a nipple so that it is both phallus and breast. The orthostat from the Pierres-Plats passage grave brings all those features together in a single figure which also has the three envelopes of the psyche: the physical, emotional and mental bodies, together with the four lunar and two solar lords of the centres or chakras (Fig. 10D). The lunar quaternio are also found at Knowth (Fig. 8C) and West Ray, Orkney (Fig. 8D).

The very simple cosmic principle that is being set out in this crop circle formation is the essential bisexual nature of Gai, the Great Mother, and this principle extends to the Solar Logos and all the other great Entities (the 'Heavenly Men') of which

our own system forms a miniscule part. This bisexuality is also true of the nature of every human person, even though the physical expression is predominantly one sex or the other. This may be a clue to the marked sexual differentiations of the classical deities, a problem that troubled Appolonius of Tyana. He asked Iarchas "shall I then call the universe female, or of both the male and the opposite gender?" "Of both genders," said the other, "for by commerce with itself it fulfils the role both of mother and father in bringing forth creatures; and it is possessed by a love for itself more intense than any separate being has for its fellow, a passion which links it together in harmony."[8,309]

This bisexual nature is interestingly confirmed by different researchers who by dowsing have assessed the sexual features of the crop formation. The lower circle registers as male, whereas the ringed circle is female and the boxes of the 'neckline' are male on the left-hand side and female on the right-hand side.

Exactly the same sexual dichotomy is evidenced by a crop formation that occurred near the seven barrows near Litchfield, Hampshire, at the summer solstice 1990 (Plate 40, Fig. 10C). The figure is a composite of the Solar and Earth Logos types, containing the lateral boxes of the quaternio with solar haloes and a lip. It is a reminder of the essential unity of the Earth with that of the wider solar system. The essential bisexual nature of the dumbbell form is reflected in many ancient symbols which consist of two circles which are linked in some way or other, most noticeably as eyes of the bird 'guardians' or deities (Fig. 8B), particularly of the Great Mother.[9] The type represents the dual aspects of positive/negative, spirit/matter, and male/female and their need for synthesis in deity. The symbol occurs on a Celtic bronze from Tal-y-llyn (Fig. 10E) and a Pictish stone from Aberlemno (Fig. 1A,A). The lightning strike appears in the 1990 Fordham crop formation (Fig. 1A,B).

THE COSMIC DRAGON

The Alton Barnes crop circles (Fig. 11A, Plate 48) is now paralleled by similar formations from Allington White Horse (Plate 50) and East Kennett (Plate 55). Each shows a linear arrangement of four main circles which are linked together as pairs, with smaller circles grouped at either end. The main circles are in most cases distinguished by attributes which take the form of claw-like projections giving the formation an asymmetrical appearance. The Cheesefoot Head formation (Plate 67) is a different version of this type.

The identification of the seven planets in relation to the crop formations have been discussed above. In the traditions of the Ancient Wisdom[2,506] there are seven sacred planets (i.e. the chakra centres of the Solar Logos) namely, Vulcan, Mercury, Venus, Jupiter, Saturn, Neptune and Uranus. There are five non-sacred planets (i.e. linked with subsidiary nodal points of energy of the Solar Logos) namely Mars, the Earth, Pluto, the Moon (veiling Uranus) and the Sun itself (veiling Vulcan). Of these various planets, both sacred and non-sacred, Vulcan, Neptune, Uranus and Pluto have yet to be covered in the symbolism of the crop circles, and it is these which appear to be represented in the new formations. Starting at the head (i.e. west end) of the Alton Barnes formation, the identifications are as follows, Neptune, Vulcan, Uranus and Pluto. The trident of Neptune is particularly evident on the Allington White Horse formation (Fig. 11B).

The significance of these four planetary principles in the order shown at Alton Barnes is that they symbolise great initiatory stages in the progress of humanity and indeed the life of the individual person.

Neptune represents the emergence from the sea of lifeless matter (*annwn*) of the three-fold life-force of spirit (life), soul (wisdom) and personality (matter), symbolised by the trident. Vulcan, working through the zodiacal house of Taurus (hence the horned symbol) represents life-growth, or individuation in the Jungian sense. This ends the two-fold development of natural man. The dual aspect of the new man begins with Uranus which represents spiritual transformation and service, and carries a similar circle symbol to Venus, which in this context represents spiritual rebirth. The last sign, Pluto, constitutes death and transformation to a new level of reality. At this stage the individual leaves the Wheel of Life carrying with him a fully integrated three-fold persona, symbolised by the three-fingered hand.

But this is not all. The overall form of the figure is that of a dragon or serpent with clawed limbs, an eye to one side of Neptune and a tail of three diminishing circles beyond Pluto. As the Tibetan states "the cycle is completed: the serpent of matter, the serpent of wisdom and the serpent of life are seen to be one whole and behind the three stands the Eternal Dragon for ever spawning forth the triple serpent for ever saying: 'Go forth and come thou back'.[2,630] Petroglyphs on the stone of Tully, Ire-

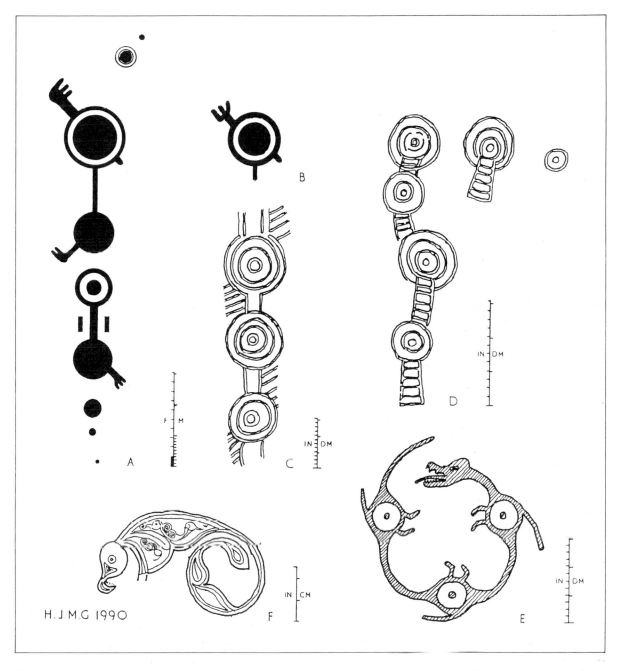

Fig. 11. Symbols of the Cosmic Dragon

land (Fig. 11C) and the panorama series on Ilkley Moor, Yorkshire (Fig. 11D), show the same idea as do an Eskimo glyph of the dragon spirit or *palraiyuk* (Fig. 11E and a Celtic figure of a dragon on a bronze found in the River Thames (Fig. 11F).

WHO IS CREATING THE FORMATIONS?

I use the word who, rather than what, advisedly, for it is my contention that the force or power that is at work exhibits intelligence, and that the phenomenon as a whole shows a planned progression of ideas. Moreover the use of ancient symbolic types, related to the areas where they occur, to convey their message is extremely clever; for the symbolism is not immediately intelligible to the modern occultist, let alone scientist, but is not beyond recall for the student of the Ancient Mysteries. It is obvious that they must be the creation of some natural aerodynamic force, combined probably with an electromagnetic charge, but such force is consciously controlled and not merely the accidental product of a plasma vortex effect, however defined. If the crop formations are then "a child of earth and starry heaven" as the Orphic prayer states, then their origins must be sought in "Heaven alone".

In the ancient world the gods are iconographic representations of cosmic energies, and in particular the Seven Gods constitute the septanate of the macrocosm, the first differentiation of the Divine Triplicity of Spirit-Consciousness-Form, and provide the entire field of expression for the Manifested Deity. For everything that exists is energy, vibrating at a certain frequency in relation to other energies. Each of the Seven Energies is expressed as a musical harmonic and a particular colour, indeed the seven colours of the rainbow express precisely this aspect of Deity. Such energies can be studied and measured by the scientist, but they are not impersonal events. They have in varying degrees consciousness, identity and intelligence, and they are capable of communicating at a human level. In short they are an expression of the hylozoistic structure of the cosmos (from the Greek 'ule', matter; 'zoon', animal; and 'ism', concept). Hylozoism is the doctrine that all matter is endowed with life. As J. P. Allen states of another tradition "the (ancient) Egyptians lived in a universe composed not of *things*, but of *beings*. Each element is not merely a physical component, but a distinct individual with a unique personality and will".[19,8] The appreciation that we are dealing with living, intelligent energies is the next major hurdle that researchers of the circles, and indeed the scientific community as a whole, have to surmount if the phenomenon is to be understood.

The seven spirits of Manifested Deity plan and order every facet of the universe through the equivalent of an enormous cosmic civil service, which at the lowest level comprises elementals who construct matter out of their own bodies.

Knowledge of this great structure of Being was well understood in the ancient world and is the bedrock of the Timeless Wisdom. In recent times there have been very few studies which have dealt in detail with this field of knowledge, but one of the most useful are the various works of the Tibetan Master, Djwhal Khul, as transmitted by Alice Bailey. I believe that these give us a key to an understanding of the circle phenomena as expressions of functional units of the *Agnichaitan* civil service, if I might put it like that.

The *Agnichaitans*, or *Alphas* as they are sometimes known, are a high grade of fire spirit. These are spirits or devas who construct and build matter of the densest kind in connection with Logoic manifestation. They function on the seventh subplane of the cosmic physical plane, and are the producers of the greatest concretion. In the planetary body of Gai (the Great Mother or the Earth Goddess) of whom the spiritual aspect is the Earth Logos, they are the builders of the Earth in its densest form. Throughout the entire solar system they are the sum total of that activity and vibration which demonstrates through what we call solid substance.

There are seven sub-planes of the physical plane: atomic, sub-atomic, super-etheric, etheric, gaseous, liquid and dense matter. The devas who operate in those spheres of activity fall into three groups, 'management' (*Agni*) who transmit the will of God: 'administration' (*Vishnu Surya*) who manipulate the initiated energy: and 'operatives' (*Brahma*) who are the recipients of force and operate on the lowest three subplanes.

The group that is contacting humanity through the circle phenomena I believe may be the second group, the 'administrators' or 'Transmittors of the Word' who operate on the second, third and fourth subplanes, particularly the last which functions as the synthesising level between spirit and matter.

Each sub-plane is further subdivided into seven classes making a totality of forty-nine departments on the physical plane (this may be the esoteric significance of the seven and forty-nine divisions of the Corhampton Triskele circles (Plate 10) which appeared in 1988). There are four classes of Agnichaitans who are particularly concerned with man's treatment of the planet in ecological terms. These are respectively:

1. The 'Green' Devas of the vegetable kingdom with special responsibility for the magnetic points of the Earth, which might be termed the 'acupuncture' nodes of the etheric, geodetic grid of Gaia.

2. The 'Red' Devas concerned with the centres of energy, (*Kundalini*) of all sentient beings, which includes the plant world.

3. The 'White' Devas concerned with air, water and the atmosphere. These create the force-field which make the circles.

4. The 'Violet' Devas who are builders of the etheric double and auras of the plant, animal and human kingdoms.

All Agnichaitans operate with and through the Seven Spirits of manifestation. Each Spirit or Ray

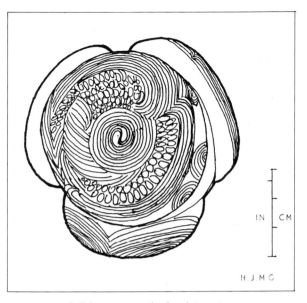

Fig. 12. Stone ball from Towie, Aberdeenshire

has a particular character, vibration and effect; and all Seven are numbered (Fig. 2) in accordance with the accepted identification of the planetary Logoii, who too are great living entities. Now certain planetary Logoii are concerned with particular kingdoms of Nature as a consequence of the energy frequency on which they operate. For instance Mars (Ray 6) is connected with the animal kingdom, Mercury (Ray 4) with the human kingdom and Venus (Ray 5) with the vegetable kingdom.[1,245] It is these kingdoms of Nature which are particularly affected by the adverse world ecological situation, and thus are appearing in symbolic form with certain subdivisions representing in numerical form the four classes of Agnichaitans outlined above.

The Devas operating within these great Ray fields of energy leave therefore, not only the logo, so to speak, of that particular ray in the form of a crop formation symbol, but also a personal monogram of their subclass expressed in terms of the satellite pattern and number.

Furthermore these Devas, or another department, have now launched into a new series of symbols concerned with certain great cosmic truths, one might term them articles of faith, which I have discussed above.

WHY ARE THE CROP FORMATIONS APPEARING?

Critics may well object that even if Djwhal Khul's belief-system is correct, my assessment of the causative factors is entirely speculative and unprovable, at least in current scientific terms. This is in part true at present, but may not remain so much longer if the phenomena continue to develop at the rate, and in the complexity, that is now evident. What I am proposing is a model, indeed a 'scientific' model, against which new information can be assessed.

What follows now is both speculative and subjective, even if not inherently improbable. Why are these other levels of Being going to such extraordinary lengths at this time to communicate in this way? First I believe that they are desperately worried at the worsening ecological state of the planet and are trying to communicate not only to express this, but to suggest ways of collaboration which will improve matters. If indeed these are 'Rings of Time', as they have been described, then time is running out for humanity. They appreciate the difficulty that the scientific world would have in believing in their existence, and therefore have initially chosen to communicate in certain places on a regular, non-harmful basis which will attract those sections of humanity who are most likely to respond in a positive manner. Furthermore such communications are of a character which, while expressing their essential nature, can be checked against information of a recondite kind, and is thus unlikely to be the work of hoaxers. But this is only the beginning. Since 1989 the crop formations have on certain occasions given off high frequency signals which may be the next level of communication.

Special equipment to monitor these signals is being prepared, and even by the end of 1990 it may be possible to study the transmissions that are being sent.

Is there any significance in the distribution of the crop formations? This field of study is crippled by the failure of researchers to publish their results so that it is difficult to prepare even schematic distribution maps. However, what little we do know suggests that the distribution in certain specific areas is not fortuitous or random. It appears to be related to the geodetic energy matrix of the planet through which the life force (*Prana*) is transmitted. Each circle is related to others which act corporately as markers to nodal points of energy along a geodetic field-force line (or leyline as some might term it), and indicate subsidiary lines of the etheric matrix. Many of the nodal points, which have been emitting fields of energy since time immemorial, are sacred places, and this is one of the reasons why the phenomena appear to group round prehistoric religious sites such as Silbury Hill. This site is a good case in point. Crop circles of Ray 4, class 4 have been appearing in alignment on both sides of this sacred site for several years, and in 1989 for the first time a further circle appeared in the very top, marking the nodal point of a force field which sweeps through it southwestwards towards Somerset. At intervals along the Michael leyline, as it has been called, are similar groups of crop formations marking the position of further nodes. If an analogy from the biological sciences might be used, it is as if they act as topographical aminoacids along an enzyme chain giving the leyline its particular character in the Gaian geodetic matrix. At present only short sections of these leylines are being identified in this way as pilot projects, but once mankind has caught on and is prepared to collaborate, much larger sections of the geodetic matrix will be revealed.

But will mankind be prepared to communicate and collaborate with other levels of Being? This imperative to work in harmony with conscious intelligent entities of the natural world is the great challenge of the late twentieth century to the scientists and politicians of the international community.

Acknowledgements: I am indebted to Mr Alec Down for illustrative material in connection with the Chilgrove pavement. Grateful thanks are given to investigators of the crop formations who have kindly provided drawings and information prior to publication: Mr Richard Andrews, Mr R. Armstrong, Mrs Beth Davis, Ms Isabelle Kingston, Ms Lucy Pringle, Ms Leonie Starr, Mr F. C. Taylor and Mr George Wingfield.

REFERENCES

1. Bailey, A. A.: *Esoteric Psychology I* Lucis, New York, 1936.
2. Bailey, A. A.: *Initiation Human and Solar* Lucis, New York, 1951.
3. Bailey, A. A.: *A Treatise on Cosmic Fire* Lucis, New York, 1962.
4. Bailey, A. A.: *The Labours of Hercules* Lucis, New York, 1974.
5. Bailey, A. A.: *The Treatise on Cosmic Fire* Lucis, New York, 1982.
6. Chadwick, N. K.: *The Druids* Univ. of Wales, Cardiff, 1966.
7. Conway, D.: *Secret Wisdom* Cape, London, 1985.
8. Conybeare, F. C. (trans.): *Philostratus: the Life of Appolonius of Tyana* Harvard Heinemann, London and Harvard, 1969.
9. Crawford, O. G. S.: *The Eye Goddess* Phoenix, London, 1957.
10. Delgado, P. and Andrews, C.: *Circular Evidence* Bloomsbury, London, 1989.
11. Down, A.: *Chichester Excavations*, Vol. II, 1971.
12. Fortune, D.: *The Cosmic Doctrine* Weiser, York Beach, Maine, 1976.
13. Graves, R. (trans.): *Apuleius: The Golden Ass* Penguin, London, 1950.
14. Green, M.: *Symbol and Image in Celtic Religious Art* Routledge, London, 1989.
15. Gusman, P.: *Pompeii* Heinemann, London, 1900.
16. Halevi, Zev ben Shimon: *Adam and the Kabbalistic Tree* Gateway Books, London, 1974.
17. Hartley, B. and Fitts, L.: *The Brigantes* Duckworth, Gloucester, 1988.
18. Helshog, K.: *Hellleristningene, 1 Alta* Alta Kommune, 1988.
19. Hinkley Allen, R.: *Star Names, their Lore and Meaning* Dover, New York, 1963.
20. Lauer, J. P.: *Les Pyramides de Sakkarah* l'Institute Français D'Archeologie Orientale, 1972.
21. Mallery, G.: *Picture Writing of the American Indians* Vol. 1, Dover, 1972, ex. 1889 ed.
22. Malone, C.: *Avebury* Batsford, London, 1989.
23. Mead: *Thrice Greatest Hermes* Vol. II, Hermes Press, Detroit, 1978.
24. Meaden, G. T.: *The Circles' Effect and its Mysteries* Artetech, Bradford on Avon, 1989.
25. Michell, G. (ed.): Arts Council Catalogue: *In the Image of Man: Indian perception of the Universe through 2000 years of painting and sculpture* Weidenfeld & Nicolson, London, 1984.
26. Reynolds, D. J.: Swathed circles effect damage in Staffordshire, a totally new form of crop damage: *Circles Research 1* (1990). Meaden, G. T. & Elson, D. M., eds.
27. Scullard, H. H.: *Festivals & Ceremonies of the Roman Republic* Thames & Hudson, London, 1981.
28. Sheldrake, R.: *The Presence of the Past* Collins, London, 1986.
29. Skinner, R.: The Crop Circle Phenomenon: *Fortean Times 53*, 1989.
30. Tester, F. J.: *A History of Western Astrology* Boydell, Woodbridge, 1987.
31. Waring, J. B.: *Stone Monuments, Tumuli and Ornament of Remote Ages* John B. Day, London, 1870.
32. Williams, J.: *Bardass Vol. 1* Longman, London, 1862.
33. Allen, J. P.: *Religion and Philosophy in Ancient Egypt*, Newhaven, 1989.

Where two worlds meet

JOHN HADDINGTON

I hope that this short piece will be of some help to those seeking to find an explanation for the appearance of the strange circular imprints in fields of standing crops. This is not intended as a ready answer for their creation but rather a pointer towards the existence of something else far more important and eternal than the world itself. The Crop Circle Phenomenon is probably only a small part of an overall exercise to raise the consciousness of humanity and prepare us for coming events whatever they may be.

The mechanics of the creation of Crop Circles and the guiding force behind them, still remain a mystery. It is much too early to make definitive statements about their origin, as the research into the phenomenon has really only been continuing for ten years or so. The mystery must be allowed to unfold by itself. Our only duty is to wait, to observe, to record, and most importantly to listen to what may be imparted to us.

My feelings on first visiting the circle sites was of wonder and puzzlement. The sheer perfection in the way the corn had been laid flat from the very definite centre to the outer perimeter of the circle without affecting the stalks that stood inches away at the cut off point, was indeed remarkable. No whirlwind would have left such a mark, as the corn would have been plucked from the ground in an upward spiral, and an awful mess would have been left. These circles were to my mind caused by a downward vortex of a force hitherto unknown. I had only a great desire to find out the truth of the matter, and I did have a strong sense that here was something of unique importance to be researched.

I looked for evidence of circles having appeared in Britain in early historical times, and found, along with other researchers that the ancient Celts had incorporated exact replicas of what we were now seeing on the ground into their art work both in manuscript form on artifacts and standing stones. This seemed to be a good lead and it was not long before it became evident that a vast majority of circles were choosing sites close to ancient Celtic ceremonial sites, and in particular White Horses, Steeps, and burial mounds. Many of these so-called burial mounds are in fact energy nodes, sources of spiralling energy, of which Silbury Hill is by far the largest in the country.

The connection between the ancient religious sites and crop circle activity became even more evident with the advent of dowsers on the scene who found lines of force running from the ancient sites to the crop circles, and indeed that the crop circles perched on known ley lines, particularly at their junctions. In order to have first hand experience of this, I renewed my interest in dowsing, an art which I had only superficially dabbled with in previous years. Funnily enough I attended a talk given by Michael Green on the subject of dowsing and got some very useful information that evening. I utterly failed to get a reaction from his angle rods but when I returned home and made my own set, I found that after some months of practice I had a workable ability in dowsing. Lines of force popped out of the ground all over the country and I traced many lines running from burial mounds to the circles.

It was just before the 1989 season that my dowsing activity progressed into the field of healing, and I found that I had the ability to channel healing energy successfully into sufferers of arthritis and sciatica. I like to think that this new-found faculty of mine has something to do with the energies present in crop circles. Certainly, had I not started research into crop circles I do not think that I would have ever uncovered this gift.

As time went on I felt that more needed to be known about the significance of the patterns made on the ground by the circles, and it was not until I contacted a group in Malta that this element has been satisfactorily explained.

Johann Blomeyer is a diviner of great experience. He is acknowledged by the Dalai Lama himself to be one of the great diviners of today, and his thoughts on the subject of the circles need serious consideration. The circles are, in his view, two dimensional fingerprints of an incoming beam of consciousness. This incoming consciousness affects people not only at the actual point of contact with the earth but for hundreds of miles around. The Earth is similarly affected by this incoming energy. The Rings at Avebury and the great mound of Silbury Hill are of vital importance. The Megaliths that are abundant in that area are in fact laid out in the form of a serpent. In Hindu philosophy the base of the spine chakra is the residence of Kundali — the serpent — so it follows that Avebury could represent the Base of The Spine Chakra on the body of Gaia.

All healing work of a Spiritual nature to a Physical body should start at the Base of The Spine Chakra. This releases energy to work on the other chakra points. If this theory is correct, does this indicate that the Earth is being healed or stimulated in some way from above by the incoming energy which we see in the form of crop circles, and is the process being effective? Have a look at what is happening in Eastern Europe. Maybe there has been violence there, but arguably in a just cause, as people have risen up against tyranny and defeated it more swiftly than seems believable.

When Johann tested the source of power of the circles in our presence with his Aurameter, he got knocked clean off his feet by the energies that he picked up, and for a man of some seventy-eight years of age this did not seem to be too wise a procedure to repeat. This energy he has divined as being directed through the Solar Logos and is, according to Johann, a double cone or diamond-shaped beam of consciousness, ultrasonic in nature above ground and infrasonic below, with electro-magnetic properties. This beam is even more powerful at altitude and below the ground as the energy travels to the core of the planet.

The crop circle is a two-dimensional cross section representation of the incoming beam, and Johann feels that more experiments should be conducted with a sensitive Gauss meter to try to establish whether indeed there is an electro-magnetic element present as a residual effect some time after the formation of the crop circle or, indeed, at the exact time of its inception. A time and space slot almost impossible to predict.

However, one can say something about the other side of the nature of a crop circle if one can visualise them in terms of Mandalic structures. I will now enlarge on this subject as it proves extremely relevant. I have drawn largely from José Arguelles' book *Mandala* to illustrate my point and my apologies for gross plagiarisation but, with only a short time to swot up on the subject and only a little personal knowledge of Buddhism, I did not want to give a garbled version of what is extremely important knowledge.

In Sanskrit the word Mandala literally means circle and centre. In traditional design the circle represents that which is external and the square represents the Earth or the man-made temporal world. The Tibetan monks achieved the most complex and full development of the Mandala. Their Thankas are most highly prized works of art and meditative ritual tools.

At the centre of the Mandala is the abode of the Deity contained within a square — the palace of inner being. This in turn is surrounded by a circle or series of circles, each representing a particular phase of initiation or level of consciousness, suggestive of a passage between different dimensions between macrocosm and microcosm, between man and the universe. The Mandala is the gateway to the otherworld through which each world may interpenetrate the other.

The one universal constant of all Mandalas is the principle of the centre. The centre symbolises the beginning of time, of space, of creation itself. Here at the centre is the origin of all things, the centre of the Mind of the Creator, the Abode of Eternity. It is from this centre that all things are made manifest and it is to this centre that we shall all one day return.

If you study Nature and the many complex patterns that appear in every living thing you will see that there is a law to which all animate life forms and inanimate life forms such as crystals and atomic structures conform. These are structures of immense beauty and symmetry and every atom of matter in the universe obeys this law of nature.

We are each of us at the centre of our own Mandala. In the Eternal Present our physical being is interpenetrated by our conscious being, and we are conscious of the needle point of the eternal NOW. Only by virtue of the undefinable and eternal do past and future exist at all. We are at the centre of our own compass with North, South, East and West, the cardinal points through which we experience the world on the physical plane.

Each Mandala and the separate parts that go to make up the whole contain a variety of inner meaning. The Mandalas of even numbers are built up from a centre consisting of four blocks. This group of blocks represents the rhythm of the quaternity of ages, seasons, elements, compass points, etcetera.

It is also the Mandala of Shiva the Divine Transformer, whose ceaseless dance reflects the ever-changing flow of Nature. This type of Mandala has no central square, the centre of time being the eternal present. It is one of the Vastu Purusha group of Mandalas; a group used as models in the construction of early Hindu Temples. It is the symbol of the unconditioned essence (Purusha) in so far as this essence is capable of lending itself to existence (Vastu). It is this structure which has appeared many times in the form of crop circles.

When the essence takes on existence it is given the form of a Mandala. This was considered by the Hindus as being literally a Divine incorporation and the individual Mandalas as symbolic of Earth or the Earth Principle. Originally the Vastu Purusha Mandala corresponded to a live sacrifice symbolising the beginning of a New World System. A broken or imperfect Mandala represents a lack of harmony.

A block of the Vastu Purusha Mandala has appeared on Earth at Goodworth Clatford as illustrated on the front cover of Colin Andrews' and Pat Delgado's book *Circular Evidence*, and the March edition of *Fortean Times*. That which is of great significance is the fact that this Mandala is specifically symbolic of the incorporation of Earth of the New Age. We have moved from the Piscean age to the Aquarian age in the last three years and the new energy has arrived.

Carl Jung in his book on Flying Saucers made a prediction that at the change of the Age there would be a change in the Psychic levels and conditions of the planet. He predicted portents and events that would be incomprehensible to people, and which were allied to a world of which we had no knowledge. This was a remarkable thing for Jung to come out with in 1959 but he felt strongly compelled to do so even at the risk of his professional reputation.

Carl Jung was a modern student of Esoteric Hinduism and the Tibetan Tantra and, although he could follow the Eastern tradition much of the way, he could not bring himself to see a world in the future bereft of suffering, nor could he see the prediction of the end of duality in Man or the attainment of 'at-onement' with the universe. However, he revived the interest in Mandalas and their meanings, in particular that of what he called the Quincunx based on the Vastu Purusha Mandala.

This representation of Consciousness has at its centre a circle representing the Divinity, the four other circles, symbolizing the four functions of consciousness, are placed in the form of a square enclosing the central circle, one of these outer circles being different in some way to the other three. This formation is a symbol of the Quinta Essentia or Philosopher's Stone. Carl Jung foretold of this event appearing on Earth as a portent at the change of the Age.

Had Carl Jung been alive today, he would have been amazed and delighted to have seen the giant Quincunx formations of crop circles lying below Silbury Hill as living proof of his predictions. Had he walked into the field and examined the circles closely, would he not have leapt with joy to have found that of the four satellites only one was turned in an anticlockwise direction, thus dotting the 'Is' and crossing the 'Ts' of his own theory?

The other crop circle that illustrated the growing complexity of design within formations were the two circles that appeared at Winterbourne Stoke in August 1989. This extremely ancient and universal symbol is an emblem of the sun and of good fortune. "The centre of the Swastika is the centre of the Great Spirit, the Great Mystery, from which all things emanate". (David Villasenor). If this phenomenon has something to do with the sun then how appropriate that this symbol should appear to confirm that suspicion. How clear a message is

The Dunnichen Pictish stone.

written here in the fields of England and yet how obscure.

Why should a message take this Oriental form, why are there no Christian symbols, you ask. The answer to that is that there are Christian symbols to be found in the crop circle phenomenon in the form of long crosses and the triple formations which are evocative of the Trinity. I have dwelt on the Hindu/Buddhist interpretation simply because the Christian tradition does not make great play with the different aspects of consciousness nor indeed with the significance of Mandalas in spite of the fact that it uses them extensively in stained glass work in cathedrals such as Chartres. There, the great rose window is a classical example of a Christian Mandala, to mention but one in passing.

There is a strong spiritual connection between England and India. This lies in the distant history of the migration of the Celtic tribes from the region we now call Afghanistan and Northern India to Europe and finally the British Isles. It was from there, too, that the Hindu and Buddhist cultures originated and spread Eastward.

There must have been considerable dialogue between the Bon Pos and other groups around that time and certain knowledge would have been shared between different groups. T. A. Wise, in his book *A History of Paganism in Caledonia*, written in 1884, makes many references to the many Hindu and Buddhist symbols to be found inscribed on Sacred Stones in Scotland. He seemed to be under the impression that Buddhist missionaries had visited the country rather than that the Picts and Celts had brought the culture here themselves.

Carved on these stones are Vajras, and sceptres, common ritual tools among the Hindu/Buddhist people, and glyphs symbolic of the elephant, boar, serpent, bull, deer, etc., all animals that appear in the Eastern tradition. Also circular patterns such as the three circles within a ring — similar to the formation which appeared in the punch bowl at Cheesefoot Head, and at Corhampton in 1988. I have also found a drawing of a French Celtic sculpture from Bouches-du-Rhône, now in the Musée Borely in Marseille, of a priest sitting in the Buddha position. Is this just another coincidence or is there a deeper meaning to be drawn from these discoveries?

There is a standing stone in the churchyard of Aberlemno in Angus, Scotland, that has amongst the many figures carved upon it an object that is described in the text on the stone as a mirror, but which looks to me extraordinarily like a circle configuration that appears on the front cover of Dr. Terence Meaden's book on the subject of crop circles.

Not more than eight miles away from the Aberlemno stone the first crop circle was reported to have been seen in Scotland. Indeed it was one of the first circles that one can believe was seen in the process of formation. When I visited the site I saw two large burial mounds in a neighbouring field some 300 yards away. No mention had been made of these mounds in previous reports and the person who had reported the circle site had no idea of the significance of their proximity to the crop circle.

It has just come to my attention that the crop circles that have been located in Australia are close to ancient Aboriginal ceremonial sites of great importance, and that the Crop Circles in Kentucky, U.S.A., which have appeared in the same field for five years running, are placed right next to a Red Indian tribe's ancient burial mounds. This illustrates the point that all researchers covering this topic must be aware of recurring constants.

Burial mounds and ancient ceremonial sites are high on the list of recurring features that should be noted when examining the surrounding neighbourhood of crop circle sites as they are now beyond a shadow of a doubt an integral part of the mystery. These new facts, along with all the evidence from England, should encourage those who are unwilling to come down this path of the cosmic significance of the circles to take a closer look at what is being said. It is becoming clearer by the day that there is an interpenetration of our existence with something of a Divine nature which may have a message to convey to us.

The symbol of the Age of Aquarius is the Cornucopia; the spiralled horn of plenty, the horn of the goat that suckled Jupiter, placed among the stars as an emblem of abundance. The Mandala can be likened to a Cornucopia as everything in Creation is made manifest from the centre of Being.

What conclusions can be drawn from this research and indeed what can one say for certain about the crop circle phenomenon that is not of a purely subjective nature?

First of all one can say that many of the configurations are archetypal images of extreme antiquity.

Secondly that they appear next to sacred sites on an international scale.

Thirdly that there are both visual and aural phenomena in association with the crop circle phenomenon.

Fourthly that the phenomenon is still a mystery but as time goes by that mystery will unfold itself.

1990 seems to be the beginning of that great unfolding.

PART

4

THE ENIGMA

The way forward

ARCHIE ROY

Well, What are we to make of it all? No doubt readers of this book and of previous books and articles on crop circles will have formed their own opinions about the crop circle enigma. At this stage perhaps I may be permitted to give you my own.

In an interview on Radio Solent some five years ago I said:

"I think that in all scientific investigations which are starting out from some seemingly unknown phenomenon, you simply have to enter the stamp collecting phase. In other words, you collect as many varieties as possible, record them, get all the information you can and then you begin to classify them. After that, if you're lucky, you'll hit on some sort of test, some sort of theory that you can apply and, if it is a good theory, it has predictability and you should be able to predict, in certain circumstances, what the phenomena should be. At the present state, you see, we haven't the faintest idea, but I must say that some of the explanations that have been put forward. . . like whirlwinds or viruses or down-draughts from helicopters. . . seem to me to be totally inadequate with respect to the beautiful symmetry of these rings and the regularity."

Later, the interviewer asked:

". . . if you find out what causes the rings, can it have any implications for us, do you think?"

I replied: "It is impossible to say. All actual phenomena have implications and in this particular case, I don't see any reason to doubt that it might have far-reaching implications. The trouble is, you see, at the beginning of any scientific investigation, you really don't know where it's going to lead."

To me, the most astonishing feature of the crop circle enigma is that my words so many years ago still reflect accurately my present opinion.

Many hundreds of circles later, I believe we are still at the beginning of our attempt to understand why and how these fascinating phenomena appear. And yet there has been progress. The invaluable pioneering work of Colin Andrews, Pat Delgado, Terence Meaden, 'Busty' Taylor, George Wingfield and others has accumulated a large body of data.

It seems to me that it has been established, beyond reasonable doubt, that the circles phenomena have been increasing, in numbers of circles, in complexity of pattern and in the number of places of occurrence.

The increases are too striking to be totally accounted for by the fact that as more and more people learn about the phenomena more and more people are looking for them. There therefore is an active evolutionary process about the circles phenomenon.

It seems to me also that all theories of origin so far put forward as 'the last word' have been either totally disproved by the phenomena or rendered less and less credible as the years pass. In particular, Terence Meaden is to be applauded for his long and strenuous efforts to accommodate the crop circle phenomena to atmospheric physics. No-one else has come near his ingenious attempts to give us a scientific working model of what may be happening. In addition, his observation and recording of events has been meticulous and we owe it greatly to him that most events can be taken as not the result of hoaxes. And yet the phenomena of 1989 and particularly of 1990 have shown us that Meaden's theory at best remains unproven and for many observers is no longer plausible. Among the phenomena leading to such a conclusion are the *White Crow* Project, and the completion or alteration of circle patterns previously measured or photographed from the air. One such example, recorded in the Epilogue, is the appearance of a gigantic fourth ring round a three-ringed circle some days after the latter occurred. The precision involved is staggering.

The growing data file of letters from many correspondents, indicate that circles have been appearing in a variety of places world-wide for many years. See also Delgado and Andrews' book *Circular Evidence*. How far back in time these circles have been appearing is something we would like to ascertain. Anecdotal accounts suggest two or three generations. The Hertfordshire pamphlet is dated 1678 and describes a typical crop circle with one ring in a field of oats, together with a mention of familiar visual night time phenomena prior to its discovery. It would be of value therefore, though undoubtedly a major piece of work, to examine old aerial photographs taken over the past 50 years — for example by the RAF, or for archaeological or historical research — to see whether any reveal the presence of crop circles.

But the overall conclusion that emerges from a study of the material in this and in previous books on the crop circle enigma is the need for a full exchange and timely publication of data, regardless of whether it embarrasses any particular hypothesis. To do anything less is simply not being scientific. If some researchers were to withhold some facts lest they provide comfort to rival theorists that would be petty in the extreme, mean-minded and perhaps the best way of setting up barriers against progress towards a solution of this intriguing mystery. For that progress to be made it is imperative that all serious researchers should pool their information at the earliest convenient stages. This need not — indeed *should* not — deny any researcher that valuable scientific reward, priority of publication. But priority is quite different from concealment and in scientific enquiry concealment is an unforgiveable sin!

In their beautiful book *Circular Evidence*, Pat Delgado and Colin Andrews make relevant statements that have my full agreement.

"If an event occurs which causes substance or material to be displaced, then science, and physics in particular, is involved. When it occurs regularly to produce circles and rings in crops, then high-level scientific investigation should be carried out and in such a way that interested parties, the world over, are kept informed of events and progress. . . It is our hope that the scientific establishment at large will realise that the puzzles encountered in the circle phenomenon are already part of the very fabric of science, so that serious research can begin."

In the Foreword I tried to show that their hopes of the 'scientific establishment' becoming involved is unlikely to be straightforwardly fulfilled. The contents of this book and the fast-swelling flood of data makes it more and more probable however, that the provision of a readily-accessible data base scientifically set up as planned by the Centre for Crop Circle Studies, is the best way in which to involve scientists of diverse disciplines in the goal of finally understanding why and how the crop circles appear. In that understanding must come increased knowledge not only about our environment but also about ourselves.

Headaches or healing

LUCY PRINGLE

I am of the opinion that we are, as indeed are all living things, composed of energies. These energies ebb and flow depending on a number of things, i.e. our emotional and physical wellbeing. They extend to varying degrees *beyond* our actual physical bodies. I wonder how many of you understand why you react the way you do if you are in close proximity to another person? Your energy fields (or aura) are in fact overlapping and you will find that you are on the same wavelength (vibrations or energies) as that person, to a greater or lesser degree, having the possibility of varying from one extreme to the other. Hence you may register abhorrence, dislike, being vaguely uneasy, neutrality, right through to total compatibility.

How often we put on a façade in order to appear as we *think* others would like to see us, for we are all chameleon-like and in order to survive and adapt we so often disguise our true self. However, from those who can feel or see the energy field there can be no concealment. They will be able to know intuitively the physical and emotional well-being of each individual. So it is with all living things; even leather and wood breathe. The Earth is a mighty energy force of a complexity not comprehended by many. The Earth's responses are controlled by many interacting and interdependent conditions, the planetary influences being a force of great importance. Remember, the planet is a living, breathing organism which we with great temerity would try and harness for our own greedy benefit.

Now for the crop circle energies. Where these involve ley lines, and indeed it would seem that this is the case with all (apart from the hoaxed ones), the energies present are powerful. Thus the reactions of individuals will relate to their own personal energies. Some may be unpleasant, others extremely harmonious and beneficial. In all events it is a *very personal* experience and I have seen a number of people come quietly out of a circle with a look of awe and humility: a far cry from the person who went in! For this reason I would like to say that the likelihood of this occurring will be greatly, if not completely reduced, if with a *group* of people. There would be too many different energies present. It is also important to point out that should you feel in any way uncomfortable you should leave as quickly as possible. There is no point in persisting and indeed it could be harmful. Experiences have varied from healing to headaches!

I would like to tell you about what happened in a crop circle in the Winchester area in July this year. My sister and a close mutual friend were with me. The latter has the great misfortune to suffer from Raynaud's Phenomenon. We went into the crop configuration and I proceeded in my usual way recording the YIN and YANG and noting the strength of the different energy forces, also the manner and direction in which the crop lay. Having almost completed this, I sat down on a strong energy point on the perimeter of the YANG circle with great relief as I had badly damaged my right

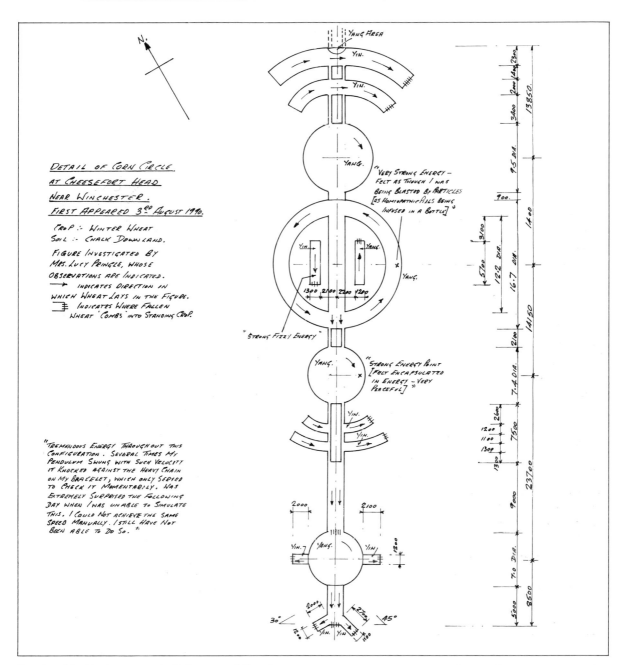

Drawing of double pictogram at the Gallops, top of Cheesefoot
Head, near Winchester, by Peter Baillie.

shoulder playing a ferocious set of mixed doubles at tennis the previous evening. I had been unable to use my right hand to clean my teeth that evening as the pain in raising my arm was considerable.

As I was sitting relaxing in the circle, I became aware of energy rippling through my shoulders. I gently moved my right shoulder and found to my amazement that I could move it without pain. I stayed where I was and let the energy continue to flow, until my shoulder was completely mobile and free of pain. Going from being full of doom and gloom at the prospect of being out of tennis for the rest of the season, I was joyful at my recovery and am back playing as before. What happened to our mutual friend was no less dramatic; on becoming aware of what was happening to me, I called her and suggested she should come and sit close by me. I did not tell her what had happened to me, I simply suggested she might find it a 'good place' to sit. She immediately expressed a feeling of tremendous well-being and said her fingers were tingling. She said, "I can't explain the tingling I experienced in my finger tips, except to say it was as if my fingers had been cold, as in a Raynaud's spasm, and that they were warming up, i.e. the blood was beginning to flow properly again. But my fingers had *not* been cold — quite the opposite when one remembers that that Sunday was probably one of the hottest days of the summer so far!"

I still had a few things I wanted to check in the configuration so I left her there and when I returned found her lying happily on her side with a blissful smile on her face. This she cannot normally do, for as she says "It is rare that Raynaud's Phenomenon is an 'illness' by itself; ususally there is an underlying cause and in my case it is scleroderma. Scleroderma in turn can be of two types: (i) morphoea which is localised and (ii) systemic sclerosis (which is what I have) and can affect different organs. One of the commonest organs to be affected is the oesophagus; the sphincter muscle to the stomach becomes slack and consequently allows the stomach acids to flow up, thus causing ulcers which, when healed, form strictures and thereby narrows the pipe. This is why I have trained myself to lie propped up otherwise it is like having perpetual heartburn! And I didn't get 'heartburn' when lying flat in the crop circle!" She was most reluctant to leave the circle after lying on her side for at least 20 minutes.

I have been in touch with her regularly since then and she has now become accustomed to her new found sense of well-being. She is sleeping extremely well and her energy has increased noticeably and in general there has been a continued marked improvement. It will be interesting to see what the medics have to say when she goes for her next routine check.

My friend Margaret Randell and I will never forget that day at the Hazeley Down circle, near Morestead, on 15th July 1990.

Epilogue: What happened in 1990?

GEORGE WINGFIELD

The Crop Circles in 1990 excelled themselves in every conceivable way, and, indeed, in many ways which could not have been foreseen. The total number of circles recorded was far in excess of the preceding year and may well approach 1000, though this is only a guess. Unprecedented new shapes such as 'dumb-bells', rectangles, triangles, 'scrolls' and semicircular rings were found. The size of some individual circles also far exceeded what had been recorded before. But most staggering of all was the appearance of elaborate formations, which were dubbed pictograms — some up to 150 yards long — whose complexity and varying combinations of certain distinctive features, exhibited an articulateness which the circles had never previously shown.

This rapid growth in the complexity of the circles during the year 1990 was so marked that none but the most hardened self-deluding sceptic could possibly seek to deny it. It is an aspect which had been clearly apparent in earlier years, but one which accelerated with seemingly increased urgency in 1990. Theories which claim to explain the circles cannot afford to ignore this unmistakable evolution, however unwelcome it may be to those explainers whose fixed ideas have failed to appreciate the real nature of this phenomenon. Nevertheless it is true to say that an explanation of what is happening, in terms generally acceptable and understood, seems as remote as ever in 1990. But the idea that some intelligence is at work now gained considerable ground.

The first 1990 circles started in late April and early May to the north of Devizes. In addition to a plethora of small circles, several large ringed circles appeared in the young crops. All of these exhibited very precise narrow rings, usually 6 to 9 inches wide, of a variety not seen in earlier years. The first ever triple-ringed circle had appeared in late 1989; now we had two more of these near Devizes, one with 4 small satellites on the second ring. These giants were all accompanied by 'grapeshot'. (pp. 92–3).

The largest of the giant triple-ringed circles was the one which amazingly 'grew' an extra outer (fourth) concentric ring one week after the initial event, as described in my article. A few days later the first recorded 'four-rings-at-once' circle (with 4 satellites on the second ring) appeared within a mile. (Plate 28). This reinforced the idea, expressed in Richard Andrews' article, that it is the developing dowsable pattern at the time of formation which determines the actual pattern of the resulting circle. Immediately adjacent to this prodigy, a new 'Celtic Cross', with four satellites on its widely-spaced ring, appeared a month later (Plate 29). One satellite was neatly positioned at one of the two points where its orbital ring intersected the outer ring of the older formation.

On May 23 the 'pictogram' series began at Chilcomb near Cheesefoot Head. The basic component of these formations is a 'dumb-bell' consisting of two circles joined by a straight avenue of flattened crop, can be seen in Plates 37, 38 and 39. This first one also had the feature of two narrow rectangles on either side of its avenue, and these were often repeated, in pairs or singly, in subsequent pictograms. Other features, such as semicircular rings concentric with one circle, followed and many of the series had one or other of the dumbbell circles ringed. These pictograms constitute an extraordinary development in the circle saga, and again and again, the researchers shook their heads in disbelief as they repeated the familiar litany for 1990, "Never seen anything like this before..."

Roughly every week or so a further pictogram appeared near Cheesefoot Head (with one at Litchfield, an old circles site 17 miles north, unvisited since 1985) until Pictogram 7 on July 6 (Plate 51). Many incorporated a tractor tramline as the dumbbell's shaft, making it into part of the design. This unmistakable characteristic, though not the invariable case, confirmed a frequent tendency of many circle formations, such as quincunxes in previous years, to align themselves with the tramlines, though this was questioned by some observers. The fact that the agency which causes the formations is 'aware' of the tramlines, and makes use of them, must cast serious doubt on the notion that the circles forming agency descends randomly from the sky.

In June John Haddington organised a circles watch lasting ten days between Silbury Hill and Wansdyke. During this the 'trilling' noise was heard again by several people and some of the observations are described in the first issue of the Cereologist. To increase the chances of seeing a circle form, the watch group consulted medium Isabelle Kingston, who claims to have received many channelled communications relating to the circles. After doing some map-dowsing she recommended that the fields below the great tumulus, Adam's Grave, near Alton Barnes, be watched as she said that circles would form just there. It was not a place that circles had formed previously and was nearly two miles from the nearest site of last year. It was the only place which she specified. As a result several nights were spent by the group watching from Adam's Grave for circles which never arrived.

A month later, on July 12th, the most remarkable, and what was to become the best known ever, set of circles appeared in the wheatfield below Adam's Grave at Alton Barnes. This spectacular giant pictogram, the eighth to form, is illustrated on the back cover of this book. It consisted basically of two dumb-bell formations in line close together, with several additional circles in line, about 130 yards long over all. The major circles in the dumbbells, either ringed or plain, were all swept clockwise (as with Hampshire pictograms), but these exhibited additional features never previously seen. Variously referred to as 'keys' or 'claws', these resembled rudimentary hands with either two or three 'fingers'. On the same day a further similar giant pictogram was discovered near Milk Hill, less than 2 miles away. This too had 'keys' or 'claws'.

A villager in Alton Barnes, half a mile away, had heard a strange humming noise on that night, and the village dogs had all started barking during the night. Other stories were of cars in the village which would not start that morning. The beauty and mystery of this huge labyrinthine hieroglyph drew visitors like a magnet. Many people travelled from all over the country to Alton Barnes during the next month to see this new wonder of the world. Their sense of excitement and awe was often quite tangible to many who were there and few of them doubted that this was some intelligently produced, but obscure, symbolic message. Many of those who went seemed deeply affected by what they found, and some observed that this pilgrimage had all the makings of a new religion. Farmer Tim Carson quickly and helpfully anticipated the public interest, and responded by charging a small admission fee to enter the field.

In view of the massive press coverage of these events, there is no doubt that the government was fully aware of, if not alarmed by, public reaction to

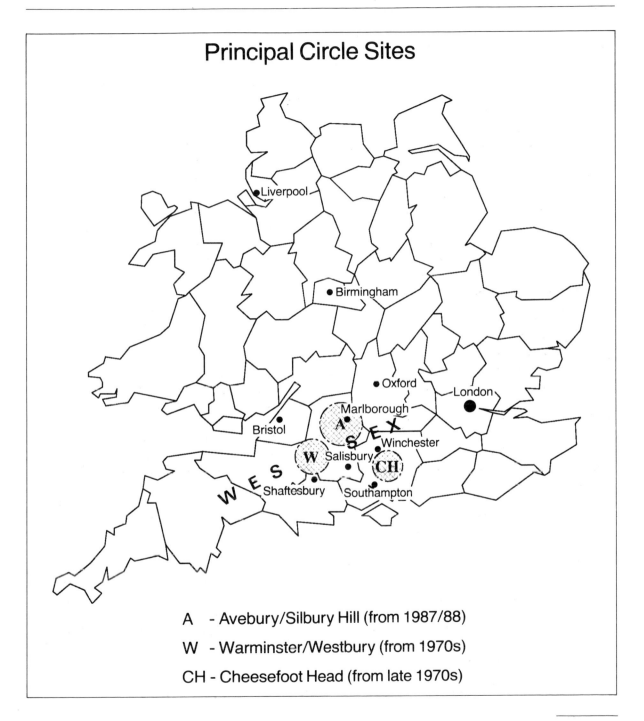

Principal Circle Sites

A - Avebury/Silbury Hill (from 1987/88)

W - Warminster/Westbury (from 1970s)

CH - Cheesefoot Head (from late 1970s)

all of this. The Army were seen to take a great interest in the new circles, and much activity, especially with helicopters, was observed in the Silbury Hill area in the following month. The military also became closely involved with Colin Andrews' and Pat Delgado's Operation Blackbird circles watch at Bratton, which ran from July 23 for 3 weeks. Sponsored by BBC TV and various others, this was a hi-tech attempt, like the previous year's White Crow, to film a circle forming. At times however it risked turning into a media circus.

On July 25, amid fanfares of media hype, the Blackbird team announced via the BBC that they had video recorded 'a major event' — flashing orange lights in the sky above a field where a large new formation of circles had appeared during the night. But within a few hours, the crowning glory of success crumbled into dust when it was found that the roughly fashioned 6 circles were no more than an elaborate hoax, and that the unknown deceivers had left an ouija board and wooden cross at dead centre of each.

It has been suggested that the hoax may have been perpetrated by a special detachment set up by the Army for this purpose. The purpose was said to be to defuse the situation which was verging on public hysteria. In this the hoax was to a degree successful. But why ouija boards and crosses? Any other hoaxer (and there were several other claimants) would hardly have left tell-tale objects behind in the circles. The Army, unable to admit to its gambit, would have had to leave behind indications of a hoax, in case Andrews and Delgado proclaimed it genuine, thereby redoubling public enthralment. The objects chosen were clearly meant to implicate New Agers and occultists as the perpetrators, suggesting that really they made all the circles. At the time of going to press CCCS is seeking further information about this allegation.

To some extent this operation had the desired result, and the Sunday papers vied with each other to proclaim all circles were hoaxes. The Mail on Sunday irresponsibly carried instructions on how to make your own circle, and another tabloid produced Fred Day (59), who had been making circles for 47 years. At last, the mystery was solved and they claimed the £10,000 offered by another paper for a solution! Such facile reasoning demonstrated little else than the idiocy of certain journalists.

Meanwhile the genuine circles continued with almost redoubled vigour. On the same day as the Bratton hoax, an extraordinary set of new circles appeared near Beckhampton, 15 miles away (p. 156). These were 'scrolls' — circles joined by a sinuous flattened path like a reversed S, and the first reported triangles. All were strongly dowsable. The Army showed much interest in these, photographing them from a small unmanned helicopter known as a WISP. This it omitted to do at the Bratton hoax, for obvious reasons.

More pictograms were to follow the Alton Barness prodigy. On July 27 a similar but even larger double dumb-bell pictogram, 150 yards long, was found one mile from Silbury Hill, at which it pointed almost exactly. This lay precisely half way between West and East Kennett Long Barrows, and, unlike the other two, was athwart the tractor tramlines. Despite several hoaxed circles which various jokers were now producing, there is no suggestion that this or any of the other pictograms was a hoax. And it is rumoured that Operation Blackbird did eventually catch a real circle forming, very rapidly, on its video recording equipment.

From June CCCS received many reports of circles from all over England and from Scotland. Many were from places where circles had never previously been found and sometimes they were of formations not previously known, such as a circle with seven satellites at Bickington, Devon, and new pictograms in Sussex. As the circle season drew to a close with the August harvest, reports arrived with increasing frequency. Now we can only wait agog to see what new surprises the 'Circlemakers' have in store for 1991.

Appendices

THE CENTRE FOR CROP CIRCLE STUDIES — ITS AIMS AND OBJECTIVES

The CCCS was founded in April 1990 in the belief that the crop circle phenomenon offers remarkable challenges to understanding which will only be met by drawing on a wide range of insights and expertise in many different fields. The principal objectives of CCCS are to encourage this interdisciplinary approach and to ensure that it is sustained by sound research and reliable information.

In furtherance of these objectives CCCS will aim:

1. to establish a comprehensive data base containing the numbers, types, geographical distribution and incidence in time, world-wide, of crop circle occurrences, together with such other factual information as may seem relevant in the light of research;

2. to facilitate study of the phenomenon by serious and competent researchers;

3. from time to time to publish, or to assist in the publication of, research papers in suitable outlets;

4. to encourage all who have a serious interest in the phenomenon and share our objectives to join CCCS or to affiliate with it.

Membership forms and further information about the Centre for Crop Circle Studies can be obtained by sending a stamped, self-addressed envelope to CCCS c/o Specialist Knowledge Services, 20 Paul Street, Frome, Somerset, BA11 1DX, United Kingdom.

A sample copy of The Circular, the quarterly journal of the CCCS, can be obtained post free by sending a cheque for £1.75, made payable to Specialist Knowledge Services

Professor Archie E. Roy
President CCCS

CODE OF PRACTICE

The main objective of CCCS is to conduct well organised research into the crop circle phenomenon, both in the United Kingdom and overseas, and to publish its data and research findings at suitable stages in CCCS publications and other serious outlets. We are very conscious, however, that the crop circles occur almost invariably on private land, for the most part land owned or cultivated by the farming community. In its search for a better understanding of these events, CCCS will encourage all its members and affiliates to adhere to the following strict Code of Practice, which was agreed on 17th May 1990 between the CCCS and the National Farmers Union.

* Always get permission from the owner or farmer before you go into a field. *If you can't get it, don't enter.* You will be committing trespass if you do.

* Shut gates behind you. Do not damage hedges or

other barriers. Do not take a dog with you. Respect all notices. Treat land and livestock as you would your own property. Don't smoke in a field. Don't take a vehicle.

* The circles are delicate and fragile scientific evidence. *Never enter one out of idle curiosity.* Enter only if you have a specific research purpose and are properly qualified to carry it out. Always take a photograph from *outside* the circle before you enter. Do as little damage as possible to the occurrence while studying it.

* Cross fields only by way of 'tramlines' if they exist. If there are no 'tramlines', make only a *single* track by the shortest path. Make sure that the farmer is willing for you to do so, and continue to use only this track for any subsequent investigation.

* Leave no litter in fields or circles. If you station any equipment at a circle for scientific purposes, make sure you have the farmer's permission to do so, as well as his agreement that you may return at a later date for monitoring.

* If a farmer has been good enough to tell you of an event which has not yet come to public notice and wishes to keep the occurrence confidential, *report the event only to a senior CCCS officer and in no circumstances to the media.* [CCCS will not publish such information until the risks of disturbance by the public are well past.]

NOTES ON FOUNDER MEMBERS OF THE CCCS WHO HAVE NOT CONTRIBUTED MAIN ARTICLES TO THIS BOOK

Alick Bartholomew, the publisher of this book, has worked in publishing for nearly forty years. His last imprint was Turnstone Press which he founded in 1971 (its first title, *Jonathan Livingston Seagull*). He is a graduate of Cambridge University in geography and geology, followed graduate studies at the University of Chicago, and is a trustee of several organisations concerned with healing and the environment.

Richard Beaumont, a graduate in Philosophy and co-

editor of the national magazine, *Kindred Spirit*, has been keenly interested in psychology, philosophy, psychic phenomena and spiritual advancement since an early age. He has travelled widely about the world and studied at first hand many of the techniques for developing the human potential, drawn from both Eastern and Western practice, which have so greatly blossomed since the mid-1970s.

Barbara Davies, Welsh with a Breton streak, but now (as she says) "adopted by Cornwall" after many years as a librarian and English teacher, has a Gemini's wide interests: Cornish archaeology and mythology, astrology, medicine-wheel teachings, healing, dowsing, ceremony and drama, art, music, science, travelling, "making things", and cats. She has published an annotated *Hamlet* and a pamphlet on reflexology and herbalism, and helped found the Oak Dragon alternative education camps.

Beth Davis is a conservation officer dealing with historic buildings in Cambridgeshire. She lectures on building history and more particularly on landscape history. She has also used her dowsing skills to identify and interpret ancient sites with groups of students. She is a watercolourist and photographer.

Christine Insley Green, an honours graduate in Egyptian and Nubian studies, has excavated as an archaeologist at Saqqära and Luxor, Egypt; served as Hon. Assistant Keeper (Egyptian Gallery) at the Fitzwilliam Museum, Cambridge; taught at Khartoum University; and published *The Temple Furniture from the Sacred Animal Necropolis at North Saqqära, 1964-1976* (London, 1987). For several years Head of the Antiquities Department at Christie's, cataloguing objects from Ireland to the Caspian Sea and from the Prehistoric to Late Roman Periods, she remains a Consultant to Christie's in this field.

Leonie Starr came to England from Australia in 1979 after formal studies in both Fine Arts and Drama. She has been studying the esoteric generally, and astrology in particular, since her teens. She started channelling in 1989 and co-wrote and edited transcripts of received material. Through this work with psychic energies she became increasingly drawn to the possible links between astrology and the phenomena of earth energies and sacred sites. Of these phenomena, she believes that the crop circles may be one manifestation.

Index